European Studies in Social Psychology
Perspectives on minority influence

European studies in social psychology

Already published:

The analysis of action: recent theoretical and empirical advances, edited by Mario von Cranach and Rom Harré

Current issues in European social psychology, volume 1, edited by Willem Doise and Serge Moscovici

Social interaction in individual development, edited by Willem Doise and Augusto Palmonari

Advances in the social psychology of language, edited by Colin Fraser and Klaus R. Scherer

Social representations, edited by Serge Moscovici and Robert Farr

Social markers in speech, edited by Klaus R. Scherer and Howard Giles

Social identity and intergroup relations, edited by Henri Tajfel

The social dimension: European developments in social psychology (2 vols.), edited by Henri Tajfel

Perspectives on minority influence

Edited by
Serge Moscovici,
Gabriel Mugny
and
Eddy Van Avermaet

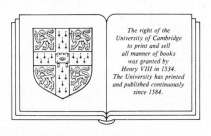

The right of the
University of Cambridge
to print and sell
all manner of books
was granted by
Henry VIII in 1534.
The University has printed
and published continuously
since 1584.

Cambridge University Press
Cambridge
London   New York   New Rochelle
Melbourne   Sydney

Editions de la Maison des Sciences de l'Homme
Paris

Published by the Press Syndicate of the University of Cambridge
The Pitt Building, Trumpington Street, Cambridge CB2 1RP
32 East 57th Street, New York, NY 10022, USA
10 Stamford Road, Oakleigh, Melbourne 3166, Australia
and Editions de la Maison des Sciences de l'Homme
54 Boulevard Raspail, 75270 Paris Cedex 06

First published 1985

Printed in Great Britain by
the University Press, Cambridge

Library of Congress cataglogue card number: 84 – 23859

British Library cataloguing in publication data

Perspectives on minority influence – (European
studies in social psychology)
1. Minorities – Social aspects
I. Moscovici, Serge   II. Mugny, Gabriel
III. Avermaet, Eddy van   IV. Series
305   HT1521

ISBN 0 521 24695 4
ISBN 2 7351 0106 1 (France only)
ISSN 0758 7554 (France only)

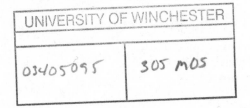

Contents

Contributors

VERNON L. ALLEN
Department of Psychology, University of Wisconsin

JEAN-PIERRE DECONCHY
Laboratoire de Psychologie Sociale de l'Université de Paris VII, associé au CNRS

MACHTELD DOMS
Laboratorium voor Experimentele Sociale Psychologie, Katholieke Universiteit, Leuven

HAROLD B. GERARD
Department of Psychology, University of California, Los Angeles

MICHEL GUILLON
Université de Lille III

BIBB LATANÉ
Institute for Research in Social Science, University of North Carolina at Chapel Hill

JOHN M. LEVINE
Department of Psychology, University of Pittsburgh

RICHARD L. MORELAND
Department of Psychology, University of Pittsburgh

SERGE MOSCOVICI
Ecole des Hautes Etudes en Sciences Sociales, Paris

GABRIEL MUGNY
Faculté de Psychologie, Université de Genève

CHARLAN NEMETH
Department of Psychology, University of California, Berkeley

STAMOS PAPASTAMOU
Faculté de Psychologie, Université de Genève

BERNARD PERSONNAZ
Laboratoire de Psychologie Sociale, Groupe de recherche du CNRS, associé à l'Université de Paris VII

EDDY VAN AVERMAET
  Laboratorium voor Experimentele Sociale Psychologie, Katholieke Universiteit,
  Leuven
SHARON WOLF
  Department of Psychology, California State University at Long Beach

Preface

SERGE MOSCOVICI

One particular phenomenon represents the touchstone of relationships between groups and individuals, and beyond that between majorities and minorities. This phenomenon is influence. In practice and from time immemorial all psychologies of people in society have been based on some vision of influence. It constitutes the common denominator in medical, religious and political activities. Virtually no peoples exist, however primitive they may be, who do not call upon some magical formula or technique for modifying the consciousness of individuals and incorporating them within the common consciousness. Through various means, which may take any form ranging from spirit possession, to spirit cures or to ceremonies organised around dance or music, individuals are brought closer together and more intimate contact is created. For us analogous functions are served by debates, mass meetings, gatherings and rallies of all kinds. In each case we may observe the presence of a group or individual that tries to convince others and achieve acceptance of a feeling or an action by a greater or lesser number of individuals. What is the goal? All the evidence suggests that the aim is to bring people closer together, to create a community of thought and behaviour. Without such convergence and such community nothing can be achieved, anymore by two people than by a great social movement.

The above mentioned examples manifestly involve influence. The most banal and least spectacular example one could imagine would suffice to illustrate this phenomenon. But whether the example is ordinary or extraordinary is of little account. The principal lesson to be drawn is clear; it is possible to exercise a hold over people's beliefs, emotions and even their behaviour. Moreover, these may be modified without their voluntary consent. Thus individuals who have been influenced in this way often consider as their own, as the product of their own minds, an idea which in reality has been inculcated in them by others.

There are several different ways in which one can examine the nature and particular characteristics of this phenomenon, but there is one dominant factor: influence represents for everyone the power of ideas, if not the omnipotence of ideas, as Charcot put it. Whatever meaning you give the word 'power' – manipulation, communication, propaganda, etc. – the intuition remains that through influence a mental cause produces a physical effect. It thus has a utility which derives uniquely from its psychological properties. These properties allow intellectual factors, and particularly language, to operate as if they were organic, as if they had bodily form. That this is possible has always astounded people. This is why influence is considered a gift, an extraordinary phenomenon.

When social psychology came into being, relatively recently, it took up this inheritance. This is not to say that it did not also provoke a kind of revolution in our understanding of what happens when people confront one another in a group. The revolution consisted in considering the power of ideas and thus influence as an elementary and normal phenomenon. From this we have come to regard the essential feature of collective action as being influence. And the essence of individual action is itself to be found in the way influence is resisted. But in another respect the tradition is maintained. It is assumed that influence is exercised by a group upon an individual, by the majority upon the minority, or even by an individual who has authority over those who do not. In other words, social psychology continues to regard influence as leading to conformity. Now in a society like ours, characterised by change and innovation, such a point of view seems rather limited. It does not allow us to understand how opinions or behaviours are modified, why people come to accept beliefs or ideas that originally appeared unacceptable, indeed absurd.

To overcome this limitation some researchers have begun to treat the phenomenon of influence from a less traditional point of view, namely in terms of its minority origins. They are concerned not with *any* minority but with that minority which undermines the order and vision of the majority. How can such a minority make its ideas convincing in the eyes of those who would otherwise reject them as nonsensical? Yet this is true of the influence exercised by a dissident minority, a heretic in his break with the church, an ethnic group asserting its rights, and even a new scientific school. These researchers have tried to respond on a general level to the question the German physicist Heisenberg judged to be paramount in understanding scientific revolutions:

We must now ask how such radical alterations have come about, or – to put it in more sociological terms, though also quite misleadingly – how was a seemingly small group of physicists able to constrain the others to effect these changes in the structure of science and thought. It goes without saying that these others first resisted change, and were bound to do so. (Heisenberg, 1975: 157.)

The initial results of this research have been encouraging. They have allowed us to establish that a solution is possible and that interesting discoveries can be made in this area. An entire view of reality is revealed to those prepared to examine it. Little by little we have seen more social psychologists become interested in the problem, in Europe and in the United States. Some have made empirical or theoretical studies. Others have pondered upon the consequences of this way of viewing influence. It obviously throws a new and different light upon the classical notions of deviance, the group, and so on. The idea began to grow of organising a conference to bring together all these social psychologists so that they might share experiences, debate their various viewpoints and establish closer relations.

The European Laboratory of Social Psychology at the Maison des Sciences de l'Homme (Paris) reacted favourably to this idea. S. Moscovici (Paris). G. Mugny (Geneva) and E. Van Avermaet (Leuven) were given the task of bringing it to fruition. Closely associated with this group was S. Barriga (Barcelona), who played a vital role. Following preparatory meetings the conference was held at L'Escuela de Formacion 'La Caixa' in Barcelona between 10 and 12 September, 1980. It was organised with the financial aid of the Fondation de la Maison des Sciences de l'Homme, the University of Barcelona, and also la Caixa de Pensiones 'La Caixa'. The generous support of these institutions enabled the conference to proceed under excellent conditions. However, the key figure, perhaps one should say the alchemist who brought together all the necessary but sometimes incompatible elements for such a conference, was Adriana Touraine. By her intelligence, her sensitivity to social relations and her patient tenacity, she untangled the most delicate situations and smoothed the life of all the participants. The following is the list of those attending: V. Allen (University of Wisconsin), E. Van Avermaet (Universiteit Leuven), M. von Cranach (Universität Bern), J. P. Deconchy (Université de Paris VII). M. Doms (Universiteit Leuven). W. Doise (Université de Genève), H. Gerard (University of California, Los Angeles), J. P. Di Giacomo (Université de Louvain), M. Guillon (Université de Lille III), B. Latané (Ohio State University), J. Levine (University of Pittsburgh), G. de Montmollin (Université de Paris V), S. Moscovici (Ecole des Hautes Etudes en Sciences Sociales, Paris), G. Mugny (Université de Genève), C. Nemeth (University of California, Berkeley), A. Palmonari (Universitá di Bologna), S. Papastamou (Université de Genève), B. Personnaz (Université de Paris VII), S. Reicher (University of Bristol), J. Rijsman (Katholieke Hogeschool Tilburg), S. Wolf (Ohio State University), M. Zaleska (Université de Paris VII), and S. Barriga, T. Ibañez, P. Gonzalez, F. Munne, P. Noto, M. D. Riba (Universidad Autonoma de Barcelona), F. J. Burillo (Universidad Conplutense de Madrid), P. Ridruejo (Universidad Autonoma de Madrid), G. Serrano (Universidad de

Valencia), M. Siguan (Universidad de Barcelona) and J. R. Torregrosa (Universidad de Valencia).

The chapters assembled in this volume can represent only a part of what was presented at the conference in Barcelona. Those we have chosen deal with minority influence from a variety of perspectives, and are organised into two broadly based parts. The first is devoted to analyses of the process of influence as such. It contains both the research paradigm which has emerged and some of the results it has yielded. The second is more concerned with the place given to the processes within the context of groups. The influence of minorities is thus located within the cognitive and social field in which interaction between minorities and majorities occurs. But between the two parts there is only a difference of emphasis, not an absolute separation. Indeed, in Part I there are frequent references to the social and cognitive field, and in Part II there are several analyses of processes of minority influence. And it goes without saying, though it is preferable that we do so, that the different authors express points of view that do not always agree. Consequently, one may be struck by the critical standpoints they adopt and by the vitality of the debates. When one considers the ground which remains to be covered in understanding these phenomena it is the degree of agreement which is surprising. After all, we have studied minority influence and innovation for only 20 years. We have simply not yet examined enough concepts, nor integrated enough information, to choose between the various explanations. In any event, the interest of a book such as this lies in the differences between the authors and in the perspective each one offers. For the moment, it is less important to decide who is right and who is wrong than to lay bare this *terra incognita* of the mind of man and of human groups. In the last analysis it is social psychology that will be the winner.

It would be impossible to end this preface without acknowledging gratitude to Silverio Barriga, friend and colleague. I am pleased to acknowledge that without him this book, like the conference on which it is based, would not have seen the light of day. His personal and intellectual energy has been a stimulus to everyone and I would like to thank him.

Part I
The process of minority influence

Introduction

Work on social influence has been concerned with the multiplicity of situations in which the behaviours, perceptions, opinions, attitudes, etc. of an individual (or group of individuals) are modified by the behaviours, perceptions, opinions and attitudes of another individual (or group of individuals). Two contrasting categories of influence situation can be identified. In the first, the source of influence is a majority, or is attractive or is competent, etc. – in brief, it possesses some resource capable of ensuring its ascendancy over the target of influence. The latter, in a complementary fashion, is a minority or is deviant or is unattractive, or lacks competence. In practice most classic work has studied this side of the coin only, where the dynamics of influence are underpinned by one form or another of dependence which ensures the influence of the superior party and confines the subordinate party to conformity and submission. Certainly, this is sometimes, and perhaps even frequently, the case.

However, a second category of situations can also be envisaged. In this, minority individuals (or groups) viewed as deviant, and to begin with lacking any power, attractiveness, or competence, or indeed any resource capable of inducing dependence, succeed despite all this in modifying what the majority thinks, or in overturning social rules; they succeed in effect in bringing others to share their convictions. In the first chapter Serge Moscovici makes a strong plea for the study of minority influence. Such study is in fact novel in two ways. First, it introduces a fundamental theoretical shift, from a functionalist model of society to an interactionist model; from an asymmetric conception of influence processes (which reduces them to the mechanics of dependency effects) to a symmetric conception in which minorities are not simply targets but also sources of influence; from an exclusive focus on conformity processes to a model in which innovation phenomena occupy a central place. Having defined the basic theoretical options, a second question is raised which requires an equally novel answer: how can the influence of minorities be explained if it cannot be derived from any form of dependence, minorities being by definition seen to have no resources of dependence at their disposal? Here a new perspective on deviance is advanced. For too long we have considered only the marginal and passive deviant. Here we are concerned with active deviance or active minorities in particular because they alone are capable of generating the potential for social change. On what is their influence based? On the only resource which a minority in practice possesses – its own behaviour. To exercise influence a minority must employ styles of behaviour, it must organise and plan its actions in space and time. The minority must be, in a word, consistent; it must be coherent, sure of itself, steadfast in negotiation. These styles have the power to create conflict in circumstances where uniformity would otherwise prevail. By its consistency the minority introduces an alternative into the social field with which the majority must come to terms. This is a theme which will be encountered frequently in this volume; if minorities have a social impact, it is by virtue of their capacity to create social conflict, through their potential for blocking all negotiation. In other chapters it will be seen that the induction of such conflict does not, however, exclude a certain attitude of compromise.

But let us look first at another important aspect of minority influence processes, taken up in the second chapter: minority influence is rarely public, rarely displayed in a direct social manner. While the hidden character of minority influence will be discussed in subsequent chapters (which deal with its indirect effects), the problem Machteld Doms and Eddy Van Avermaet consider is why public influence is so problematic for minorities, as compared with the strong public influence of the majority. One of the principal reasons, examined here in detail, is the lack of social support that a minority secures relative to the majority. In a majority influence situation, the target is, in effect, exposed to a degree of influence which exceeds the social support available for its own initial response. In a situation of minority influence, by contrast, minority pressure is largely counterbalanced by the support that the target receives from the other (majority) subjects in confirming the same (majority) response that the target initially defends. If this social support mechanism is effectively responsible for the contrast between the rather feeble public effects of a minority and the somewhat stronger ones of the majority, it should be possible to equalise their respective capacities for influence by holding constant the social support given to the target's own 'spontaneous' response. In a series of experiments, the authors contrive to do this through an experimental artifice: by simulating a breakdown in the measuring apparatus, they attempt to isolate the experimental subjects from the social support they would otherwise have received from the majority of other subjects (responding in the correct or popular direction), thus rendering the minority and majority conditions effectively equivalent. It emerges that, other things being equal, the social support factor does effectively explain the difference between the majority and the minority in their relative degree of direct influence. Moreover, this demonstrates that what is important is the entire social context created by the minority influence situation; even within the experimental situation subjects can escape minority influence, particularly if they have the support of individuals who in some way represent their reference group and who socially reinforce their own initial responses. This relational dimension is particularly important since it is necessary to recognise that minorities appear, almost by definition, to be numerically more feeble, and at odds with the consensus.

In the third chapter Charlan Nemeth examines the public aspect of minority influence but also introduces measures of indirect or latent influence. What determines whether influence is direct or indirect? It depends on the nature of the compromise offered by the minority, not withstanding its behavioural consistency. There is no contradiction here. Everything depends on the level on which the minority seeks to exercise influence. Thus, to take the example of a bargaining or decision-making situation, it is evident that the goal is public influence in the sense that a choice has to be made; influence on this level can only be achieved by compromise in the course of negotiation. However, most of the time active minorities are studied in situations where they do not aspire to, or even realistically expect to achieve, public influence, and in which their behaviour is structured with strict consistency. Influence then will be indirect. Does a third possibility exist in which indirect influence closely matches public influence, in which compromise and consistency are reconciled? These two aspects of minority activity, in reality more complementary than contradictory, can effectively give rise to a two-fold influence, one overt and the other latent; this requires that minority compromise does not appear as a change in the private response of the minority (in which case the minority would be *ipso facto* perceived as inconsistent), but as minority tactics to facilitate collective agreement on the public level. By compromising, the minority is publicly influential; by its consistency, it is a source of latent influence.

The fourth chapter more directly examines this other specific dimension of the minority influence process, conversion, that is the indirect, latent form which minority influence often takes. Bernard Personnaz and Michel Guillon first of all describe the various experimental techniques, from the most simple to the most sophisticated, which have been used to demonstrate the effects of conversion. These effects routinely emerge as specific to minorities;

majorities have the greater influence on public responses but no latent effects. In contrast, minorities find their influence taking the following pattern. At the public level their influence is undetectable, almost zero, or at the most very feeble. At the same time, some change occurs in responses that have some link with the object directly involved in the influence attempt, which, although not a direct acknowledgment of the minority, does indirectly result from it. Confronted with majorities, target subjects make a social comparison of their responses with those of the majority and tend to resolve the social conflict at the most socially overt level of response. Faced with minorities, on the other hand, such a comparison of responses at the public level is no longer made. Instead, one finds a focus on the object, a search for a valid definition of the object in which the minority alternative is considered and thus becomes a source of change, often unsuspected by the individuals affected. Why these contrasting reactions? The authors argue that these effects are linked to the dynamics of the representations generated in the course of a conflict-laden interaction between source and target. Faced with a majority, the subject would be preoccupied by his own 'minority' position as a deviant in relation to a majority and would pay attention to the interpersonal relationship thus made salient at the expense of more intellectual considerations. The external social conflict remains to a certain extent psychologically externalised, and becomes increasingly so as the conflictual interaction develops. When faced with a minority, however, this external social conflict is internalised by the target subject; it is projected inwards so that the subject factor becomes a redefinition of the object of dispute.

Chapter 4 is also concerned both with the dynamics of the representations linked to conflict and with the mechanisms involved in the gradual consciousness of internal changes that is characteristic of conversion. The changes and influence processes examined here prove to be exciting and surprising, taking forms which have been rarely studied in the past. This little known type of influence has only come to light because of the emergence of research on minority influence. Although several experimental attempts have now been made to demonstrate its existence and uncover its mechanisms, much still remains to be explained.

Minority influence thus proves to be a particularly fertile research field. On the one hand theories about the mechanisms of influence which have been taken for granted for too long now need to be modified. On the other hand processes are now revealed which have previously been hardly considered. Thus we find that social conflict is sought by the minority, is indeed the sole weapon of active minorities; they can thus exercise influence only by consistently resisting any negotiation with the majority. Their influence, moreover, takes the form of private conversion.

The apparent failure of minorities at the public level is the basis for the research programme described in chapter 5, which concludes Part I of this volume. Stamos Papastamou and Gabriel Mugny develop the idea that the social context of innovation is a particularly complex one. When one considers ideological minorities (for example, anti-militarist, or anti-nuclear factions), it may be seen that the minority is confronted on one side with power (pro-militarist, pro-nuclear factions) and on the other with the population, which is the real target of influence. Within this framework, consistency defines the oppositional relation of the minority with respect to the established powers; consistency is indispensable in this relation if the minority is to appear as an alternative in the social field. In the face of power, blockage of negotiation is the most adequate strategy. To influence the population, however, a minority does better to show itself open to negotiation, to avoid inducing the appearance of too great a divide through any behaviour that the population would perceive as rigid.

Several dimensions of research summarised here are located around the functioning of such rigidity. Following a definition of flexible *versus* rigid negotiation styles in relation to a population (in contrast to more or less consistent behavioural styles in relation to power), a study is made of the effects they have on the representations induced by the minority. However, these representations do not derive solely from minority styles; they also depend substantially on the normative context that prevails in a particular situation. Thus the same minority behaviour takes on a different meaning according to whether it is judged in terms of conformity, objectivity, independence, or social originality norms. These normative contexts are to a large degree established by the powers that be, which thus defend themselves against minorities by a tendency to promote a psychological interpretation of their deviance. Their behaviours then cease to reflect an alternative in the social field since they are seen simply as revealing the psychology of the minority. These highly potent context effects thus explain the difficulty minorities have in achieving direct public influence, since they render salient the social costs of the identity which would be involved in movement towards, or acceptance of, the minority thesis, as the evaluative connotations associated with it are often highly negative. But this does not imply total absence of influence since, even if rigidity diminishes public influence, it often induces a more marked conversion effect!

One of the important consequences of the approach the authors advocate is to redefine the relationship between majority and minority influence in a more dynamic and dialectic manner. The experimental study of one without the other can only be an abstraction. It is only by locating it within the overall social field (which includes both power and population) that minority influence can be understood for what it is. Moreover, this idea will be encountered in other chapters. Hence, for example, does not a consideration of the effects of social support in resistance to minority influence also derive from a dynamic and integrated conception of minority and majority influence?

To sum up, processes of minority influence are based on two key notions, those of conflict and conversion. They are based on conflict first because it is the weapon available to the minority to unsettle, particularly by a display of consistency, a group or a social system. However, this is a conflict which the minority also has to negotiate to some extent with those it wishes to influence. Secondly, they are based on conversion, a gradual mechanism of internal, covert change, the outcome of a cognitive activity whose details have yet to be researched. Paradoxically, a minority derives its power to influence indirectly from the very conditions which inhibit its direct or public influence, in other words those of conflict. Here is an idea with which we must become familiar even if it does overturn the framework to which we have become accustomed in the classic treatments of social influence processes. It also implies that the entire dynamics of social change should be considered; the social context of innovation points to the need to take account of minority and majority influences simultaneously within a single dynamic model. And the theoretical elements developed so far with regard to the mechanisms entailed in minority influence provide the scope for such an integration.

1. Innovation and minority influence

SERGE MOSCOVICI

1. The parable of the lonely minority

In beginning the preparation of this chapter two events immediately came to my mind. One took place in the real world and one in the laboratory. During a recent conversation, Fritz Heider revealed that his ideas were publicly presented for the very first time in 1921 to a kind of popular science group at Graz in Austria. He recalled that his colleagues, with one exception, merely laughed and departed without further comment. And this brings me to the other event. Every student in psychology knows of the famous experiment by Asch. Individuals, who find themselves in groups of eight to 15 stooges who assert that two visibly unequal lines are in fact equal, naive to the deception, adopt this manifestly incorrect judgment. But what most students do not know is that at the end of his series of experiments and out of curiosity Asch reverses the situation. A single stooge affirms in front of 14 or 15 'naive' individuals that these visibly unequal lines are equal. These other individuals, like Heider's colleagues, begin to laugh, perhaps embarrassed by what this crazy person claims (Harvey, Ickes & Kidd, 1976).

Laughter, then, is a common reaction to a minority of one individual, whether encountered in real life or in the laboratory. However, the resemblance between the two events ends there. In the real life example, strong in his convictions and obligated by standards of scientific inquiry, Heider stuck resolutely and consistently to his position. He exposed himself to indifference and isolation until he was ultimately acknowledged and accepted. He, in effect, followed the path that all minorities have followed since time immemorial to establish innovations and alter majority opinion. In the laboratory, on the other hand, with his exploration of the phenomena of conformity accomplished, Asch published his now widely known conclusions. The subsequent experiment he has recounted only to the privileged few, like a savoury, an ambiguous closing comment on his research. And each has been

9

able to take or leave it in his own way. It seemed to lie outside the proper territory of social psychology and touched limits beyond which trespassing would be risky, if not punished.

But why the laughter? Why does the same judgment create difficulties for individuals when expressed by a majority but provoke mirth in them when introduced by a minority? It is as if the first condition represents a 'natural' state for individuals in society while the second is an 'artificial' state; being in this condition is maladaptive, abnormal and even comic. But let us note for a moment that our minority of a single individual has made more progress in the real world than in the laboratory. He began his task at the point where the experiment left off.

I do not know how clear my parable is. What I want to show is simply that the aim of research on minority influence is to reduce the discrepancy between events in the laboratory and those in the real world. Its aim is to push back the limits imposed by existing theory and include phenomena relating to innovation in groups and in society (Moscovici & Faucheux, 1972; Moscovici & Nemeth, 1974). We have sometimes suggested that in this sense our research represents an inversion of Asch's. We have said that it is the exact contrary of his own. At the level of experimental procedures this is, strictly speaking, true. But taken as a whole, it raised questions which go beyond those posed within the social psychology of conformity. And it is also characterised by the view that the minority state is as 'natural' as that of the majority. It explores what happens when the laughter ends and examines the conditions under which the 'crazy' individual ends up the winner. Or, we might say, how does he get the others to laugh *with* him ('he who laughs last laughs longest')? In exploring these questions we enter a no-man's land of uncharted psychological phenomena and problems.

2. The paradox of conformity

These preliminaries are intended to raise basic questions and to tackle fundamental issues. In depriving myself of the comfort and security an author may derive from the presentation of specific research, I am taking the calculated risk that this chapter may seem too elementary or general. As I have just indicated, the gap that separates the manner in which influence is exercised in the real world and the way it has been analysed in the laboratory has finally led to the study of innovation and minority influence phenomena. Justifications of this kind based in experience are often necessary, but they are never sufficient grounds for launching into a particular area of research for they do not indicate the direction in which one should go or the assumptions one should make. Indeed, in so far as I became preoccupied with these kinds of phenomena it was because I had earlier been struck by certain theoretical problems. More exactly, I was struck by a paradox inherent in the dominant paradigm in social psychology. This paradox indicates not only why innovation and minority influence have not been analysed but why they could not. Or, in other words, it marks a limit to theory in the same way that Asch's results mark a limit to experiments.

This then is the paradox. If you examine the literature and the textbooks closely you will find they contain two simple ideas, presented as established postulates. First, individuals are motivated to achieve correct judgments of things, to bring valid judgments to bear upon them. When, for objective reasons, they cannot do this, they turn to others. Second, the conformity of individuals to a group facilitates movement of the group towards its goal, and thus conduces to its success and its adaptation to reality. Everything else, or almost everything, is deduced from these two ideas. They explain why groups try to achieve unanimity and why similar individuals are drawn to one another. They also define deviants as sources of difficulty, as obstacles to the progress of the group and its adaptation to the external world (Festinger, 1950; Schachter, 1951; Jones & Gerard, 1967). An impressive number of experiments have illustrated the *consequences* flowing from these postulates in the most diverse areas, conferring upon them the solidity of a mental frame of reference. And, time after time, it has been observed that even if one rewards individuals for correct responses, even if they are informed that all erroneous judgments, although they conform to those of the group, will lead to collective failure, their reaction remains the same. They prefer to say what the group says rather than what they see themselves (Duetsch & Gerard, 1955). We do not find this surprising.

For a long time it has been known that men bend more towards the consensus of all than towards the truth of a single person. They choose being with others against reality in preference to being with reality against others. All organisations and all propaganda take this for granted and use it as their lever. Consciousness of this impasse has directed other experiments, such as those of Kelley & Shapiro (1954), towards the potential deviant. Attempts have been made to combat the conformist propensity, to stimulate the individual to prefer reality and to counter group pressure, to influence the group by telling others what he sees and what he believes to be true. But experiments such as these did not serve their purposes because they left untouched the theoretical facet of the paradox which served as a kind of certification of the individual's powerlessness. Nonetheless, the impression grew that conformity to the group did not have the beneficial character once attributed to it, and that it could precipitate, among other effects, an inability to adapt or to solve objective problems. Finally, the famous experiments by Milgram (1966) ruined the entire edifice by carrying to extremes the effects of obedience to authority. Individuals in this case submitted as if neither internal morality nor external reality any longer existed for them.

In my opinion the principal reason why researchers in our area have for 30 years abandoned collective phenomena and turned instead to individual phenomena lies within this paradox. In the absence of a solution to the paradox it was not possible to renounce the dominant theoretical model. Neither was it possible to continue in the otherwise fertile direction it had opened up (de Montmollin, 1977). The odds are that there will be a return to these phenomena when another model is established and another way of viewing the problems is accepted (Moscovici, 1976). Our research on innovation and minority influence is viewed by some of us as a means of overcoming the paradox and as pointing the way to a necessary shift in perspective. It may be argued that it still fails to fill the gap in the literature (Latané & Wolf, 1981) or to correct its bias towards conformity. But this would presuppose that the existing paradigm is untainted by any contradiction between what is claimed in theory and what is shown by experience. It also presupposes that it is sufficient to set forth a new class of facts – innovation and minority influence. But this will not do. It is not sufficient to shift the limits described above. It is vital to consider these facts in a way which will allow one to overcome the paradox in the theory itself.

To summarise: for both empirical and theoretical reasons studies of minority influence must be located within a different perspective. Such an approach often proves to be necessary: in mastering a difficulty or solving a problem, it eventually ceases to be economical simply to accumulate information and make further minor adjustments to established ideas. The most effective procedure is to go to the heart of the matter, and adopt a new conception of the set of realities with which one is concerned.

3. Deviance and minority

It was thus neither from exhaustion nor from lack of imagination that studies of influence and group phenomena declined so rapidly in the 1950s. It was because there was no longer any wish to build on foundations which the paradox described above had shown to be so unsteady. There has been no open debate on the subject. Rather, people have, as it were, voted with their feet and abandoned the centre of social psychology. Concurrent with this decline has been the recognition of the point of departure for any new approach, namely the issue from which the difficulties arose, that of deviance and the deviant. Though it may not be a systematic and rigorous approach, there is something to be said for the idea that to overcome the contradiction it will be necessary to allow the deviant to do what the old conception forbade and to consider the consequences. Now, within the terms of the theory the individual was permitted, although barely, to resist the group. And according to experience he was supposed to lack the power to act upon this group. In brief, he was by definition the target of influences that derived from the majority, and what is more, a passive target. This provoked the failure of the group when it needed his positive participation and contribution. Up to now, only what happens on the majority side has been considered. The moment has come to look also at what happens on the deviant side.

Deviance was actually envisaged as a defect in the majority and not as a potential trump card. It was not recognised as an asset which could improve the group's chances of success (rather than cause its failure); nor was it recognised that correct judgment (and not just error) could depend on the capacity of group members to deviate when necessary rather than conform on every issue. Without deviants a group can neither adapt to reality nor achieve its goals. In seeking to eliminate them it eliminates one of its resources, one of its chances of success. Consequently, the only way it can progress is through a capacity to acknowledge, rather than to exclude or eliminate, them.

Progress occurs according to a kind of socialised version of Gödel's Theorem. In a great many social and psychological theories it is implied that the system changes according to an internal law of development from one state of equilibrium to another. It is also implied that *all* individuals belong to, or become members of, this system, or again that the system can explain and identify *all* those included within it. Now, according to Gödel, a logical system includes propositions which cannot be proved true or false. They can only be proved by generating another system. The system has to change. This is principally because the undemonstrated propositions are, if I may express it this way, 'in search of' a system which can decide their truth or falsity. They are thus at the same time the agents, and the seeds, of discovery and change. By analogy it follows, as we have just seen, that it is not possible to have social systems, and thus groups, without deviance, without minorities, any more than it is possible to have systems without paradoxes or systems which prove all the propositions that they generate. If one has such a system in social psychology it is only by considering the group as closed.

On the other hand, change and adaptation to the external world, even if its remote cause lies in a general law of development, has as its immediate and obvious source the presence of active minorities. Without law there can be no system, and without minorities no change or adaptation. If my interpretation of the evidence and the difficulties of which I have written here is correct, the problem is yet more simple than that: how must the deviant individual or minority behave in order to achieve an impact on the group? At first sight the solution is just as simple. It consists of considering the deviant individual or the minority as a source of, and not just a target of, social influence.

Put like this, the question is in fact too simple. To understand why, it is necessary first of all to get rid of a confusion. It arises from my use of the words 'deviant' and 'minority' as if they were synonymous. Now, despite the deeply rooted habits of language and thought, they are neither synonymous nor do they designate the same thing. In order to re-establish their meaning we are obliged to ask ourselves what we understand by 'deviance', or again what is it that distinguishes a deviant from a minority. It will be seen later that we give to minority influence a larger meaning than to the influence of deviants. We must not lose ourselves in the labyrinth of definitions. Everyone knows, or believes he knows, the meaning of these concepts. A few intuitive observations will suffice. Upon reflection, it seems evident that deviants are individuals or groups who stray from the norms and beliefs of the group or society to which they belong. They may be recognised by their non-conforming behaviour, their challenging attitude to institutions or to those who embody them. To put it another way, they locate themselves at the fringe of the majority. They transgress laws and established values and resist all pressures upon them to conform. When one draws up a list of deviant individuals or groups one finds jumbled all together delinquents, drug addicts, the socially handicapped, gypsies, prostitutes, sexual deviants, and so on (Becker, 1963). They are all, according to the hallowed expression, *outsiders*. If one considers the different elements, one sees that what they have in common – what characterises them – is that they are, in Durkheim's terms, 'anomic' individuals or groups, that is, they trample beneath their feet accepted judgments, behavioural standards and opinions in spite of possessing few of their own. In brief, they oppose but do not propose. They transgress the norms but do not invent others. They disorganise without organising. They are characterised by an extreme or excessive indulgence in what society tolerates in small doses but forbids in large ones.

Now social minorities, in the political sense of the word in the last century, are individuals or groups that occupy a particular position, that have a clear preference for specific values. They defend something rather than being against something. They offer an alternative to existing opinions and beliefs, a different solution to the major problems of society. Such would have been the case then with Protestant sects and workers' organisations. Such is the case with *avant-garde* movements, with unorthodox currents of thought, with dissenters and protest movements. They pursue a definite goal. They are committed to a system of beliefs or ideas and act accordingly. One may fairly see them as challengers or adversaries, the more so in so far as they are active minorities. English historians call them 'antinomians'. The term is appropriate because we are in effect concerned with *antinomic* groups or individuals, opposing the dominant norms with contrasting norms. Moreover, they seek not to disorganise but to reorganise with respect to what they oppose. In brief, they wish to overturn the existing order of things so as to substitute not chaos but a different order.

In the course of the evolution of a group, and even in the life of an individual, one can clearly observe the passage from the situation of deviant to that of minority, and occasionally the reverse. But the two situations are distinct. They entail quite distinct attitudes, behaviours and psychological qualities. This was shown in a comparative analysis of the cases of Solzhenitsyn and Twardowski, the one an active dissident and the other a deviant in relation to the Soviet system (Moscovici, 1979).

I believe that these various brief considerations clarify the distance which separates deviants from minorities. We can define a minority by its antinomic position or by its numerical inferiority, but most accurately by both. Neither the positions adopted nor the number alone are sufficient to specify a minority. And to this it should be added that the label, by historical tradition, has the symbolic power of evoking images and giving rise to particular reactions. Taking these observations into account leads to our first conclusion. Most of the important concepts in social psychology envisage closed social systems without rivals or alternatives, located within a perspective of group–deviant interaction. On the other hand, the concepts which interest us concern the dialectics of relations between majorities and minorities. This presupposes open collective systems in which alternatives and rival social actors exist. But these remarks are too general in character. I will return to a more concrete level.

First, it is important to emphasise the distinction between deviants and active minorities and the necessity, ultimately, of exploring their respective psychologies. Next, the paradox to which I alluded may be resolved if one acknowledges that individuals and subgroups may be minorities and thus antinomic and not only, as has been the tendency, deviants and therefore anomic. Until such time as the contrary is proved, we should recognise, as history has taught us, that antinomic and anomic phenomena are quite different in nature. For us this represents a plausible and well-founded hypothesis. Finally, bearing this in mind, it seems unlikely that one would be able to transfer or extrapolate the basic results obtained in the classical studies on elimination of deviance or on conformity (de Montmollin, 1977), as they stand, to the study of minorities and innovation. In the same way, the influence of minorities should be recognised as possessing the capacity to change the group itself, to alter its norms and judgments. Or, to put it another way, it can make more acceptable what is rejected by the group, and transform what was the exception into the rule.

4. Some conceptual modifications required by the existence of minority influence

(i) We must accept the need to modify some concepts if these new elements are to be introduced into the field. There are two particular concepts which matter to us here. Let us describe them briefly. On the one hand, in classical theory the process of influence is identified with that of conformity, despite the limitations mentioned here – or at least conformity is regarded as fundamental. Thus other forms of influence are seen as being forms of conformity or else realised through conformity. In these terms innovation, for example, is presented or analysed as deviance or simple non-conformity. In this, social psychology follows sociology and particularly Merton's (1957) theory. For Merton, all behaviour directed to producing change is a form of deviant behaviour. When he studies deviant groups he takes as examples anomic groups: criminals, adolescents and so forth. But if social psychology is to follow sociology on this point it cannot acknowledge any place for minority influence, in the form we have just considered, nor for the type of innovation to which it tends. To put it more bluntly, such a view is circular. By taking conformity to be a fundamental and normal state, one is forced to see in each innovation a transgression and a deviation. Nevertheless, this reasoning can be reversed. Following Tarde, one can thus see in innovation a fundamental or normal state. Then conformity becomes a repression or regularisation of change, a derivative and secondary process.

On the other hand, the majority of theories have tended to associate influence with power. Accordingly, the more power one has the more influence one has. The same idea is expressed in the concept of dependence (Thibaut & Kelley, 1967). In this view, individuals are dependent on the group either for the information they need or for recognition of their competence or status. And these three resources, information, competence and status, are distributed in a very uneven manner. Or, to recall a well-known phrase, some individuals are more equal than others in these respects. Given such a state of social relations, it is natural to expect that those who depend on others to obtain one or all of these three resources will be influenced by those who possess them: the less competent by the more competent, people lower down the ladder in the group by people higher up, and so on. So, theoretically, minorities are lacking in both power and resources. It would follow that they could never exercise sufficient influence and would never be in a position to reverse the established hierarchy of values or opinions. This, in a very simplified form, is the case that I have put forward elsewhere in a more complete and documented fashion (Moscovici, 1976). Nevertheless, I hope to have said enough now for it to be clear why it was necessary to reject the identification of social influence with conformity – i.e. the conformity bias – and the equation of the phenomena of power with those of influence. Let us next look at the proposed modifications.

(ii) From its very beginnings social psychology has been dominated by a conformity bias. Social psychologists have held tenaciously to the idea that what they must explain is the undeniable fact that most people do, to some degree or another, submit to the pressures of society. It is presumed that people do so because doubt is a disquieting and unbalancing condition. Everyone will try to overcome doubt and achieve the certainty from which he or she can derive peace and satisfaction. And people will evidently not want to lose a balance once achieved and succumb to doubt again. Some people may arrive at this kind of certainty by their own means but those who cannot must rely on others. At this point they submit to others' influence, accept the judgments of others. Conformity could thus be defined as a kind of learning in situations of doubt or uncertainty.

But we can view doubt from another angle. It can arise from differences and disagreements, from conflicts of beliefs or ideas. Everyone is likely to have had this kind of experience since everyone does not necessarily think alike. And at a given moment one may come to admit that another's opinion is better than one's own. This shakes one's confidence and seems to put one's own ideas into question. This situation is sufficiently familiar for us to regard the following proposition as a basic assumption: influence is rooted in conflict and strives towards consensus. Once this consensus has been attained it produces what the American philosopher Peirce has called 'the fixation of beliefs' – a stabilisation of judgments and opinions and a feeling of internal and external control. To make things clearer, let us quote directly. In the famous article in which he asks the question of how beliefs may be fixed, he writes 'unless we make ourselves hermits, we shall necessarily influence each other's opinions, so that the problem is how to fix beliefs, not in the individual merely, but in the community (1934: 235). The underlying implication in this, quite remarkable from a philosopher of science, is that we cannot fix them alone. We are always obliged to rely on others. I will be returning to his ideas further on.

At the root of influence, therefore, is to be found a conflict that openly erupts when disagreement comes to light. Conscious of the disruption this tends to bring, men try to redefine their opinions, hoping thus to reduce the divide which, in one way or another, separates them. By so doing they open themselves to the influence of their fellows. Thus one could say that influence very much resembles a *tacit* negotiation. It is curious that the link between influence and negotiation has not been acknowledged before, though analogies immediately come to mind. One should not lose sight of the fact that the real issue of discussion is agreement or consensus. The majority puts all its effort into preserving the existing consensus. The minority, which can be very small indeed, is always free to reject it and to aspire to changing the order of things. When consensus is finally established it is clearly always in favour of one of the two parties, so each puts all its efforts into establishing the consensus in its favour. All its strength is required to marshal the decisive arguments, and this is just as true when conflict arises from opinions as when it concerns objective judgments. It necessarily provokes a controversy and a new shared decision.

What are we aiming for when we strive to persuade someone, if it is not to end a conflict we have provoked or to which we have been exposed? Most research in social psychology, whether concerned with decision making or influence, entails negotiation, be it internal or external to the group. In the course of these negotiations each participant tries to ensure that his point of view prevails. He therefore explores the grounds for consensus even though consensus appears to be out of the question. In this case, each type of conflict, depending on the factors which give rise to it and the adversaries involved, corresponds to a specific type of negotiation. Just as there are several results to which conflict can give rise, so there exist different modalities of negotiation tending towards these ends. I will describe them in a moment but I should first say that the assumption of conflict and negotiation has a further significance. Social influence is not to be equated with one of its forms. On the contrary, each of the modalities envisaged is as fundamental as the others; none has priority. Everything depends on the nature of the conflict and consequently on the nature of the negotiations that occur between members of the group or between the groups in a society.

(iii) Certainly no single modality of controlling conflict will be employed alone. In real life they will be applied in combination and they will act in concert, since groups and societies are engaged in several conflicts at once, pursuing multiple aims. Thus one group may try to increase the conformity of its members in the cultural domain but follow an innovating course in the political domain; for another the opposite may be the case. A group may wish to innovate at the level of social relations or at the intellectual level, while at the same time displaying conformity to the point of total inflexibility on the economic or religious level, and so on. In our analysis we have identified three modalities of influence: normalisation, conformity and innovation. I will describe each separately, to give an idea of their phenomenology.

Normalisation tends towards the avoidance of conflicts *via* compromises between individuals with divergent opinions. One may define it as a progressive change of behaviours or beliefs with the aim of establishing a shared norm. It is evident that an individual or group that observes an event or situation or object, whether ambiguous or not, may form a particular impression of it and establish its own norm. This judgment, once formed, is bound to be confronted with the judgments or norms of other individuals or groups, given that it will not exist in a social vacuum. The various parties then discover that their viewpoints do not coincide; to their great surprise they disagree precisely when they thought they would find agreement. This plurality of norms creates the possibility of conflict and with it two negative consequences. First, the disagreement has a tendency to change the external opposition into internal tension and from this doubts and instabilities in beliefs and norms are born. Second, reality is now tainted with ambiguity where once it seemed to be clear, and it appears to become more ambiguous than it is. This is a very disturbing situation from which the individuals or groups concerned will want to escape. They attempt to reduce their disagreement and to mitigate its effects *via* a consensus which satisfies everyone.

There is one point here that I must emphasise. What constrains people to bring their viewpoints closer together is the prospect of conflict and its potential repercussions. Each person is either disposed to, or resigned to, concessions as far as his own 'truth' or beliefs are concerned, as soon as it is apparent that others are not going to try and impose their 'truths' or beliefs, and in so far as no 'external' or 'impersonal' force intervenes to constrain the participants to accept an 'objective' truth. The concessions these individuals make are thus founded on reciprocity and lead progressively to consensus.

Another decisive factor, in the absence of a clear majority, could be the search for a balance between majority and minority in an attempt to reach a mutual compromise. There is thus a twofold reason for avoiding conflict. On the one hand, no particular path to a solution appears to have any preferential status; and on the other, psychological and social factors prevent the different participants from imposing their own views. In his pioneering work, Sherif (1935) studied this modality of influence with great insight. He actually showed how beliefs or norms are formed or fixed just by studying their averaging through gradual compromises and their successive stabilisation. The best analogy I can conceive of for normalisation is market force. Prices are fixed by a game of offers and counter-offers, by subtle negotiations, until a price emerges. Once this is established it regulates all the subsequent buying and selling transactions.

Conformity is a modality of influence which develops in situations where there are definite majorities and minorities and clear differences between legitimate and illegitimate opinions and beliefs. As soon as a human group allows certain things and forbids others, labels certain ways of seeing things as 'normal' and others as 'deviant', as soon as the failure to think like everyone else is categorised as an antisocial act, then it becomes difficult to arrive at compromises. Thus one finds oneself in the presence of a conflict between mutually exclusive perspectives. The orthodox viewpoint of the majority clashes with the heterodox viewpoint of the minority. The usual way of resolving this conflict is by submission of the latter to the former. Deviance is re-absorbed or limited. Conformity is the process which allows this to be accomplished.

It is not necessary to discuss this further here since it is given detailed treatment in many textbooks. Asch's (1956) work on majority effects, that of Festinger and his colleagues on pressures to uniformity (1950), that by Schachter (1951) on the re-absorption of deviance and, finally, the work of Deutsch & Gerard (1955) on informational and normative influence, are now classics. All deal in detail with this submission to the group and the rejection of individuals who resist or deviate.

The process of innovation in its 'authentic' form is located at the other end of the spectrum from conformity. It can be found in various forms but it is at its most straightforward when a minority, with no advantages in terms of social status or resources, tries to secure the dominance of its own beliefs, opinions or behaviours. These are obviously going to be beliefs, opinions or behaviours which are in the context regarded as unorthodox or new. In this case two types of situation may occur. In the first there is either no explicit consensus or only a vague consensus. Under these conditions individuals tend to waver or to be indifferent towards the other party. As they become conscious of the differences which separate them, and if they have no reason or incentive to adopt an aggressive stance in support of their own viewpoint, their first inclination will be to try to avoid a conflict by offering to compromise. The process of mutual concessions will nevertheless be blocked if one of the parties, a group member or a minority, refuses to move in the direction of compromise and sticks to its own judgments, beliefs, etc. By taking such a position this individual (or minority) not only challenges the 'logical' solution, which would be to average opinions, but also imposes his own preferences. The fact that he adopts such a position is not just negative, in the sense that he refuses to compromise; it can also have a positive function. In effect, he offers a solution as valid as the other, and one which has the advantage of being clear and definite. Of course the individual or minority makes some concessions – but to be able to accept them the adversary must do rather more. Consensus is thus established in favour of the minority, and closer to its position than to that of the majority. For reasons of this kind a resolute minority that knows what it wants and is ready to accept conflict when others want to avoid it can succeed in influencing the majority. It may also influence other individuals or minorities that are less resolute and/or that hold beliefs or preferences less strongly than it does itself.

In the second type of situation the majority does hold a definite viewpoint and does demonstrate resolution. On its side the minority holds a different view and consciously tries to change that of the majority. When an individual or subgroup resists rather than conforms, and when it not only resists but proposes something different, it creates conflict. Such conflict has the effect on the one hand of rupturing consensus, and on the other of introducing an alternative to the dominant solution in the group. By maintaining a constant pressure a minority can succeed in making its own viewpoint as familiar as the well-established one. It thus forces everyone to take its alternative into consideration. In addition, by refusing to compromise the minority increases the intensity of the conflict and demonstrates its unwillingness to make concessions. In other words, it makes abundantly clear that its principal aim is to wring concessions from the majority. In view of this we could say that individuals or groups that innovate exercise influence by creating or increasing conflict. The tacit negotiation that takes place revolves around the changes the majority is prepared to make in order to arrive at a consensus with the minority. It is this that characterises innovation as a modality of influence. It is centred on the virtual or actual creation of conflicts, just as normalisation is centred on their avoidance and conformity upon the control or reduction of conflict.

By considering such varied types of influence, we enlarge the field of phenomena to be studied and comparisons to be made. Here, as elsewhere, extreme types also constitute pure types and provide for a more informative contrast. In idealised terms, innovation appears to be a creator of conflicts, while conformity tends to re-absorb them. The goal of the former is social change by means of accentuating differences, that of the latter social control by means of increasing uniformity. Or again, innovation aims at introducing new behaviours or beliefs and conformity at stabilising existing ones. A longer list of contrasts could certainly be made. But we observe that in reality our entire social and scientific system is based on a cycle of alternation between the two. A product or idea differentiating a social category is invented. This product, or this idea, is first resisted, then adopted and finally becomes commonplace. It ends by being imposed on everyone, by creating total uniformity, and this leads to further invention and thus the cycle is repeated.

Recently I have found that there is some analogy between these modalities of influence and the methods conceived by Peirce. Examining the methods by which beliefs could become fixed in philosophy and science, the American philosopher describes three possibilities in addition to the scientific method: the method of authority, the method of preference and the method of tenacity. The first, which possesses all the characteristics of conformity, is

...the path of peace. Certain non-conformities are permitted; certain others (considered unsafe) are forbidden. These are different in different countries and ages; but wherever you are, let it be known that you seriously hold a tabooed belief and you may be perfectly sure of being treated with a cruelty less brutal but more refined than hunting you like a wolf. (Peirce, 1934: 245)

The second method approximates to normalisation; one may need to fall back on it:

as long as no better method can be applied, it ought to be followed since it is then the expression of instinct which must be the ultimate cause of belief in all cases...It makes of inquiry something similar to the development of taste; but taste unfortunately is always more or less a matter of fashion. (1934: 241)

Finally the third method, that of tenacity, possesses several of the features we have enumerated with respect to innovation and minority influence. To be sure, as Peirce observes, 'the social impulse is against it' and to follow it 'we cling tenaciously not merely to believing but to believing just what we do believe' (pp. 235, 236). But in his comparison of these various methods, it is this last that he admires and approves.

I introduce this analogy between the types of influence that I have distinguished and the methods described by Peirce to add some support to the claim that they are relevant to any circumstances in which individuals or groups compare their beliefs or their visions of reality. This includes that sphere in which opinions and ideas are most rational and logical. But I also wish to give some indication of their differences. These, I believe, are clear enough when one begins to consider the facts objectively in an area where the characteristics of conformity and innovation are explicitly contrasted.

Further on other analogies will be noted, particularly between what we call consistency and what Peirce calls tenacity.

(iv) In our observations on the conditions in which a minority can exercise influence some particular points must be stressed. The first is that these minorities have either little or no power. They are dominated by, and dependent on, others. But if this is so we are confronted by a difficulty. Most current theories begin with the notion of a connection between power and influence. Whoever has power has influence, so it is implicitly assumed. Nevertheless, minorities lacking in power do still have influence. In examining what happens in the countries of Eastern Europe one finds no shortage of examples showing that power and influence sometimes run counter to one another; power can be an obstacle to influence. In any case, I am reasonably convinced that this assumption has prevented social psychology from giving much-needed attention to minorities and innovation, or even from understanding the phenomenon of deviance in all its richness.

Now one is led by the logic of the evidence to question the interdependence which is supposed to unite power and influence, to create the narrow dependence of the latter on the former. Let us say that their independence seems necessary and even self-evident. Who could fail to be aware of the number of social movements, or clearly minority groups, that have managed to make an impact quite out of proportion to their numbers or their power? We need only think for a moment of feminists or ecologists, of Protestants and Jews, to appreciate this fact. It seems, nevertheless, to judge by some reactions (Levine, 1980), that to propose such a separation contradicts the general consensus or what passes for a paradigm in social psychology (French & Raven, 1959). If it were true I would have failed completely in my efforts to be both careful and clear. I would have had no success in tracing the arguments which make this separation tenable, at least provisionally and in as much as one proceeds heuristically.

Yet it is a phenomenon we observe in present-day life. In all known societies we find a division between the apparatus of power and that of ideology. The men dedicated to the administration of power and entrusted with the task of legitimising it, and those dedicated to propagating beliefs, ideas or political programmes, are not the same. Without the latter the former could not accomplish their task in such a smooth and effective fashion. For a long time it has been said that religion and education are the *instrumenta regni*, but instruments which differ from the police, the army or the tax collector. Obviously the two types sometimes go hand in hand, but this is far from being the rule and it does not mean that the actions of one are in direct proportion to the actions of the other. On the contrary, whenever the machinery of authority and that of ideology confront one another, as was the case with the Catholic church in the middle ages, or the Bolshevik party in the present century, the ascendancy of the latter tends to decline. It is as if there exists beyond their convergence a strong antithesis between power and influence. The aim of the former is external control, that of the latter internal control. In their pure or ideal forms one presupposes inequality and dependence while the other excludes them.

In reality, if influence as we envisage it is basically negotiation, then having power, far from representing an advantage, can in the long term become a disadvantage. In one of the most famous studies on the question, Shelling vigorously criticised those theories which suggest that the final result always favours the powerful, the strong or the clever.

It does of course if these qualities are defined to mean only that negotiations are won by those who win. But if the terms imply that it is an advantage to be more intelligent and more skilled in debate, or to have more financial resources, more military resources then the term does a disservice. These qualities are by no means universal in bargaining situations; they have often a contrary value (1956: 282).

They are, to employ a familiar term, counterproductive.

This then encourages us to consider, instead of the association between the two phenomena which the current paradigm demands, their contrasts. I would argue that the contrasts are much more significant because they show us much more clearly the nature of the relationship between power and influence. Let us however backtrack for a moment and examine the consequences of associating them. By setting up power and influence as cause and effect we logically end up with the idea that where there is more power there is more influence. This means that only the powerful are influential. They enjoy the enviable capacity to control and change everything. This position excludes or limits the possibility that influence can be exercised by a minority, and in a quite logical fashion. The consequence underlies the only attempt in social psychology to come to grips with the process of innovation, that of Hollander (1958). He raised the question of how it is that an individual can become a leader and innovate. According to Hollander, this individual must first acquire power or competence (idiosyncrasy credit) if he is subsequently to have the right to reject the existing norms without being immediately accused of deviance. And he acquires this credit by conformity to the group. Once invested with authority he can introduce his own changes and also encourage others to change and follow suit. Here relations of dependence are a necessary preliminary to innovation and the latter is a direct extension of conformity. Power then appears as a reserve of influence and influence as spent power. At no point is there any question of minorities. Indeed the concepts involved allow no place for them.

It is obvious that this vision of the phenomena is limited. We have seen in recent times too many individuals regarded as 'incompetent', or minorities without power or credit overthrow political regimes or overturn cultural values, not to be conscious of the limitations here. The history books contain many thousand more examples. But no great effort is needed to see that by making influence dependent on power and innovation on conformity, this kind of hypothesis expresses an elitist conception of change: it is from the top down. In other words, all innovation within a group is nothing but another facet of the submission of inferiors to superiors. It would thus abolish the distinctions between anomy and antinomy, between violations of beliefs and conflicts of beliefs, with respect to the process in which challenges to consensus lead to new and different belief systems.

A conception more faithful to the reality and variety of social situations should acknowledge first of all that individuals and groups exercise influence when they cannot exercise power, the minority because it has no power, the majority because it is prevented from exercising it by laws or internal dissension. Peirce describes this relation as self-evident. He writes:

Let the people turn out and tar-and-feather such men, or let inquisitions be made into the manner of thinking of suspected persons, and when they are found guilty of forbidden beliefs, let them be subjected to some signal punishment. When complete agreement could not otherwise be reached, a general massacre of all who have thought in a certain way has proved a very effective means of settling opinion in a country. If the power to do this is wanting, let a list of opinions be drawn up, to which men of the least independence of thought can assent, and let the faithful be required to accept all these propositions, in order to segregate them as radically as possible from the influence of the rest of the world (1934: 236).

This statement carries the distinct flavour of the dissenters who founded America. It retains all the vigour of a new, unencumbered perspective on the undiluted reality of human affairs. He describes, without pulling any punches and with great simplicity, the choices that confront groups and he indicates what the choice has to be for those who respect both individuality and collective freedom. That these choices can be brutal in character we all know, though they are not in any concrete sense specifically envisaged in our theories. But if account were to be taken of this character it would be seen that something basic separates power from influence and renders all reduction of one to the other superficial. The former has, in truth, a deep affinity with violence while the latter, beyond any accidental association, excludes it almost entirely. We are thus led to recognise a plurality in the relations between power and influence.

The four possibilities are shown diagrammatically in figure 1. The first case is clearly recognisable as that of a society or party in which a dominant minority retains all the means of coercion and reward. But its hold on the

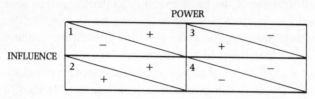

Figure 1.

beliefs and judgments of the population is either nil or negative. There is a plethora of illustrations in the contemporary world. Today's Poland would be an exemplary instance, given that it is a country where issues of ideology and persuasion are part of the official doctrine and practice of the regime. Case 2 is that of political or prophetic minorities at the point when they reach the summit and attain their ultimate goals. This would have been the case, at least if we are to believe the history books, of the American Independence movement, the Russian Communists and most nationalist movements. It is even more often the case when a scientific or artistic school triumphs, at the moment when it is imitated to the point of turning into a fashion, when rewards, positions, honours are accumulated in the hands of those who were a short time before unknown (or shunned) outsiders. Within psychology the psychoanalytic movement has been and remains the classic illustration of influence without precedent in history.

Case 3 has already been mentioned. It represents the circumstances of most active minorities in our time (ecologists, feminists, radicals, students, racial groups, etc.) that have achieved a profound transformation in existing values and perspectives. In the future it will be seen that one of the failures of Western democracy resides precisely in the gulf between the profound hold minorities exercise and the tiny share of authority conceded to them. The result will be a growing estrangement between systems for the government of men and those for the management of their beliefs. Finally, case 4 represents sects, deviant minorities, miniparties, rejected or isolated groups. Their deficits on both levels separate them from the rest of society, isolating them in the interstices and margins when they are not broken up or reduced to pure and simple delinquency.

The plausible correspondence between the four cases in figure 1 and real events argues in favour of a less rigid view of relations between the two fundamental phenomena we have been examining here. In any case, we may conclude that there is some justification in viewing the phenomena of minority influence, its causes and its effects, as distinct from power and dependence in relation to the majority.

The entire set of arguments on which we base this conclusion is perhaps shot through with errors and mistakes, but for the present we will assume that it is evident and sufficient.

5. Influence and styles of behaviour

(i) If the theory of minority influence does include some new concepts, as I have suggested here, the most important is without doubt that of behavioural style. Although it is easy to grasp intuitively, to appreciate its centrality one has to begin by understanding the theoretical questions the concept seeks to resolve. Let us start with the minority as it appears within the group or within society. We have in mind, of course, an active minority here. It defends a position and has something to say. Why give it any attention? It has no recognised competence. Nobody has any confidence in its declarations or its actions. Its judgments cannot be considered as offering any valid information. What is more, the content of its utterances is bizarre. At first glance, then, it seems to concern no one. It is laughed at or ignored. Those who happen to give the minority further attention nevertheless continue to require further reasons why it should be taken seriously. What then can it offer others? On what grounds can it suggest ideas contrary to accepted reality? Why does it hold out against the drift, against the spontaneous good sense of men, against the evidence? There are many questions of this kind which serve as excuses for rejecting everything that comes from the minority. The chances of it piercing the solid bastion of the majority seem minimal. And yet it succeeds.

Such success cannot be explained by recourse to the familiar concept of dependence as the origin of any influence exercised in a group. This is purely and simply because dependence on the minority is feeble to non-existent – indeed it is negative. Besides, we are not likely to find among the properties of this supposed cause anything which could make an individual or subgroup without credibility more credible, or anything which would make universally rejected judgments more convincing. It certainly could not be numbers or authority; the minority, by definition, possesses neither. We must therefore look for some other cause capable of producing such a 'miracle', such a total turn-about. It may be found without difficulty by recalling that a long-established method of persuasion does exist, namely rhetoric, and by envisaging change as an internal psychological process. If it is also accepted that this process is to a large degree 'irrational' and symbolic, it is not thereby deprived of its efficacy – quite the opposite.

Without going into further details, we may see that the origin of a minority's influence is its behavioural style. The concept refers to the organisation of responses according to a particular pattern which has recognisable meaning for those to whom the responses are addressed. One can codify and learn behavioural style in such a way that it is clear to everyone and elicits the appropriate reaction, in exactly the same way as does placing stress on a particular word or making a particular gesture. Repeating the same word or the same gesture can indicate rigidity in one context, certainty in another. Each style of behaviour projects an internal state of mind or feeling (thoughtfulness, anger, etc.) into the environment. Everyone can interpret and make predictions about an interaction with a person on the basis of behavioural style. One could say that each message presented, whether in the form of a judgment or a behaviour, produces in us a twofold impact. On the one hand, it furnishes us with information about the belief or perception concerned: this person is for or against nuclear energy, believes that two lines are equal or unequal, etc. On the other hand, behavioural style allows us to infer that this is a person strongly committed to his pro- or anti-nuclear position, who is prepared or reluctant to revise his judgment about the lines, etc. The recipient of such a message is thus affected at one and the same time by what is stated explicitly and by what is transmitted implicitly, by the content of what the person says and by its relation to the form (commitment, conviction, etc.).

Furthermore, style of behaviour exercises two types of psychologically connected pressure, a referential pressure related to the response advocated by the source and an inferential pressure linked to the manner in which the responses are given or transmitted. It is quite obviously one thing to have an extreme opinion and another to uphold it consistently, to make it clearly understood that one will make no concessions. The secrets of behavioural style may seem futile to some people, but surely not to any individual sensitive to the ways in which languages and cultures function. We usually place the emphasis on the informational (or content) elements in behaviour, but its symbolic and stylistic features represent another dimension worthy of study. We are only at the beginning here and we are sometimes reproached for a lack of precise proposals; the familiar and already understood always seems to be better established. However, a critical examination reveals that this is scarcely the case. We are still a long way from achieving a clear picture of the nature of dependence, of competence, and so forth; and it is to be hoped that with the progress of research we shall also arrive at more detailed conclusions about behavioural style.

(ii) We have elsewhere described (Moscovici, 1976) several behavioural styles – autonomy, objectivity, loyalty, etc. The most significant is consistency. It always indicates strong conviction, commitment. It shows that the minority believes in what it says and that its belief is fixed. Let us suppose that an individual or group expresses the same idea or preserves the same form of behaviour in all circumstances. This provides evidence of an undeniable conviction in what is said or done. Such singleness of purpose, such confidence, never fails to make an impression or indeed to attract others. Everyone recognises that a consistent individual or group knows what it wants, is willing to pay the price of its actions, will reject any concession to the majority, and will in no case give in to pressure. By the same token this behaviour preserves the internal strength of the minority itself. Such, for example, was the attitude of the Baptists, Quakers and other dissident English groups in the eighteenth century when the government approached them:

for they offered to the more yielding and undecided members among them the temptation or possibility of forming intermediate positions or at least of attenuating their contrasts. Every concession of the other side, which is partial anyway, threatens the uniformity in the opposition of all members and hence the unity of their coherence on which a fighting minority must insist without compromise. (Simmel, 1955: 97)

It is as if the individual or the group has renounced all freedom of choice. It can no longer be shaken or induced to make concessions. Since it can no longer give in, it is therefore up to the adversary (the majority) to give in if there is to be any consensus. We think of the, often silent, demonstrators who chain themselves to a railing to express their intention not to be moved. But here the chains are mental, more difficult to break. The position is impregnable. In general their manner of speaking or acting clearly indicates that they expect the other to give in to their wishes and make the concessions. With respect to the tacit negotiation pursued, the minority, by appearing fully engaged, applies the procedure described by Shelling:

In bargaining, the commitment is a device to leave the last clear chance to decide the outcome with the other party, in a manner that he fully appreciates; it is to relinquish further initiatives, having rigged the incentive so that the other party chooses in one's favor (1956: 294).

One can say the same of all consistent behaviour. It confers an advantage on the group or the individual that displays it, for two reasons in addition to those I have already described. On the one hand it bears witness to an unusual capacity to brave a conflict and pursue it to its end. On the other it rejects responsibility for resolving this conflict and places it on others. It thus exercises a strong pressure on them to change and make concessions. 'The power of a negotiation', Shelling wrote elsewhere, 'often rests on a manifest inability to make concessions and meet demands' (1975: 19). This incapacity derives from the conviction of the minority. It is certain it knows the truth, sure it is correct. Thus, as a dissident in a socialist country declared:

I have always believed that it is not unimportant that one should be resolute, sure of oneself and one's cause, and that deep within oneself one will not hesitate when the time comes to take decisions. (Bahro, 1979: 62, trans.)

To return to the question with which we began, we know that the majority has every reason to ignore, to distrust or laugh at, to regard as false or invalid, the positions or opinions of the minority. In the eyes of the majority this is as it should be; the minority is regarded as deviant and thus dangerous. Now the consistency of the minority, the fact that the same positions and the same opinions are maintained, its degree of commitment, all these have a meaning. Whatever reservations we have, there is nevertheless something sufficiently valuable in these judgments or these opinions for human beings to devote to them much energy and to take many risks. Unless one assumes that these individuals or minorities are dishonest or foolish – and this may happen – one feels constrained, if not to go along with them then at least to consider what in other circumstances one would reject. This is why behavioural style, and above all consistency, transforms the worth of the substance of what the minority asserts so that it may occasionally achieve some impact. Besides the fact that in the long term the minority does attract attention through its behavioural style, it also projects a distinct social identity. For a group as for an individual, 'the identity of man consists in the consistency of what he does and thinks, and consistency is the intellectual character of a thing; that is, it is expressing something' (Peirce, 1934: 264). This may be one of the reasons why dissenters are viewed as more dynamic, confident and even more accurate, than conformers (Morris & Miller, 1975).

Consistency also has its limitations. It may take on negative connotations – narrow-mindedness, obstinacy, rigidity, etc. (Mugny, 1982). But on the other hand it strikes a chord and meets a desire people have for simple and clear opinions to explain the world in which they live. In the light of these considerations we can understand why Cato the elder, concluding all his speeches with the famous exhortation 'We must destroy Carthage', ended by convincing the Roman Senate. An extensive series of experiments (Nemeth, Wachtler & Endicott, 1977; Mugny, 1982) have confirmed our hypothesis here; behavioural style produces influence and is one of its origins. Most of this research has considered only the minority but we have shown that this proposition is generally true. In other words, consistency even explains conformity to a majority. This has previously been erroneously attributed to the dependence of the individual on the group, as in the famous Asch experiments discussed above. On average, the naive subjects conformed to the group in one out of every three responses (32%). Asch himself, together with all other social psychologists, attributed this significant degree of yielding to the individual's dependence on the group.

On the basis of our own hypothesis we can offer another interpretation. We would regard this conformity as due to the consistency of the majority responses. This consistency is manifest in the fact that each one of its members gives the same response. On the one hand this transmits information about the stimuli – they are unequal. This information is incorrect. On the other, the response is unanimous. It expresses the conviction of the group regarding the correctness of its judgment and the fact that it will not change, no matter what the response of the naive, and thus deviant, individual.

Now the interesting question is the following: is conformity due to the effects of being the majority in the group or to its consistency? If the first alternative is correct, then no matter what the number of individuals above three, the number of conforming responses should remain about constant or be very slightly reduced. If the second of these alternatives is correct then, we would anticipate a rapid fall in influence when the majority becomes inconsistent. Let us suppose, as has been the case in some experiments, that there are two kinds of group. In the one the majority members are unanimous. In the other they are not. Their respective effects are consistent with our hypothesis. In the first kind of group, *regardless* of the size of the majority, there is no change in the percentage of conforming responses. In other words there is no relation between the quantity of dependence and the quantity of conformity. In the second kind of group, when a stooge is instructed to break the unanimity the percentage of conforming responses falls rapidly to a very low level. Briefly then, the evidence supports the conclusion that behavioural style, whatever its modality, is a reasonable candidate as the cause of influence.

If this claim is accepted then some important questions can be given a fresh treatment. Why do behavioural styles have such an impact? What is the relationship between behavioural styles and status? Are there behavioural styles specific to a majority or minority? Does the meaning of a behavioural style change depending on whether it is adopted by a minority or a majority? And so on. The fact that it does raise so many questions demonstrates how seminal such a concept can be. In any event, a minority can change a stigma into an asset by its consistency and its resolution.

6. The hidden persuasion of minorities

When we seek to construct a social psychological theory we should first choose from amongst the properties accessible to observation those which we take to be primary and submit them to experimental test. This is what we have done with behavioural styles, and particularly with consistency, with the aim of redefining the causal factor in influence. We have seen that it is a general property and thus independent of power, competence or type of influence. Furthermore it has a psychological character (as have prestige, charisma, commitment, etc.) and it has a conventional meaning and thus a social value. This first step has been accomplished in the three preceding sections in which we have considered the causes of minority influence.

The next step is to define the effects, and thereby the manner in which change in opinions and judgments is produced. The specific character of minority influence may usefully be examined by contrasting it with that of majority influence, but it must be clear from the start that it is not a matter of deciding which of the two has the greater influence. Firstly, the meaning of this quantity is not identical for a minority and a majority. Thus a minority that influences 10 or 15 per cent of people may be judged to have had a considerable impact (and could win elections on this basis). However, a majority which influences 30 per cent clearly has had a lesser impact than would have been expected. Secondly, quantities alone give us no clues as to the structure of a phenomenon. Mechanical phenomena are not distinguished from thermal phenomena by the fact that the latter involve more energy than the former, but by the fact that one kind is reversible and the other irreversible and that they therefore obey different laws.

Let us begin our conjectures with the observation that majorities and minorities both produce conflicts of opinions or beliefs and that both exercise influence. The conflict does not proceed in the same fashion in each case. In the case of a majority the individual on whom influence is exercised feels deviant. He wonders why he is failing to see or to think like the other members of the group. Usually he makes no serious attempt to solve this problem by going back to the disputed object or reality, since this is already familiar to him. And in principle the responses of the majority to the object or reality should be accepted. As the proverb says, several pairs of eyes are better than one. All he can reasonably do to discover the reasons for the disagreement is to undertake a process of *comparison* between his responses and those of the others, particularly if these others are unanimous. As in principle he cannot exert pressure on them, he is tempted to make concessions. He feels impelled to find a consensus, even if this consensus is not in fact justified.

This is not all. It may be supposed that each individual who finds he is deviant forms the conjecture that the majority is 'right' and he himself is 'wrong'. Thus his doubts increase and he comes to believe that his concessions are merited. When, on the other hand, the individual is confronted by a minority he assumes from the outset that it is the minority's responses that are 'deviant' or 'incorrect'. He has no reason to doubt his own responses; by definition they are correct, they conform to reality. His first reaction would therefore be to laugh off the minority, to reject what they say. But if they persist, and do so in a resolute fashion, then the group member may begin to ask 'How can this minority see what it sees and think what it thinks?' To resolve this problem members of the group engage in a process of *validation*. That is to say, they compare the responses of the minority with the reality to which they refer. By trying, in the course of interaction, to see what the minority sees and to think what it thinks, they change without really being aware of it. As a consequence, when each member of the majority finds himself confronted with the same object alone, he perceives it and judges it in a way that is closer to the minority point of view. It appears, in other words, that his own point of view is modified without him being conscious of it.

It may be an overstatement, but not a complete misrepresentation, to say that when an individual is in disagreement with the majority his attention centres on what people *say*. When, on the other hand, the individual is in disagreement with a minority, his entire attention is directed towards what they *see* or *think*. One may therefore suppose that majority influence will be confined primarily to the period of social interaction. The individual subsequently finds himself relatively unchanged with respect to the object of controversy. Minority influence, in contrast, persists beyond the social interaction. The individual has changed in a positive or negative direction and no longer perceives the object in the same way.

To this conjecture must be added another. In the negotiation and resolution of a conflict people are inclined to follow the most direct path. If this path is blocked then they follow a less direct one. In influence situations there always exist both a public and a private path to change or yielding. All the evidence suggests that in conformity situations the public path is the more direct. Confronted with a majority, the individual may debate with his own conscience. But the best way for him to resolve his external and internal conflict is to give in, to change his public response. At the same time nothing prevents him keeping his private opinion intact. It is thus possible to conform and resist conformity at the same time. He gives to the group what is due to it and preserves his individuality. This is what we call *compliance behaviour*. A large number of experiments confirm that public responses, those which can be observed by other individuals in the group, are more conforming than private responses (Jones & Gerard, 1967). So, to put it more concretely, people change their opinions or judgments and they give in to the group during social interaction, but after the interaction, when they are alone again, they tend to return to their own opinions and judgments.

When we are talking about an innovation advanced by a minority the individual member of the group finds himself in the inverse situation. Now it is the public path to a resolution of the conflict that is blocked. It is difficult to make an open concession, to change his behaviour or his opinions in public. On the one hand, people, even when they waver, feel that they are 'correct' since they belong to the majority. On the other hand, they want to avoid becoming 'antinomic' or 'deviant' and particularly to be seen as such, even if they are inclined to accept the views of the minority. Thus the only acceptable way for them to reduce the conflict is in the private domain, through a change in private responses. We have called this *conversion behaviour* (Moscovici, 1980).

(i) Before considering any experiments or drawing any, necessarily provisional, conclusions, some details require clarification. The problem of detecting what type of change is produced by social influence has been around for a long time. In particular it has been asked under what conditions this change is 'internal' as opposed to 'external', 'superficial' as opposed to 'authentic'. In a classic article, Kelman (1958) distinguished three forms of change: internalisation, identification and compliance. According to him, the first results from acceptance of information from a competent source. This type of change is regarded as relatively durable because of the process of integrating the new information into the cognitive system. The second, identification, represents a change of attitude produced when a person feels linked to an attractive and likeable source. But his change of attitude only continues so long as the attractive source remains salient. Finally, compliance is a change of attitude produced by a powerful source. It only persists while the source retains control over the recipient of the message through its power to administer rewards and punishments.

It may be seen that we are dealing here with a taxonomy of phenomena and an analysis of processes. It is possible to link internalisation and conversion behaviour, for the latter also appears to involve a lasting change in which individuals internalise the judgments of the minority. But although this link has some justification it should not be allowed to obscure the differences or the particular character of conversion. The reasons are obvious. First, the minority is not considered an expert or an attractive or likeable source (Nemeth & Wachtler, 1973). It is found to exercise its influence when it is no longer present. From this follows our hypothesis that *conversion is a means of resolving a conflict which has been internalised*. Moreover, it should not be forgotten that real behaviour can be involved here in the sense that it has a social meaning in the religious, political and even scientific areas (Kuhn, 1962), whereas internalisation as such refers to a condition without obvious social meaning.

(ii) Having settled these details we may now consider the experiments. Here two types of data are relevant. In a series of investigations, Mugny (1982) presented his subjects with one message reflecting a 'rigid' position and another reflecting a 'flexible' position, both extolling a minority point of view. The effects of the messages on individuals' attitudes were assessed by two series of questions: direct questions relating to the content of the message that had just been read, and indirect questions dealing with connected subjects not directly included in the message. A change of response in the first category thus reflected a direct influence. A change in the second category indicated an indirect influence. Conversion is reflected in the differences between direct and indirect influence. This means that though individuals may have been persuaded by the minority they do not give in, but they do modify their opinions following a kind of internal debate on a much larger cognitive scale.

All these experiments had the following result (Papastamou, 1979): the flexible minority produced almost as many changes of opinion on direct as indirect questions. In other words, its direct and indirect influence were just about equal. There was as much private change as public. Wolf (1979) has obtained a similar result in an experiment concerned with decisions taken in small groups. In contrast, the rigid minority produced little change of response on the direct questions, in fact none, but considerably more change in the indirect responses. Its indirect influence was thus always significantly greater than its direct influence. This clearly shows that the less individual members of the majority reduce the difference at a public level, the more they reduce it at a private level by a shift towards the connected content. On the whole, where the path to direct change is blocked we witness a process of influence, of more widereaching cognitive change.

The second set of data concerns perception of colours. In a series of experiments a minority consisting of two stooges asserted in front of a majority of naive subjects that the blue slides presented to them were in fact green. One result was particularly striking. Individuals subjected to this influence had a tendency to give more 'green' responses in a private context than in a public one (Moscovici, Lage & Naffrechoux, 1969). It is as though while they were assembled together in a group they continued to call 'blue' what they had begun to see as 'green'. What is more, the less they gave the deviant reply in the public situation, the more they gave it when they were alone. To determine whether this attitude involves an authentic perceptual change, Moscovici & Personnaz (1980) conducted a further experiment. Subjects were shown a series of blue slides which the experimenter's stooge publicly identified as green. Depending on the instructions given, this stooge was made to appear to represent the majority in one condition and the minority in another. A measure of 'authentic' influence on perception was derived from the chromatic after-image. We know that if an individual fixates on a white screen after having fixated for a few seconds on a particular colour, he will see the complementary colour on the screen. In this case the relevant complementary colours were yellow-orange (for blue) and red-purple (for green).

From our knowledge of this effect two predictions can be made. Firstly, if subjects have been mainly influenced in their public verbal responses, the chromatic after-image will be in the yellow-orange range of the spectrum. Secondly, if subjects really have modified their perceptions, even though not influenced in their verbal responses, the chromatic after-image will be closer to red-purple. The chromatic after-image judgment was obviously given in private. As expected, we found a very low percentage of 'green' responses (5%). However, subjects that had been confronted with a minority actually saw the colour complementary to green with a significantly greater frequency than subjects that had been confronted with a majority. In this latter case, in fact, we found no modification in the perception of the colours. This effect confirms that we had achieved a 'hidden' influence of which the subjects were not aware. Personnaz (1981) examined this paradigm again, this time measuring perceptual responses with a spectroscope, and replicated these results. Doms & Van Avermaet (1980) have also replicated the experiments and found the same phenomena. But they note that, when the source of influence is a majority, there is also a significant degree of chromatic after-image effect. This result presents us with a problem because it shows that we have yet to identify the exact conditions under which conversion behaviour occurs. As we have remarked elsewhere following this experiment (Moscovici, 1980), this behaviour is likely to be associated with minority influence without necessarily being exclusive to it.

A parallel series of observations is of interest here. In an earlier experiment (Moscovici & Neve, 1971) we showed that 'those absent are in the right': that is, a minority is less influential during the interaction than afterwards. In most of the experiments based on the chromatic after-image, we asked subjects to make a series of judgments after which the experimenter's stooge left the testing room and they found themselves alone. Now we have established quite systematically that instead of reverting to their individual judgments, as happens with compliance, the subjects tend on the contrary to shift closer to the responses of the experimenter's stooge, which is to say the minority. In sum, the individual is more influenced when the source is less salient than when it is more salient. This demonstrates the contrast between compliance and conversion behaviours. In the former those absent are wrong and in the latter the absentees are correct.

These analyses, like the experiments they have generated, certainly have other dimensions, but these need not concern us here. They offer a conclusion which, despite its hypothetical character, has some significance for this area of research. It is that the influence of the minority is associated with conversion and that of the majority with compliance. In more concrete terms, we understand by this that minorities begin by exercising on the majority a hidden influence, an influence of which the latter need not necessarily be aware. In effect they produce an unconscious influence which emerges and becomes conscious only after a certain time. If one had the means to examine things in detail one would perhaps perceive that, in reality, members of the majority do not resist at the outset, because they are convinced that their opinions are right and those of the minority wrong and not to be taken seriously. They only become acquainted with the latter's views out of curiosity. This facilitates the unobtrusive penetration of deviant or antinomic opinions up to the point that this produces a sudden change in their favour. But here we are on slippery ground; speculations and observations are confused and uncertain. It remains to be seen whether the particular effects associated with minority influence have been adequately demonstrated. In social life and from a logical point of view these effects are not exclusive to it, but they are nevertheless highly characteristic of it.

7. On some criticisms

(i) Many findings in this area of research have not yet been mentioned. There remain Nemeth's research on preferences, juries and group creativity, Mugny's research on communication, the research by Paicheler on decisions, by Personnaz on conflicts of influence and, last but not least, the work of Doms on social support. However, it is not my aim to provide a comprehensive review here, not only because it would be beyond the scope of this volume but because it would be rather premature. If I have singled out hypotheses to do with the causes and effects of minority influence, it is because they convey the nature of the underlying theory. However it is also because they have been the targets of criticism. Criticism is certainly necessary and indeed it is welcome, but the tenor of the arguments has sometimes been surprising. Moreover the apparent aim of the critics has been to maintain the position of the dominant theory, despite the hopeless plight in which it finds itself.

The principal objections, obviously, have concerned behavioural style. There has been a reluctance to abandon the idea of dependence. There have also been doubts about the possibility that influence could be due to minority consistency. Thus the theses of Biener and Wolf compared the two kinds of variable directly and, in my view, the new theoretical position could be said to have been vindicated. More recently Latané & Wolf (1981), on the basis of their social impact hypothesis, have tried to show that influence is proportional to strength of numbers. That of the minority is obviously less than that of the majority. Here one is confronted with a truly formidable difficulty for, no matter what theory I or anyone else might envisage, the assumption underlying their hypothesis remains the same – numbers create influence. Now, up to the present the experiments that have tested this assumption have on some occasions given a positive answer and on other occasions a negative one. On the whole the evidence remains both fragile and ambiguous. I do not believe that all the evidence based on this assumption is sufficient to overturn the evidence accumulated to date in favour of consistency. And there is a further point, to which we will return. For us a minority is defined by two characteristics, an antinomic position and numbers. For the theory these two characteristics are inseparable, as they are in reality. Or to put it another way, a minority contrasts with a majority in distinctive features. There is a qualitative rather than a quantitative (less *versus* more) difference. To seek to define the minority by numbers alone is to consider it from the most abstract point of view. At the same time this deprives it of its most concrete property, the content by which it operates in the world.

Let us go one step further. As Doms has commented (personal communication), Latané and Wolf's hypothesis is located directly within the earlier theoretical framework; the minority is presented in a restrictive, and indeed negative, fashion. In practice it has for a long time been acknowledged as a source of influence but has always been seen as subordinate to the majority, given that its influence must always remain qualitatively weaker. From the majority point of view an increase in minority influence is seen as a decrease in conformity. In remaining faithful to the assumption of dependence, therefore, this hypothesis leaves no possibility for positive influence and thus for innovation deriving from an active minority. Now this contradicts most of the experimental results so far mentioned, including the fact that minorities have a greater influence than majorities at a 'covert' level. We come back to the point that consistency produces a stronger and more authentic influence than dependency. That said, it is true that Latané and Wolf do adopt a more open-minded position and have attempted to modify the existing theoretical model so as to bring it closer to that presented here.

With similar open-mindedness, several researchers have attempted to compare the influence of a competent minority with that of a consistent minority (Bray, Johnson & Chilstrom, 1982). Thus they have set out to test both Hollander's hypotheses and the alternative that we would support. But one observation immediately springs to mind. Hollander's hypotheses are concerned with leadership and not with minorities; they deal with innovation from the point of view of authority. This is not the case with our hypotheses. Therefore the two are not, as they have been represented (Bray, Johnson & Chilstrom, 1982), alternative models of minority influence. One can obviously show that in certain cases a competent minority will exercise as much or more influence than a consistent minority. I do not believe anyone would claim otherwise. But such superiority does not demonstrate that an explanation in terms of 'status', 'competence', etc. would be more appropriate than one in terms of behavioural style. It no more proves such a case than (to take up an earlier analogy) does the superior quantity of heat produced by thermal phenomena prove that the laws of heat explain the phenomena better than the laws of mechanics. Each one relates to different phenomena and to specific hypotheses. It should also be added that problems really arise at the point where the 'normal' conditions of influence are not fulfilled. That is, they arise in so far as minorities in reality have no recognised advantage in competence, knowledge, status, etc. And they arise in so far as the majority regards itself as properly on the side of reality, law, common sense. Yet we have shown in our own research that the minority influences the members of a majority group *in spite of* the fact that the latter judge it less competent (and less attractive). Thus they are influenced *in spite of* the fact that they regard themselves as more competent. It is this 'in spite of' which makes the problem so interesting and which has for so long surprised people. I admit that the difficulty would have been greater if it had been shown, as Doms (1983) tried to do, that only those individuals closest in space to the minority are influenced, or that competence, completely independently of all behavioural style, produces significant influence of the same kind.

Since the researchers who have worked in this direction have, as I have said, shown a genuine openness of mind, it is appropriate to stress once again two important points. On the one hand, even though numbers are manipulated in the laboratory (though this is not always so), the minority should be defined in terms of the position it takes. On the other hand, the 'ideal-typical' case, in Max Weber's terms, of an active, innovative minority is one in which it enjoys no recognised assets, power or competence. By extension, therefore, a competent minority represents something else, an *élite* or power group. And this latter case probably does not reveal to us the phenomena of innovation from the most significant direction.

These remarks are designed to clarify certain assumptions in the theoretical model. It is true that, according to this model, behavioural style represents the causal factor in influence in as much as the exercise of influence is considered as distinct and separate from the exercise of power. But this does not mean to say that power is not involved, that it has no effect. Dependency is entailed in all social ties; we always encounter one another within relations of dependence. All are in agreement on this point and no one would deny anything so obvious. The critical difference then is not at this level. Rather it comes down to the fact that the theoretical model described here treats dependency as a parameter and not as a variable, an external element and not one intrinsic to influence. It is an element which should be taken into consideration in the same way as, when we construct a clock, we have to take account of the nature of metal, of atmospheric humidity and of other physico-chemical properties. It nevertheless remains a fact that the laws governing pendulum movement as such concern only mechanical variables such as length.

On the other hand, and for good reasons, the elements of dependency which have been considered up to the present as intrinsic variables should be preserved as parameters. They reinforce or diminish the effect produced by the ways minorities or majorities behave or the forms of the messages they transmit. What I propose is not a compromise and it will not end the debate. It is nevertheless a move towards a more complex and accurate vision of reality.

(ii) Other critics touch on the distinction between conformity and innovation. They accept all the objections we have made against the conformity bias and acknowledge that it should be modified. For them the study of innovation represents a useful addition to previous knowledge. But having recognised this, they assume and try to show that the psychological processes underlying these two modalities of influence are the same. In short, whatever may be said about majority influence is taken to be equally valid for minority influence. From this position one sides towards more tortuous logical reasoning: as these processes are the same, no new theoretical viewpoint has been posited. Although we who explore innovation believe we are studying something different, our critics seem to be saying 'thanks for pointing out that minorities exist but you have not uncovered a new process of influence. If there is, as you maintain, some difference between innovation and conformity then it is a difference of degree and not of kind.' These critics have thus returned surreptitiously to the dominant theoretical model, without seriously considering the differences I have mentioned; the minority becomes once again simply a matter of numbers, of just one or two individuals who are simply outnumbered in the face-to-face group.

The consequence of this position is obvious. Since neither specific processes nor genuinely new concepts are involved, it is enough to apply the old here as elsewhere. Research on innovation, while needed to cover reality adequately, immediately becomes useless as a means of understanding it. The ultimate reaction might be that we have made much ado about nothing. What is even more splendid about such reasoning is that it is unbeatable! But it is also self-defeating. I will therefore not try to fight it even though it appears to me to be introducing a certain traditionalism into the field of social psychology. It is as if one is supposed to remain faithful to a paradigm which no longer serves any purpose except to teachers or textbook writers. At least this is what one might suppose, given that the number of scholars studying influence, attitude change or group dynamics has fallen off so drastically. The only possible response to this is the one we have given *via* our hypotheses and the experimental results these have predicted, particularly those concerning conversion and compliance. They have allowed us to discover new facts and this is not something to be ignored.

They also demonstrate that conformity cannot be reduced to innovation; they cannot be dressed in the same garb. To do so would be to ignore the inherent properties of each. Experimental evidence is certainly not sufficient here and never will be since there is no way of saying what the upper limit of proof has to be. However, by comparing the current evidence with that from other areas, particularly conformity, there is no reason to be dissatisfied. Its spread and coherence are such as to convince us that we do have new and well-established effects here. Moreover, they lend continuing support to the hypotheses first suggested (Maas, Clark & Haberkorn, 1982; Moscovici & Doms, 1982). No matter how the question is examined and re-examined there can be no going back to the *status quo*; one must go on. None of the criticisms so far formulated has raised any serious doubts about the contrast between innovation and conformity. At the very most it now appears less straightforward, and the objections indicate the lines that may be followed to validate the position. On the whole we have been able to benefit from the criticisms in so far as we have been obliged to clarify a concept here, a phenomenon there, or to confirm certain of our deductions.

8. Growth points for research

We all know that no theory or experiment is destined to last very long. Neither will any controversy, if it is concerned with a problem of any significance, ever be concluded with a definitive statement. On the other hand, to have been made conscious of a contradiction or to have been shown that some aspects of reality can be explored in a more heuristic fashion can sometimes leave more lasting traces. I do not pretend that the theoretical hypotheses proposed, the experiments conducted or the critical arguments advanced are sufficient, or are the only ones possible. Much remains to be done, perhaps almost everything. Nevertheless innovation and minority influence must be seen from a preferential perspective if we are to reach a common position. We need to put ourselves in the position of a minority or individual or innovatory group and look at reality from there, and then ask the questions and look for the answers. Just as those who have gone before us have taken conformity and majority influence as their point of departure and achieved such a rich harvest, so may we. They reacted to the new ideas of their century by creating an entirely new field of research out of phenomena that appeared to be secondary, namely suggestion and crowds (Moscovici, 1981). In my opinion we should remain faithful to this line of descent by occupying ourselves with the phenomena of our time which has been marked by the appearance of a veritable archipelago of minorities, by the transformation of formerly anomic groups (homosexuals, women, youth, etc.) into antinomic groups, and by the transformation of deviant groups into active minorities. If social psychology as a science was born out of the 'age of crowds', it can continue its mission and remain in contact with the significant movements in history by studying the psychological characteristics of our 'age of protest', as it has so often been called. Otherwise, it risks becoming a science of insignificant social phenomena after the fashion of that psychology which studied language as a set of nonsense syllables. Instead of doing its utmost to maintain the dominant theory which in one way or another has had its day and which simple inertia has trapped in a *cul de sac*, social psychology should continue to advance towards the unknown along the paths that have been opened up.

Among the possible directions for research several appear to me to offer the promise of progress in the future. I will mention five.

(1) The research by Nemeth & Wachtler (1982) on minority influence in group creativity and by Wolf (1979) on decisions constitute a reworking of small group dynamics. In this area we possess a considerable accumulation of knowledge and of relatively coherent concepts. But since the work of Festinger and Schachter there has been very little progress. Now it appears

that by considering small groups as open rather than closed we may better understand who they change and how they alter their environments. To achieve this it suffices if we substitute within the classic dynamics the pairing majority–minority for that of group–deviant, so as to uncover a different functioning and different relations. No less important is the change of perspective involved in moving beyond conformity and viewing the deviant (or minority) as a resource rather than as an obstacle, as a positive rather than a negative asset. (One finds an attempt to move in this direction in Levine's (1980) work.)

These efforts will bear further fruits if they are linked to research on innovation and minority influence. We have the clear impression that united efforts can lead to a new dynamic of groups (Moscovici & Mugny, 1983). For example, it is possible to envisage pressure to uniformity not only as pressure on the minority, as has been the case, but also in terms of pressure on the majority such as may be observed in the studies by Nemeth and Wolf. In the same way, in addition to the search by uncertain individuals for social comparison which leads to uniformity, we could explore the characteristics of social recognition, the recognition to which individuals who are certain aspire in situations marked by a difference (Gordon, 1966; Moscovici & Paicheler, 1978). It is a fact of life that social recognition is a necessity for minorities and that it is universal or ubiquitous in communities changed by an innovative principle or disrupted by a conflict between the majority and a minority. Thus it is with scientific, artistic and political communities.

If social comparison is provoked by the necessity of coming to a shared and valid belief, social recognition is born of the need to give one's beliefs a stable and legitimate character. The search for validity and the search for legitimacy are both essential in a group, but they do not lead to the same thing. It is normally the case that validity is a 'rare' resource for majorities while legitimacy is such for minorities. Thus, to sum up, motivation towards comparison will predominate among members of majorities, and members of minorities will be motivated towards recognition. There are here several indications of possible developments which could help revitalise a once flourishing area and lead once more to progress. The greening of the small group area is at hand.

(2) In our theoretical analysis of influence processes we stressed that social interactions and exchanges are fashioned by social norms. This is no more than a truism but one that is transformed into a hypothesis when its precise content is defined. This can be done by distinguishing objectivity, preference and originality norms. Objectivity norms impose the obligation to test opinions and judgments according to a consensual criterion of accuracy such as

measurement, averaging and so forth. Preference norms presume the co-existence of more or less valued opinions, etc. All the values are regarded as equal and members of the group are supposed to accept them without discussion. Finally, originality norms order opinions or judgments according to their degree of novelty or their capacity for invoking surprise. In the same way they devalue everything that is familiar or trivial even when true.

We may assume that there is a probabilistic relation or analogy between each type of norm and the three modalities of influence. Thus there would be a relation between the objectivity norm and conformity, between the preference norm and normalisation, and between the norm of originality and innovation. Some research has begun to explore these relations and the way in which the norms are involved in the process of influence (Nemeth & Wachtler, 1973; Moscovici & Lage, 1978; Mugny, Rilliet & Papastamou, 1981). But again almost everything remains to be done. In particular there are the questions of why it is so difficult to activate originality norms and of how they affect behavioural styles. There also remains the vast area of problem solving and creativity (Kelley & Thibaut, 1968). By introducing the minority factor into this area we may be able to rethink the observed phenomena. In introducing this factor in an exploratory fashion, however, it is important to take account of these norms. They regulate both the interaction and the cognitive operations, depending on whether the individual is looking for a correct, or an original, solution.

(3) In the experiments we have carried out so far one thing in particular has struck us. Individuals have a social representation, or a relatively precise image, of what the majority and minority are or should be. Clearly, the very words 'majority' and 'minority' have an affective and cognitive significance independent of the particular groups to which they are applied. Hearing one or the other word used immediately provokes certain reactions and creates an impression which one then seeks to verify or disconfirm. In one of their experiments, Doms & Van Avermaet (1980) created a condition in which individuals gave responses analogous to those of the minority. The only difference was that they were not labelled as 'minority' responses. The mere absence of this label in fact reduced the impact which these individuals had on their partners. With different objectives, Mugny & Papastamou (1980) defined, on the basis of word association, the image of the minority as either flexible or rigid. They found interesting correlations, but paradoxically no systematic relation emerged between these images and the degree of influence. This raises the question of what the function of these images may be. In a similar vein I have tried to examine how minorities are perceived by others, and in particular what attitudes are adopted by those exposed to their

influence. Comparing the results we find that minorities are neither esteemed nor liked, nor are they judged more competent than other members of the group. On the other hand we find that they are admired, appreciated for their strength of conviction and for giving others a shake-up, an opportunity to escape from routine and think in new ways.

Thus there is an abundant richness of findings in almost every sense. The time has arrived to order and compare them systematically, to bring out the regularities. On the basis of such ordering it should then be possible to conceive of a whole series of studies on the social perception of minorities and majorities, of the ways in which we form impressions about their objectives and the reactions their social representations provoke among us. Going a bit further, one may speculate on the existence of distinct psychologies of minorities and majorities and on the possibility that education in different groups leads to one or the other. The thought occurs that the psychology of a minority is 'inner-directed' and that of a majority is 'other-directed'. The locus of control of the minority individual is internal, while that of a majority individual is external. Finally, the 'need for approval' is not the same in each case. This opens up an entire field of research. Furthermore, we might move in this direction on the basis of concrete problems.

(4) I have already spoken in sufficient detail about conversion and compliance but, for those interested in influence phenomena, it goes without saying that the analysis of conversion behaviour is of first importance. The progress accomplished to date is sufficiently promising to encourage further work. It has led us to some surprising and intriguing discoveries. There is a feeling of being in the presence of certain 'magic', complex and fascinating mechanisms, as complex and as fascinating as were those of hypnosis in earlier times. All the mysteries of mental life and of the action of man upon man are contained here. Its inscrutability renders conversion even more attractive. How can one fail to be fascinated by something that produces such extraordinary effects as religious, political or scientific conversion (the last of which is even more rare than Kuhn pretends). By comparison, compliance is prosaic, without mystery. Yet this is exactly what should arouse our suspicions and stimulate us to have a new look at it. We have certainly missed something essential, for it is too easy to take for granted that a man should follow the group and, to paraphrase Pascal, pray without believing. In other words, I hope that through a better understanding of conversion we will discover hitherto unsuspected aspects of compliance.

If we are to go beyond these pious wishes and generalities, however, some more specific approaches need to be framed. I foresee two. The first is a matter of taking conversion as a means of, and even a pretext for, exploring more adequately the cognitive activity involved in influence situations. We know very little of this activity and what we do know is rather fragmentary. Now here we have a specific situation (that of internal or external conflict), a relatively circumscribed mechanism (that of comparison or validation) and two categories of empirical response, the public response (overt, direct, etc.) and the private response (covert, indirect, etc.). Here is an adequate point of departure for exploring the cognitive transformations operating in an individual before or after interaction with a group.

The second direction would involve shedding light on resistance to compliance and on the specific character of innovation in the face of conformity. To embark upon this path one would have to accept the existence of this resistance and this specific character. But it appears to me to be so endemic in the structure of society, in the history of religions and cultures, that I do not see how it could be doubted. I believe that to formulate an accurate social-psychological theory to explain it and to generate the experiments to illustrate it, however, may be harder to achieve than theories or experiments disproving the existence of this resistance and its specific character. Even then I would maintain that reality is more potent than such experiments and that such theories are incorrect, pandering to our incapacity to grasp what is clearest in reality. For the moment I prefer to go along with reality rather than against it. It is a calculated risk but it accords with my interests.

Consider the alternative. If I uphold that conversion and submission, innovation and conformity are one and the same, I can immediately stop my research. If I do not take the risk of being wrong I have no further reason to come up with hypotheses or experiments. The answers are there even before the questions are asked. If, instead, I stick to the position I have taken, I at least retain the possibility of conceiving hypotheses and conducting experiments to decide their validity. It remains to me to ask such and such a question even if this ignores the chances of finding a reply. Even if I am in error I would nonetheless have the opportunity of discovering something in the process, of acquiring further insight no matter what my mistake. But in view of what we have learned so far the risk is not too great; conversion seems to me a field fertile in lessons and surprises.

(5) Ever since society has been society and the individual the individual, each has had to invent both the means of influence and the means to combat influence, just as arms for attack and arms for defence have had to be invented. Moreover, battles of will are no less bitterly disputed than physical battles. Among the means for combating influence that we know of, there is inoculation (McGuire, 1969), resistance, defence, censure and of course others. But there is one which appears to me particularly apt in guarding

majorities against the influence of minorities, i.e. psychologisation. In the modest and poorly defined area that is ours, this discovery by our Genevan colleagues has opened new horizons. They have shown that the 'personalisation' or 'subjectivisation' of a minority message attenuates its effects and its strength. Obviously we have recognised for a long time that 'dissidents' are not incarcerated in psychiatric asylums for nothing; the unorthodox or the deviant are often diagnosed as 'mad', and innovations or unusual ideas are frequently attributed to personal defects in their authors. Thus at various times rumours circulated that the bizarre character of Picasso's work was due to a deformity in his eye or his incapacity to draw. There is an entire mythology to be found here, a vast anthology to be examined. Give a dog a bad name and hang it. But it is enough to consider the language used against minorities to appreciate the nature and quantity of psychologisation.

Although these disparate elements are known to exist, Mugny and Papastamou have nonetheless brought them together and transformed them into coherent objects of research. The experiments I know of are certainly exploratory in character and the results are sometimes paradoxical. But they are also sufficiently consistent to justify studying what may one day emerge as an essential feature of relations of influence between majorities and minorities. The antidote to psychologisation is what we call, for want of a better word, 'social support'. It is a process of 'objectifying' or 'depersonalising' a message or judgment, of transforming the thoughts or words of a minority into a reflection of reality. In fact the issue of the social support given to a minority has not received particular attention until now. This is because we have needed to show that it can succeed without support or that this support is not decisive. From a given moment, however, it does become so; a minority which neither proselytises nor convinces becomes isolated and disappears. This is why, in our view, the positive contribution of Doms' experiments resides in the fact that they begin to tackle this problem. They allow a glimpse of the importance of social support in the study of influence phenomena. Although conducted from completely different perspectives, and they are all the better for that, these two groups of studies have too many points of contact not to converge in one way or another.

Such then is the range of potential research on minority influence. It offers the promise of a definite future in this area, and in social psychology generally, taking its place as an autonomous science with its own legitimate field of study. As part of this field, the phenomenon of influence without any doubt helps define its particular character, covering as it does one of the three or four elementary relations in social life.

9. The essential tension

There is no doubt in our minds that great creations in art, science and political life in general can be traced back to minorities. This is true not only because the minority acts as a stimulant, but also because it activates the mind and triggers social change. And that is not all. Some minorities generate intellectual movements; and the majority, for all its conformity, may have had a minority as its starting point. Stir the ashes of most of our now widely accepted maxims, like 'love thy neighbour', and at the bottom you will rediscover the flame of a revolutionary creation for which a handful of men suffered martyrdom. The tension between majorities and minorities, between conformity and innovation is thus a driving force everywhere, including science (Kuhn, 1977). This tension is the subject of most of our studies, as it is the prime concern of most of those who criticise our approach and who try to replace this tension with harmony. But beyond specific details it is a vision of the entire process of innovation towards which all our efforts should bend. Only then will each finding assume its true significance. As my research progressed and I became familiar with other studies, I began to create a web. This web is speculative for now, but it is open to improvement and to observations based on real cases. It foreshadows a genuine theory of innovation phenomena and the phases that they undergo (Moscovici, 1980, 1981). I shall explore these phases, illustrating them with an example drawn from Proust's *Remembrance of things past*. Of course this involves a fictional work and invented characters. Nonetheless, Proust, who was an unrivalled observer of his time, drew on his own experience of real human beings and reconstructed attitudes that he himself had been able to witness. Everyone knows what I have in mind: the Dreyfus affair, which in the final years of the nineteenth century triggered a real philosophical and political struggle in France and mobilised public opinion in its full range. Many, many people were forced to take a stand for or against the French captain (wrongly) accused of espionage. But in the beginning only a very small minority, including Proust, was convinced of Dreyfus' innocence and fought against the views of a compact majority, which included the army, the church, most political parties and the press.

To come back to our theory. In an initial phase, a consistent and resolute minority emerges and confronts the majority with a system of beliefs or antinomic practices. It overcomes criticism and the initial obstacles until it makes itself heard. Let us call this the *revelation* phase, as the minority at this point reveals something and at the same time is revealed to the majority and to itself. In Proust's novel this is clearly shown. The supporters of Dreyfus discover the illegal acts of which he was a victim, because of being a Jew, and they begin to make them public. The Prince de Guermantes admits to another character in the novel, the Jew Swann, that like everybody else in his social world, he held the same views as the majority on Dreyfus' guilt and that he persevered for a long time in these views. Similarly his wife, who happens to be Bavarian, categorically declares to someone who assumes her to be a Dreyfus supporter, 'I am now a French princess and I share the views of all my fellow countrymen' (p. 731; all quotations are taken from the Vintage Books edition of 1981, details of which appear in the Bibliography). However, a conversation with a general, who belongs to the minority, made the Prince 'suspect not an error, but grave illegalities, had been committed in the conduct of the trial' (p. 731). In short, he discovers and understands what he had failed to hear previously.

In the second phase, the new messages are repeated and disseminated. They become familiar, penetrate everyday language and are investigated by thinking individuals, who try to grasp them and gradually take them seriously. The polemics surrounding them endow them with a special intensity (the Dreyfus trial becomes the Dreyfus affair, for instance) and imbue them with passion. At the same time individuals begin to rely on minority arguments, often inadvertently, just because they are so prevalent and repeated almost everywhere. They are mixed and interwoven with old messages. Collective thinking and collective memory become saturated with them. In other words, they fuse with existing opinions to create new ones. Behavioural models, especially consistency, are decisive in this regard. Consistency endows words and gestures with additional psychological meaning and emotional density. Unintentionally and often unconsciously, people incorporate minority beliefs – and practices – into their concrete experiences, feelings and judgment. We shall term this the *incubation* phase, during which what has hitherto appeared shocking and unorthodox infiltrates into the arena of collective life. This penetration into everyday thought can be condemned, but it cannot be ignored.

In the third phase, the members of the majority change their minds, adopting the minority point of view without overtly yielding. At first they may not be aware of what has happened, because of the taboos in place, and yet everyone begins to see, think and even act differently. The same thing occurred with the subjects in our experiment, who continued to call a blue slide blue when they had begun to see it as green. It also happened with the subjects in the experiments by Mugny and Papastamou; these subjects continued to respect the content of the message while adopting new attitudes suggested by the minority on related questions. This is the *conversion* phase, whose psychological aspect we explained previously. It is crucial in so far as what was repeated is now accepted, what was external becomes now internalised. The process manifests itself in Proust's character. The Prince de Guermantes, haunted by what he now considers an illegal act, undertakes a thorough study. He now reads newspapers he had refused to read. And now he comes to doubt not only the legality of the proceedings but the condemned man's guilt (pp. 734–5). He refrains from discussing this with his wife because he feels deep shame at the thought that French officers could have been responsible for such a vile action. He learns during another conversation with the general that proof of Dreyfus' guilt exists. And right after that it is found that this piece of evidence is a forgery. The Prince de Guermantes is now torn by an inner conflict, suffering from insomnia. He is compelled, forced, in truth and without realising it, to side with Dreyfus deep inside. He thus begins, secretly so to speak, to read the newspapers supporting Dreyfus, Le Siècle and L'Aurore. Gripped by a sort of guilt feeling, and in order to express his approval of the minority stand, he asks his friend Abbé Poiré (who, he was 'astonished to find, held the same conviction' (p. 735)), to say a mass for the intention of Dreyfus and his family. As the Prince moves from revelation to incubation and at last to conversion, he experiences all the expected agonies and undergoes all the different phases.

In the wake of the conversion phase there is a fourth phase, during which each individual separately recognises his changed views and accepts them. He puts all his zeal into the consolidation of the new beliefs in the private sphere. And he fails to realise that others – his relatives, his friends – have undergone an evolution similar to his own. In the process, he maintains in public his former beliefs and behaviours as though nothing had happened. People individually side with the minority but collectively continue to belong to the majority. A state of 'pluralistic ignorance' prevails. Private knowledge of accomplished change is coupled with public ignorance of this change. Until someone, still in the minority of course, unveils this ignorance. Let me return once more to the Prince de Guermantes. He has, we know, mentioned nothing to his friends nor even to his wife. He believes that the Princesse de Guermantes is against Dreyfus, like the majority, on the basis of what he sees from the outside. But when the Prince asks Abbé Poiré to say a mass, the latter turns him down. For just this very day somebody else has asked him to say a mass for the unjustly condemned captain. The Prince is dumbfounded to hear that another Catholic as well as himself is convinced of Dreyfus' 'innocence'. He urges the Abbé to name this person who was already asking him to say masses when he 'still believed Dreyfus guilty' and then learns that it is someone of his own world. 'This rare bird' is none other than his own wife, the Princesse de Guermantes (p. 737). While he was afraid of offending his wife's nationalist views, she feared to upset her husband's religious beliefs and patriotic feelings. Which did not prevent them from sharing the same ideas and reading the same pro-Dreyfus newspapers, the Princess having her chambermaid secretly buy *L'Aurore* for her.

Pluralistic ignorance finally gives way. Having admitted his conversion to the Princess, the Prince makes the same confession to Swann, who had long since sided with Dreyfus and openly belonged to the minority. He explains his silence by telling him that 'thinking the same as yourself must at that time have kept me further apart from you than thinking differently' (p. 737). As can be seen, once each person's secret is disclosed, private opinions become public opinions, shared by many, and the process of change is completed. At first it is imposed from the outside. Let us call this last phase *innovation* proper. What was against the norms becomes a norm, the minority of the few becomes the majority of the many. For the moment, I have nothing more to add about this sequence. I now await the evidence to confirm it.

2. Social support and minority influence: the innovation effect reconsidered[1]

MACHTELD DOMS and EDDY VAN AVERMAET

1. Introduction

Recent social influence theorising (Moscovici, 1976, 1980) departs from the assumption that the two major influence modalities – innovation and conformity – involve different processes and produce divergent behavioural effects. It has been assumed that majorities would elicit a social comparison process, direct a person's attention to the interpersonal relations and produce compliance effects. Minorities on the other hand would trigger a judgment validation process, direct a person's attention to the object of judgment and produce conversion effects. Empirical support for this line of thought can be found in numerous studies which show that majorities exert more influence on public responses than minorities, whereas the reverse holds with respect to private or latent responses (Lage 1973; Mugny, 1974–5, 1976; Moscovici & Lage, 1976; Nemeth, 1976; Moscovici & Personnaz, 1980).

Paradoxical as it may seem, part of the very same evidence may serve as a point of departure for an alternative conception of the relation between innovation and conformity, namely one that stresses their similarities rather than their differences. The present chapter intends to re-analyse existing data from this perspective and it will also introduce some new empirical evidence. It invites the reader seriously to consider an emerging parallel between both influence processes, at least with respect to their public effects.

A first section of this chapter will briefly recapitulate our earlier efforts to re-analyse the current operationalisation of the comparison between both influence processes from the perspective of the literature on the role of social support within social influence contexts. This analysis intends to demonstrate that many of the earlier experimental conformity–innovation comparisons are unsatisfactory because they inadvertently neglect social support effects within an innovation context. The larger part of this chapter consists of the presentation of new evidence which highlights the role of social support in minority influence situations and which reveals the similarity of social support effects within innovation and conformity contexts. A final section will digress on the possible implications for further innovation research and will derive, on a provisional and conjectural basis, some strategies for effectively innovating, and/or for effectively crossing, an active minority's influence pressures.

2. Empirical research on the conformity–innovation relation: a re-analysis

Unravelling the relation between the innovation and conformity processes has been a major objective of recent social influence research. Experimental studies of this matter usually involve a direct comparison of the public and private influence effects produced by minority and majority influence sources, by means of experimental paradigms that are clearly derived from the conformity literature. Majority influence effects are assessed using classical conformity situations whereby the researcher's attention is focused on the reactions of single targets to the influence attempts of numerical majority sources. Minority influence effects, on the other hand, are assessed in what might in fact be called reversed conformity situations, with the researcher's attention focused on the reactions of groups of targets to the influence attempts of numerical minority sources. The data obtained in these settings are generally interpreted to support the conclusion that majorities produce more pronounced public influence effects than minorities, the latter producing more pronounced private or latent effects. This conclusion would be justified if one could assume that in both influence situations the resulting effects could be fully ascribed to the influence source. With respect to the conformity situation there appears indeed to be no reason to question either the plausibility of this assumption or the accuracy of the picture concerning the antecedent conditions of effective influence. With respect to the innovation situation, however, there are grounds for wondering whether the final effect is indeed fully determined by the minority source's behavioural style. A perusal of the literature on the role of social support in influence situations (Asch, 1951; Allen, 1975) would suggest that the minority influence effect – its public effect at least – is co-determined by the behavioural style of a particular target's own group members. More specifically, it would suggest that in the typical innovation situation the final public influence effect will generally be less pronounced than the public influence effect obtained in the conformity situation. This is not necessarily because a minority would be incapable of producing such a pronounced effect, but most probably because the presence of several other targets would drastically reduce the final innovation effect. Previous conformity research offers ample evidence for the proposition that public influence effects reach their maximum when single individuals are exposed to unanimous influence sources, and that these effects are drastically reduced when the unanimity of a source is broken by one or more individuals. Moreover, conformity research has repeatedly shown that different behavioural styles of social supporters differentially affect a target's conformity behaviour. In the light of these well-established facts it could then be hypothesised that minority influence targets will be differentially vulnerable to the source's influence attempts as a function of whether or not the source's unanimity is broken by other targets present and as a function of the other targets' behavioural style.

A series of experiments (Doms, 1983) was designed to test this hypothesis. Within a classical Asch-paradigm the two factors that possibly co-determine a minority's public influence were rigorously controlled. The majority group, therefore, no longer consisted of four subjects, but rather of one subject and three confederates. To manipulate the source's unanimity the targets under focus responded either immediately after the source and before any other majority confederate (unanimity condition) or after the source and after the three majority confederates (broken unanimity condition). The behavioural style of the majority confederates was manipulated by instructing them either to consistently resist the influence attempts of the minority, or to go along with the minority viewpoint on a predetermined number of trials, or to always go along with the subject. The data showed differential public influence effects as a function of both manipulated factors. A consistent minority had no meaningful impact on its targets when its unanimity was broken by other targets present. This was the case independent of whether its unanimity was broken by targets who consistently stuck to correct judgments or by targets who acted inconsistently. In line with previous conformity research, the minority had no significant influence in either case. A consistent minority proved to be potentially influential only when its unanimity was not broken by other targets present, i.e. when the subject had to respond immediately after the minority source. However, even then the minority's public influence effect did not necessarily become fully expressed or pronounced. Indeed, when the targets present, although incapable of breaking the source's unanimity, consistently held to a correct judgment, the particular target on which the researcher's attention was focused did not become meaningfully affected by the source's deviant position. However, when the other targets present reacted in an inconsistent, and therefore unpredictable, manner, then the particular target under focus became meaningfully affected by the source's influence attempts. In the latter situation the minority proved to be capable of producing a public influence effect that was strikingly similar to the conformity effects regularly reported in the research literature.

These data clearly suggest, then, that the current empirical comparisons of minority and majority public influence effects are indeed ambiguous. By inadvertently neglecting the impact of a mutual influence process at work within a minority's target group, the antecedent conditions of effective minority influence have possibly been misrepresented. The impact of the source's behavioural style would have been over-emphasised, whereas the impact of the target's behavioural style would have been underestimated. By underestimating the impact of a target's own reference group, the emergence of a salient analogy between minority and majority influence processes was precluded.

3. The emergence of a *post-hoc* analogy between innovation and conformity

As we have just indicated, under particular conditions consistent minorities are capable of producing public influence effects that are strikingly comparable to the currently reported compliance effects in the conformity literature. Minority influence targets confronted with a unanimous source and unable to predict the (inconsistent) behaviour of other targets present are influenced to a very meaningful degree. The fact that both these factors – the source's unanimity and the unpredictability of the other targets' behavioural style – determine the significance of the innovation effect affords a step forward towards a salient analogy between both influence processes.

Allen (1975) holds the view that in a conformity situation targets remain independent not because they go along with the norms of another reference group, but because they are able to predict that other influence targets will not go along with the laboratory majority group. Conversely, when targets are certain or able to predict that other targets will go along with the majority viewpoint, a meaningful conformity effect has to be expected. The question of what targets will do when they are unable to predict the reactions of other targets has not been raised or explicitly tested. It is, however, plausible to assume that in such situations targets will go along with the majority viewpoint.

On this basis a plausible analogy can then be drawn between a classical conformity situation in which a single target is exposed to a numerical majority source and an innovation situation in which a particular target is exposed to a unanimous numerical minority source and unable to predict the other targets' reactions. In both situations the target is informed of the deviant viewpoint of the influence source, and is uncertain as to the reaction of the other targets to the deviant viewpoint. The only difference between the two situations concerns the way in which the target's uncertainty is created and maintained. In the conformity situation the target is uncertain because he is exposed to the source as a single individual. In the innovation situation he is uncertain because the behaviour of other targets is inconsistent and therefore unpredictable.

However salient and inviting the analogy may be, at this stage it should still be treated with caution, because it is based on *post-hoc*, and even indirect, comparisons, between our own research on minority influence and earlier conformity research. Nevertheless, on the basis of this analogy we would speculate that both influence processes, if studied and compared under identical conditions, would lead to very similar public influence effects. We would further speculate that the differential public influence effects, which in the innovation literature are usually related to differences between the two influence modalities, possibly emerge within each influence modality and relate more specifically to differences in the conditions under which the process is looked at. These condition differences would concern differences in the social support a target receives for holding a correct judgment, and perhaps more generally for holding a judgment shared by members of his own reference group. With these speculations we arrive at the core problem that will be addressed in this contribution.

4. Minority and majority influence: differential or similar public effects?

In view of the tentative but inviting character of the analogy that we were able to draw between the minority influence effects assessed in our previous research and the compliance effects regularly reported in the conformity literature, we considered it worthwhile to study further the relation between the two influence processes under as identical conditions as possible. In doing so, we mainly aimed at directly comparing both influence processes with respect to their public effects within a single experimental paradigm.

A first study served the purpose of testing the general hypothesis that minority and majority influence sources will produce similar public influence effects provided they can exert their influence under identical conditions. This was realised within a classical Asch-paradigm by exposing individuals to the influence attempts of two confederates who unanimously defended a deviant position, i.e. they overestimated the length of the standard lines by consistently selecting a too long comparison line. The minority or majority character of the influence source was introduced by giving the subjects the impression of belonging to a group of a particular size. In the conformity conditions subjects were led to believe that the group consisted of three members and that a majority, i.e. two confederates, defended a deviant viewpoint. In the innovation condition subjects were given the impression of belonging to a six-person group of which a minority, again two confederates, held a deviant position and of which the majority (i.e. three confederates and the subject himself) shared, at least initially, the correct response. However, in order to have the innovation condition as similar as possible to the conformity condition an equipment breakdown was simulated in the innovation condition. After the fifth trial subjects were told that because of a breakdown in the experimental equipment the first three group members (i.e. the two confederates and the subject himself) could no longer be informed of the responses of the last three group members and *vice versa*. Hence, from the sixth trial onwards the conformity condition and the 'innovation breakdown' condition were completely identical. The only difference related to the first five trials and was considered essential to create different perceptions of the source's position. To evaluate the significance of the effects assessed in the conformity condition and the 'innovation breakdown' condition, two additional conditions were run: a control condition in which subjects were not exposed to any influence attempts and an innovation condition consisting of two confederates and four subjects.

If minority and majority sources exerting their influence under similar conditions would produce comparable public effects, then one would have to expect equally important effects in the conformity condition and the 'innovation breakdown' condition. These effects should be more pronounced than the effect observed in the regular innovation condition, for the reasons explained in detail in section 2 of this chapter.

Do our data offer evidence for our hypothesis? The picture of the data is indeed very promising. Minority and majority sources were correctly assigned to different positions and subjects were fully aware of the source's and their own position in the group. When asked what percentage of the people would agree with the source's responses, subjects in the innovation condition thought this percentage would be 28.7 per cent; in the innovation breakdown condition they thought it would be 30.6 per cent and in the conformity condition they thought it would be 47.8 per cent. As to these data, the conformity condition was significantly different from the innovation condition ($t = 2.13$; $p < 0.05$) as well as from the innovation breakdown condition ($t = 1.77$; $p < 0.05$). Conversely, when asked what percentage of the people would agree with their own response, subjects in the innovation condition thought it would be 81.5 per cent; in the innovation breakdown condition they thought it would be 70 per cent and in the conformity condition 58 per

Table 1. *Mean percentages of influenced responses*

	Control condition	Conformity condition	Innovation breakdown condition	Innovation condition
1a (original data)	3.98	30.79	17.24	4.31
1b (replication data)	4.17	22.02	15.52	9.29

cent. In the control condition the percentage was 79 per cent. Again the conformity condition differed significantly from all other conditions (conformity *versus* control, t = 3.14; p < 0.01; *versus* innovation, t = 3.92; p < 0.05; *versus* innovation breakdown, t = 1.35; p < 0.10). Hence it is safe to conclude that the influence source was correctly assigned to the same minority position in both innovation conditions and that the minority and majority influence sources were correctly assigned to different positions.

Yet, the two minority sources produced different public effects whereas the minority and the majority source produced similar public effects when having the opportunity to exert their influence under similar conditions. Indeed, the picture of the influence data (table 1a) clearly supports our predictions. Both the innovation breakdown condition and the conformity condition differ significantly from the control condition (t = 2.31; p < 0.05 and t = 2.97; p < 0.02 resp.), whereas the regular innovation condition proves to be different from the control condition only by a non-parametric test (Mann Whitney U-test with correction for ties Z = 1.98; p < 0.02). However, the regular innovation condition differed significantly from both the innovation breakdown condition (t = 2.40; p < 0.05) and from the conformity condition (t = 3.01; p < 0.02), the difference between the latter two conditions not reaching an acceptable level of statistical significance (t = 1.37; p < 0.14).

As part of a larger design we later replicated the above-mentioned conditions, and in general the replication data were quite similar. The three experimental conditions differed again significantly from the control condition (control *versus* conformity, t = 4.25; p < 0.001; control *versus* innovation breakdown, t = 2.25; p < 0.04; control *versus* innovation, t = 2.15; p < 0.05). Moreover, the difference between the conformity condition and the regular innovation condition was again very meaningful (t = 2.87; p < 0.01) whereas the difference between the former condition and the innovation breakdown condition again turned out to be non-significant. However, and in contrast to the original data pattern, the difference between the two innovation conditions did not reach an acceptable level of significance (t = 1.18; p < 0.13).

On the one hand both sets of data clearly indicate that the impact of minorities on isolated individuals may be as important as the impact of majorities in a classical conformity paradigm. At the same time they reveal how drastically the impact of the same minority source is reduced when it is no longer confronted with an isolated majority member but rather with several members of the majority group. As mentioned in section 2, this reduction is possibly due to the social support every majority member receives from the other group members for holding to the correct judgment.

On the other hand it cannot be ignored that the innovation breakdown condition itself tends to result in less yielding behaviour than the conformity condition, although not significantly so. In addition, in the replication experiment the difference between the innovation breakdown condition and the regular innovation condition was not statistically significant. These tendencies in the data would suggest that even in the innovation breakdown condition targets receive a certain amount of social support (be it only on the first five trials of the influence phase), resulting in reduced later influence, compared to the conformity condition (where social support is completely lacking).

The fact that such a small amount of social support for holding to the majority position reduces to some extent a minority's impact detracts on the one hand from the validity of our operationalisation of similar influence conditions for minority and majority sources. On the other hand, however, it adds to the plausibility of our proposition that the possible effects of social support within a social influence setting should be taken into account. They can, indeed, no longer be neglected since they proved to be even more pronounced than assumed until now.

5. The role of social support within innovation and conformity settings

In the previous section we mainly addressed the issue of empirically demonstrating the similarity of the public influence effects produced by minorities and majorities on *isolated* individuals. This was realised by comparing the public effects obtained in a classical conformity situation with the public effects obtained in an innovation situation from which the social support factor was extracted by isolating the targets from their own reference group. In the present section our attention will be focused on the public impact of minorities and majorities on individuals who receive differential amounts of social support from members of their own reference group for holding to a correct response. The introduction and manipulation of the social support factor in both minority and majority influence situations, and this within a single experimental paradigm, may eventually serve a threefold purpose. First of all, it may provide us with an alternative test of our hypothesis that under identical conditions the two influence sources produce similar public effects, and it could possibly add to the validity of this hypothesis. Secondly, it may provide us with a test of our implicit assumption, made when drawing the analogy between both influence situations, that the social support factor functions in the same way in both influence settings and hence detracts to a similar degree from both sources' impact. Finally, in view of the rather unexpected finding that even very small amounts of social support may eventually reduce a source's impact, it may certainly enhance the similarity of the conditions under which both influence processes are studied and compared.

The study designed to compare the public effects produced by minority and majority sources under various conditions of social support basically consisted of a 2 × 3 design, with the minority–majority variable as a first factor and the differential amounts of social support as a second factor.

In both the innovation and the conformity conditions individuals were led to believe that they were members of a six-person group. In the innovation conditions a minority, consisting of two confederates, consistently over-estimated the length of the standard lines and communicated their deviant judgments in the first and second place. All subjects responded in the third place and received social support for correctly judging the length of the lines from three confederates who responded after the subject. In the conformity conditions, a majority of four confederates overestimated the length of the standard lines and gave their deviant responses in the first, second, fourth and fifth place. All subjects again responded in the third place and received social support for correctly judging the length of the lines from one confederate who responded in the last place.

As to the manipulation of the second factor, the targets received social support either on the first five trials, or on the first half of the trials, or on all trials. The cut-off of social support in the former two conditions was realised by the simulation of an equipment breakdown so that the targets could no longer be informed of the responses of the last three subjects and *vice versa*. From that moment on, majority and minority influence targets no longer received social support from their own group members and were exposed to the very same influence source, i.e. two confederates.

In view of the analogy drawn between the two influence processes, and in view of our previous research data, it was hypothesised that under each of the various social support conditions minority and majority influence sources would produce similar public effects. Moreover, and in line with

Table 2. *Mean percentages of influenced responses as a function of the amount of social support*

	Social support on first five trials	Social support on first half trials	Social support on all trials	Social support observed
Conformity condition	23.44	9.62	12.02	15.63
Innovation condition	15.63	7.81	4.69	17.79

previous conformity reseach (Allen, 1975), it was hypothesised that the larger the amount of social support targets received for sticking to a correct judgment, the less pronounced the public influence effects would be.

The general data picture (table 2) proves to be consistent with this hypothesis. As in the previous study, the targets correctly perceived the position of the influence source, of the social supports and of themselves. Indeed, minority influence targets assigned themselves and the social supporters significantly more to a majority position than majority influence targets ($F_{(1,264)} = 28.02$, $p < 0.01$; $F_{(1,264)} = 20.98$, $p < 0.01$). Moreover, minority influence targets assigned the influence source significantly more to a minority position than majority influence targets ($F_{(1,264)} = 35.59$, $p < 0.01$). Yet the two influence sources again produced similar public influence effects. Indeed, the analysis of variance revealed a main effect for the social support factor ($F = 2.75$, $p < 0.05$), but no main effect for the majority–minority variable ($F < 1$), nor an interaction effect ($F < 1$). A closer examination of the social support effect by means of *a priori* comparisons revealed, as expected, that the targets were most affected by the source's influence attempts when they received social support on only five trials. In these conditions the influence effects proved to be more pronounced than in the other two social support conditions ($F = 2.27$, $p < 0.05$; $F = 2.16$, $p < 0.05$), the latter two conditions not reaching a meaningful difference ($t = 0.10$).

These data, then, add to the validity of our hypothesis that under similar antecedent conditions minority and majority influence sources produce similar public effects. They do indeed reveal that under conditions of social support both the conformity effect and the innovation effect are drastically reduced, and that the larger the amount of social support the smaller the resulting conformity and innovation effects.

As to the interpretation of these social support data, we have to touch lightly on two problems. First of all, the conformity literature currently considers the social support factor in itself as the major determinant of non-conformity behaviour. Yet a most plausible alternative interpretation could be proposed. Indeed, the fact that under social support conditions subjects repeatedly give correct responses could enhance the subjects' public commitment to this particular response. It is plausible to assume that once targets publicly adopt a particular response – in this case the correct response – they want to appear consistent so as to avoid losing face in the eyes of others. Therefore, the fact that targets stick to this response even in the absence of social supporters could possibly be due to the subjects' public commitment to this particular response pattern rather than to the social support factor itself. Some additional data collected within the present study to some extent lend support to this interpretation. Indeed, subjects who during the first half of the influence phase merely acted as observers – they observed the social supporters' responses without having to take positions themselves either in public or in private – proved to be somewhat more vulnerable to the influence attempts of a majority and of a minority source in the absence of the social supporters than subjects in the comparable social support condition ($t = 1.85$, $p < 0.10$). However, since only a marginal difference was obtained, the conclusion that a subject's public commitment to his initial response pattern co-determines his reduced vulnerability to the source's influence attempts at a later stage should be considered as tentative and provisional. It should be noted, however, that with respect to these observation conditions the data patterns that emerged in the innovation and the conformity conditions were again quite similar.

A second argument relates more specifically to the similarity of the observed innovation and conformity effects. In the previous section we already digressed on the trend towards a difference – a statistically non-significant difference, it is true – between the conformity and the innovation breakdown conditions, and accounted for it by referring to the small difference between both conditions with respect to the amount of social support given to the targets. In the present study, again small (and in fact not significant at all) but remarkably consistent differences appear between both influence conditions. In all but one of the innovation conditions the influence effects are somewhat less pronounced than the effects in the comparable conformity conditions. Although we should not rely too heavily on these apparent differences, it may be noted in passing that these small differences possibly arise from the still present differences between the two influence conditions with respect to the strength of social support which targets receive. It should indeed be kept in mind that in the innovation conditions the target group consists of one subject and three social supporters while in the conformity condition it consists of one subject and only one social supporter. In view of these differences, which are difficult to erase because they are inherent in the two influence modalities, it could then be conjectured that the three social supporters in the innovation condition would possibly create more resistance to the cross-pressures exerted by the influence source than the single social supporter in the conformity condition. Although this conjecture should be seriously considered, at this stage the need for caution in this respect cannot be overemphasised.

6. The saliency of a target's own reference group: its impact in innovation and conformity settings

The empirical research discussed in the previous paragraphs essentially focused on the effects of social support within innovation contexts and highlighted the similarity of its role in situations of majority and minority influence. The manipulation of the social support factor served two purposes. First, it empirically demonstrated that under identical conditions of social support minority and majority influence sources would produce similar public effects. Secondly, it offered evidence for the proposition that previous comparisons of public conformity and innovation effects were weak, because of the ever-present differences in social support which by themselves can account for the differences between the public conformity and innovation effects. To serve these purposes – the second purpose in particular – in the best possible way, it was decided at the outset that the operationalisation of the social support factor should be as identical as possible to the current operationalisation in both the previous conformity literature and the recent innovation literature.

If, however, we distance ourselves for a moment from the second purpose, we can very properly observe that the particular operationalisation has its shortcomings in that it consists of several confounded variables. In the previous section we already introduced the argument that under conditions of social support the resulting reduction in the subjects' vulnerability to a source's influence attempts might not directly relate to the social support factor in itself but might be mediated by the subjects' public commitment to their initial response pattern. When extracting this public commitment factor from the current introduction of the social support factor, subjects proved to be somewhat less resistant to the subsequent pressures exerted by the influence source. In the present section we will focus on another factor that is regularly confounded with the induced variations in social support, and which might in itself be held responsible for differences in the subjects' vulnerability to the influence attempts of a source. The factor we are referring to is the target's own reference group, which occupies an active and noticeable position in conditions of social support but whose character is not rendered salient at all in conditions without social support. The argument that the latter factor might lead to differences in subsequent influence effects should be seriously considered, and for two reasons. First of all, previous research data (Kelley, 1955; Charters & Newcomb, 1958) revealed that the degree to which a specific group membership is salient for a person has an effect on resistance to a change of attitudes supported by the group. When an individual's awareness of his membership in a specified group is heightened by vivid reminders of this membership, the individual proves to be more resistant to 'cross-pressures'. If one may assume – as we already have – that by increasing the amounts of social support, the target's own reference group becomes a more salient aspect of the influence situation, then our data discussed in the previous section are highly consistent with the proposition that the saliency of the target's reference group functions as an influence parameter. The effects of cross-pressures are indeed reduced to similar degrees in both minority and majority influence situations. It becomes essential, then, to disentangle and distinguish these two factors in order to unequivocally interpret the data of our previous studies.

There might, however, be a second reason why the two factors should be separated. The experimental conditions discussed in the previous section consisted of two parts. The first part served the purpose of introducing the majority–minority variable and of manipulating the amounts of social support. During this part the target's own reference group was actively present and gave social support for sticking to correct judgments. During the second part the target's own reference group no longer gave social support and, in addition, no longer occupied a noticeable position in the situation. Indeed, the target was not merely deprived of social support, he was also completely isolated from his own reference group. Under those conditions similar influence effects were produced by minorities and majorities. The question may then be raised as to whether similar majority and minority effects would also emerge if the target's own reference group were to occupy a more salient position at the time the target's judgments were recorded. In view of the typical composition of the minority and majority target group in situations of, respectively, conformity and innovation, to which we already referred in the previous section, one could speculate that the weak tendency towards differences between minority and majority effects would become more pronounced. One could indeed conjecture that the larger target group in the innovation situation would create more resistance to the cross-pressures exerted by the minority than the smaller target group in the conformity situation.

In an attempt to test the impact of the factor 'saliency of the target's reference group' an experimental situation was created in which the character of the reference group was rendered more conspicuous without, however, introducing additional differences between minority and majority influence situations. As in our previous studies, the experiment started with the manipulation of the majority–minority variable. During this phase the own reference group was actively present. Thereafter, subjects were led to believe that because of a breakdown in the experimental equipment the exchange between themselves and their own group members would either be totally impossible or partly impossible. In the former case, as in our previous studies, the own reference group would no longer play either an active or a passive role in the influence situation (bilateral breakdown). In the latter case, however, although they still played only a passive role, they would preserve a more noticeable position in the influence situation (unilateral breakdown). This was realised by explaining to the target that he would no longer receive feedback from his own group members' reactions to the source's viewpoint, but that the other group members would be kept informed of his reaction to the influence source. In that case, the target's reference group serves, in a way, a control function, albeit in a rather passive manner. A more active participation would have interfered with the purpose of creating as identical conditions as possible for the study of minority and majority influence processes.

The resulting experiment was a 2×2 factorial design, the first factor relating to the position of the influence source (either a majority or a minority), the second factor relating to the degree of saliency of the target's own reference group. An additional control condition served the purpose of evaluating the assessed influence effects. If the saliency of the target's own reference group has to be considered as a factor contributing to differences between both influence processes and effects, then one would have to expect an interaction between both factors. If, on the other hand, this factor only functions as a parameter that reduces to similar degrees the targets' resistance to the influence attempts of minority and majority sources, then it should be responsible for a main effect.

What do we learn from the data? If one just keeps strictly to the results of the statistical analyses, the picture of the data is strikingly simple. First of all, and as in our previous studies, the targets correctly perceived the position of the influence source, of the social supporters and their own position. Indeed, minority influence targets assigned themselves and the social supporters

Table 3. *Mean percentages of influenced responses*

	Bilateral breakdown	Unilateral breakdown
Innovation	18.62	11.95
Conformity	16.32	26.67
Control		1

significantly more to a majority position than majority influence targets ($F_{(1,168)} = 12.39$, $p < 0.01$; $F_{(1,168)} = 9.67$, $p < 0.01$). Conversely, minority influence targets assigned the influence source significantly more to a minority position than majority influence targets ($F_{(1,168)} = 20.73$, $p < 0.01$). Yet, both influence sources produced similar public influence effects. Indeed, an analysis of variance carried out on the 2 × 2 factorial design revealed that neither the main effects nor the interaction effect turned out to be significant ($F_{(1,56)} = 1.34$, 0.12 and 2.52 resp.). Even a non-parametric analysis of variance allowing us to test for interaction effects (Wilson, 1956) and probably most appropriate for the analysis of the influence data obtained, did not reveal either main effects or an interaction effect ($\chi^2_{(1)} = 1.07$, 1.07 and 1.07 resp.). An analysis of variance carried out on the factorial design and the additional control condition revealed a significant difference between all experimental conditions and the control condition ($F_{(1,67)} = 7.27$, $p < 0.01$). These data then force us to conclude that the saliency of the target's own reference group does not function either as a parameter that reduces the target's resistance to a source's influence attempts in general, or as a factor that contributes to differences between both influence processes and effects.

The fact that neither the parametric nor the non-parametric statistical analyses revealed a meaningful interaction effect may be quite surprising and unexpected in view of the percentages of influenced responses mentioned in table 3. An inspection of these data would easily lead us to the conjecture that minorities and majorities lead to similar influence effects when the target's reference group does not occupy a salient position in the group (bilateral breakdown condition), and that they produce different public effects when the target's reference group plays a more essential role (unilateral breakdown condition). As a matter of fact, some data seem to lend support to this conjecture.

When we examine more carefully the difference between all experimental conditions and the control condition, there proves to be one experimental condition, namely the innovation–unilateral breakdown condition, that is not significantly different from the control condition. The comparable conformity condition, on the other hand, leads to the most pronounced effect. When both experimental conditions are compared by means of *a priori* comparisons, the difference reaches an acceptable level of statistical difference. However, the results of *a posteriori* comparisons reveal that the difference cannot be considered as meaningful. Hence, although there seems to be a tendency for minorities and majorities not to produce similar effects when the target's reference group occupies a noticeable position, one should treat this tendency with caution, because it is based on *post-hoc* analyses that do not reveal unequivocal results.

Nevertheless, in view of the data pattern, we should consider the possibility that the actual manipulation of the saliency of the target's own reference group was not strong enough to elicit meaningful differential minority and majority influence effects. The present data do indeed invite us to strengthen the manipulation of this factor so as to create optimal conditions for evoking the possibly present tendency towards a differentiation of minority and majority influence. The present tendency towards a decreasing innovation effect and towards an increasing conformity effect is indeed most interesting. If significant it would imply that in the innovation situation the target's own reference group, by merely observing the target's reaction to the source's influence attempts, would be successful in increasing the target's resistance to the source's pressures, whereas in the conformity situation the own reference group would not be successful at all in reducing the source's impact – on the contrary. It should be remembered, however, that in the latter situation the target's behaviour was observed not only by a member of his own reference group but also by two members of the influence source. The effects of the additional two members of the source could possibly have outweighed the effects of the own reference group member. At this stage, however, and in view of the conjectural and tentative character of the foregoing digression we would be inclined to base our conclusions more heavily on the data obtained in the main analyses. We would therefore provisionally conclude that the saliency of a target's own reference group does not significantly reduce the effects of cross-pressures and that it does not contribute to a differentiation between innovation and conformity effects. Our data can therefore be considered as supporting the proposition that under similar conditions of social support majority and minority influence sources produce similar public effects, and this irrespective of the salient character of the target's own reference group.

7. A recapitulation and a digression

The present chapter has basically aimed at further disclosing a remarkable parallel between minority and majority influence processes and effects by examining the role of social support within an innovation context and by focusing on the eventual similarity of the function served by social supporters in situations of majority and of minority influence. The impetus for our efforts derived from a three-fold observation. First, the innovation literature currently reports influence data derived from comparisons between public majority influence under conditions without social support and public minority influence under conditions with social support, to provide empirical grounds for proposing that majorities produce more pronounced public effects than minorities; this is done without ever considering the possible effects of social support within the innovation context. Second, the conformity literature offers ample evidence to uphold the contention that social supporters serve the undeniable function of successfully thwarting a majority source's final public impact. Third, our previous work on minority influence set the stage for serious consideration of an analogy that emerged – on a *post-hoc* basis and derived from indirect comparisons, it is true – between minority and majority influence processes.

Against this background it was proposed that social supporters serve a similar function in situations of minority and of majority influence, in that they are capable of successfully increasing a target's resistance to the influence pressures of a source and therefore effectively reduce the source's public impact. It was furthermore argued that a minority influence source, if it were given the opportunity of exerting its influence on isolated targets who were by no means socially supported for holding to their initial judgments, would be as capable as a majority influence source of producing very pronounced public effects. The implication is that the reported differences in public effects that are currently exclusively associated with the position of an influence source should in fact be dissociated from a source's position and should instead be related to differences with respect to the amount of social support received by a particular target.

Three studies were carried out to complement our analysis with direct experimental proof. The data offer empirical grounds for upholding the propositions and they invite us seriously to consider an integration, rather than a differentiation, of conformity and innovation processes with respect to their public effects. At the same time they provide indications that recent minority influence research has precluded the emergence of this parallel between both influence processes by inadvertently neglecting the possible effects of the ever-present social support factor in the innovation context – resulting in current underestimation of a consistent minority's public impact.

In view of the consistency of the experimental data reported in the present contribution, we consider these conclusions as justified, although they may still be subject to various criticisms.

A major argument might in fact concern the external validity of our conclusions. One could object that the data on which our conclusions are based have been observed under rather peculiar conditions, the most salient of which would relate to the fact that both the majority and the minority influence source did in fact defend objectively incorrect judgments. Outside the laboratory situation these judgments would unquestionably be considered as deviant and hence as minority responses. The implication would be that our efforts missed their mark since we studied and compared two situations of minority influence rather than situations of minority and of majority influence as we had in mind. With this argument one broaches a core problem concerning the theoretical definition of a minority and a majority source and its operationalisation. Beyond a few exceptions, majorities and minorities are currently defined in a relative way, i.e. in terms of the number of individuals who share certain opinions, judgments, values, and so on, relative to a salient reference group. At first glance, the definition is self-evident and unambiguous, so that everyone will agree on it. However, the vagueness of the notion 'reference group' makes the definition less unequivocal and hence debatable. We might get different answers to the question of which reference group should be focused on when defining one group as a 'minority' and another as a 'majority'. Indeed, the choice of a particular reference group depends largely upon the momentary salience of a particular social reality. The argument relating to the external validity of our conclusions reflects exactly this divergence as to the social reality that should be focused on. Whereas we focused on the social reality created within the laboratory, others would focus on the social reality outside the laboratory, i.e. on the total population out of which a random sample was brought into the laboratory. These differences of focus will naturally lead to contradictory definitions of the position of a source. The question arises, then, whether it is at all possible to define and operationalise a particular influence source's position in such a way that everyone will agree upon it.

To get round this problem one might ask the individuals involved in a given social interaction setting to define their own and others' positions in the group, and rely upon their perception of the most salient social reality. It was to this alternative that we had recourse in our own studies reported in this contribution, and it was shown that subjects in all innovation conditions assigned themselves to a majority position and the source to a minority position, and conversely that subjects in all conformity conditions assigned themselves to a minority position and the source to a majority position. These data would suggest, then, that the social reality created within the laboratory was the most salient reality to the subjects at that time. The question arises as to whether, in view of these data, one still has the right to disregard the subjects' interpretation and to state that both sources occupy identical positions because that would be the case in the social reality outside the laboratory?

In our opinion the question should be answered in the negative, because it would be unjustified to ignore the subjects' reality construct. With respect to the validity of our own studies we would therefore be inclined to state that we studied and compared minority and majority influence processes and that our conclusions are externally valid in view of the social reality definitions provided by the individuals who took part in the social interactions. The data we reported have therefore reality value, even when they go against expectations derived from facts present in a different social reality – for instance, outside the laboratory. At this stage we are therefore convinced that our experimental situations reflect exactly several real-life situations in which individuals are confronted either with majority sources or with minority sources. Nevertheless, we are at the same time fully aware of their limitations. It should indeed be kept in mind that the social reality definitions given by the subjects cannot be considered as totally independent of their own behaviour, their own reactions in the social influence situation. Their definitions are in fact *post-hoc* definitions that might be affected by the behaviour they displayed during the social interaction. As a matter of fact, some data do reveal that there exists a correlation between the subjects' definition of the source's position and their own reaction to the same source's influence attempts. In the innovation conditions there proved to be a positive correlation between the degree to which subjects were influenced by the source and their definition of the source's position: i.e., the more subjects were affected by the source's influence attempts, the stronger they considered the numerical position of the source. In the conformity condition no such correlation emerged however.

In view of this weakness, future research should seriously consider a different methodology to unequivocally introduce the position of an influence source. In our opinion this can only be realised by creating a totally new social reality that evokes as few associations as possible with existing social realities. However difficult this task might be, it is certainly a challenge to our inventiveness and one that we have to take up in our endeavour to study a complex social reality within the laboratory without detracting from its external validity.

In spite of these limitations we are still convinced, as we said before, that our actual experimental situations reflect exactly several real-life situations. Indeed, even outside the laboratory individuals take active part in several social realities and, depending upon the momentary saliency of a specific social reality, they can at one moment or another feel in a minority or in a majority position with respect to, sometimes, the very same statement, opinion, viewpoint. The data assessed in our studies, therefore, allow us to consider their implications for real-life social movements and to derive, albeit on a conjectural and provisional basis, some strategies for effectively innovating, and/or for effectively crossing, an active minority's influence pressures.

Quite contrary to what is currently assumed, in these experiments minorities proved to be capable of producing public agreement with their viewpoint up to a level that until now was exclusively reserved to a majority source. This is a most interesting and important result for two reasons. First, one can think of several real-life situations in which it is most important for an active minority to have public indicators of its influence so as, for example, to strengthen its position in the eyes of the other minority groups or of the actual majority group. If the latter is their final goal they could hardly refer to any private or latent changes they may have brought about, since in several instances (Doms & Van Avermaet, 1980; Moscovici & Personnaz, 1980) these changes may have taken place outside the target's own knowledge or awareness. If, in the end, minorities were only able to produce such private or latent effects, they would have a hard time in convincing outsiders of the numerical strength of their membership, since their adherents would not even be aware of the fact that they were converted to the minority viewpoint. Secondly, and perhaps more importantly, this finding may possibly set the stage for considering some strategies to make minority influence targets publicly express what they already privately believe. Up to now this is certainly one of the major problems minorities have to deal with: to work out strategies that turn private adherence into public agreement. In this respect our general data picture possibly offers promising clues for a digression on some useful strategies for effectively innovating or crossing innovations.

We would advise active minority groups aiming at extending their membership to isolate individuals from their own reference group and to confront them as lone individuals with the minority viewpoint. As a matter of fact, this strategy is already frequently used by some religious minority groups in their efforts to recruit new group members. However, the total isolation of the targets would only be necessary when the group to which the target belongs is very confidently and consistently opposed to the particular minority viewpoint. At times when the target's reference group is less consistent or less self-assured in its position a minority does not even have to isolate its potential targets but can exert its influence within the opposed group. If, however, the target's own reference group is very confident in its own position and if the minority for some reason is incapable of isolating its targets, they might still be quite influential by having own minority group members infiltrate the target's reference group. Through infiltration the minority members could play, in a very credible way, the role of influence supporters – i.e. support the target for going along with the minority viewpoint – and at the same time cross the impact of the target's reference group by rendering the latter group's character less confident, less consistent, and hence less influential. To active parts of the majority group whose ultimate goal is to prevent innovations or social changes, we have merely one bit of advice: break the active minority's unanimity and/or provide your members with consistent social support for sticking to the majority position. A charge history has proved to be at times heavy and difficult.

8. A caveat

This chapter has addressed the issue of the plausibility of an alternative conception of the relation between innovation and conformity, emphasising their isomorphism. A re-analysis of existing evidence and the introduction of new data have offered, in our opinion, sufficient empirical grounds for contending that majority and minority influence processes lead to similar public effects when they operate under identical conditions. To phrase it differently, we would propose that the targets' behaviour in a particular influence situation will be shaped not so much by their perception of the influence source's position – its minority or its majority character – as by other characteristics of particular influence situations, for instance the presence or absence of own reference group members and the behavioural style displayed by them publicly announcing their viewpoint.

However, there are some restrictions concerning the actual validity of this contention which at this stage cannot be overemphasised. A first restriction relates to the fact that the present series of studies merely focused on the similarity of the *public* effects brought about by minorities and majorities. Future research should also investigate subjects' private responses to both influence sources. If majorities and minorities elicit similar effects on the private level as, for instance, we observed in previous studies (Doms & Van

Avermaet, 1980), it would add to the validity of our proposition that both majorities and minorities are capable of eliciting similar kinds of cognitive processes and produce similar behavioural effects.

A second restriction relates to our assumption that majority and minority influence sources exert their influence under *identical conditions*. It should be explicitly stated that, in view of this restriction, our contention does not necessarily nor automatically imply the incorrectness of the more general proposition (Moscovici, 1976, 1980) that the two influence modalities in general involve different processes and produce divergent effects. After all, the factors that proved to shape the targets' public behaviour in our laboratory situations might not be as evenly distributed over both influence modalities in more natural influence situations. Consider, for example, the probability that targets will receive social support for their own initial viewpoint or the probability that the targets' own reference group will occupy a noticeable position in an influence situation. Everyone will agree that these probabilities will be different for both influence modalities, i.e. that they will be much higher for situations of innovation than for situations of conformity. Since in more natural influence situations there will be a co-variation between the factors we focused on and the influence source's position, it can indeed be stated on a more general level that both influence sources produce divergent behavioural effects. However, if minority and majority influence sources in reality would lead to different effects that have to be accounted for by referring to different processes, then antecedent conditions other than those presented in theoretical reviews and manipulated in recent research have to be seriously considered. The fact that it would not be the perceived position of an influence source that automatically triggers a specific cognitive process, but rather certain situational aspects of the influence settings – which usually co-vary with the source's position, it is true – possibly opens up an avenue for actively planning and arranging the environment within which influence sources will present a well-defined and coherent viewpoint, so as to evoke the desired effects.

Note

1. The present research was carried out as part of a research project (OT/VI/14) supported by the Research Foundation of the K. U. Leuven and awarded to the second author. The authors are grateful to Hilde Sas for her invaluable help in the running of the experiments and to Jos Feys for his technical assistance.

3. Compromising public influence for private change

CHARLAN NEMETH

In most decision-making settings individuals attempt to reach an agreement on what they feel will be the best, the most efficacious or the most proper position. Whether in corporate board rooms or in jury rooms this attempt at reaching a group decision generally involves a modification of judgments on the part of some or all of the individuals involved. This modification of judgment may be simply at the overt or public level; it may also reflect a real modification of attitude or judgment on the part of the individual.

The possibility that the modification may be at the overt level but not reflective of a true change in position is obvious in certain types of decisions. In jury trials (found in the Anglo common law tradition and most frequently used in the United States), 12 individuals come together to hear the evidence and to deliberate until they reach consensus on the guilt or innocence of a defendant (or compensation to be awarded a litigant). In some cases the evidence is such that the defendant either committed murder in the first degree or is 'not guilty'. Yet juries may find that person guilty of manslaughter. If all the evidence suggests premeditation but the question is 'Who did the shooting?' the defendant is either guilty of first degree murder or is 'not guilty'. The notion that he committed the crime under 'passion of the moment', for example, does not follow from the evidence. Yet, it may culminate from a deadlock between individuals who believe the defendant is 'guilty of first degree murder' and those who believe him to be 'not guilty'. Thus, the modification of judgment appears to be a result of negotiation, of overt modification, in order to reach a consensus.

From a practical point of view, the issue of whether or not public or overt attitude change is reflective of a corresponding private or latent change may or may not be of considerable importance. The hypothetical defendant can be freed or imprisoned because of the jury verdict whether or not all the jurors privately believed the verdict to be the most appropriate. A salesman may or may not care whether or not he/she has changed attitudes if a customer overtly agrees to his viewpoint (and buys the product). However, the lack of corresponding private change, even at a practical level, could be important in terms of morale, community confidence, willingness to carry out the implications of a decision, etc. At a theoretical level, the distinction is of the utmost importance.

Every area that has dealt with social influence processes, be it under the rubric of attitude change, negotiation, conformity, minority influence or group decision making, has had to contend with the importance of the public/private, manifest/latent, distinction in influence. Research on conformity, for example, tends to find public change in judgment but rarely finds private change. The attitude change literature is nearly obsessed with failure of attitudes to predict behaviour that should be consistent with the attitude. Even the distinctions between compliance, identification and internalisation (Kelman, 1958) are based in part upon a public/private dimension.

Compliance generally refers to public conformity without private acceptance. This is why compliance requires surveillance. One example is the study by Lewin, Lippitt & White (1939) which showed good performance when a leader was present but poorer performance when he was absent. A related example is given by Coch & French (1958) who found that group pressures could induce reduced productivity on the part of workers; when the group could no longer punish, however, the production increased. Internalisation, on the other hand, refers to attitudes or judgments that are incorporated into one's own value system and which then 'act as guides for one's behaviour without the necessity of surveillance. For example, political beliefs that have been adopted during early years in college can become important and internalised guides for other attitudes and behaviour (Newcomb, 1943).

1. Competing theories of social influence

The foregoing distinction between public and private change may be the reason for some competing, and even contradictory, theories of social influence. If one theory concentrates on public change while another focuses on private change one might expect the theories to be contradictory. There is no reason to assume that the mechanisms promoting public change are necessarily those that promote private change; there is even some reason to assume they may be in opposition. Let us first look at some examples.

A good many theories assume that attraction and influence go hand in hand. Such a connection is so entrenched in the literature that one textbook author considers it 'obvious' that 'attractive groups (get) more conformity' (Schneider, 1976: 247). Another (Middlebrook, 1980: 202) finds the adage 'the more likable they are, the more persuasive they'll be... almost too obvious to be stated'. Such an assumption also provides the underpinning to many versions of a balance theory. Osgood & Tannenbaum's (1955) 'congruity principle', for example, posits a balance between the source, the assertion and the concept. If the source is positive, agreement with him provides a balanced state. Empirical work has, by and large, confirmed such a proposition. Communicators who are more physically attractive, more credible or more similar to the target, for example, are found to be more influential (Hovland & Weiss, 1951; Mills & Aronson, 1965; Berscheid, 1966; Horai, Naccari & Fatoullah, 1974). Similarly, some theorists assume that behaviours that make you liked are also those that render your influence attempts more effective. Thus, one is advised how to 'win friends *and* influence people' by tactics such as emphasizing similarity (Mills & Jellison, 1968), dressing well (Darley & Cooper, 1972) or ingratiation (Jones, 1964).

There is another literature, however, where influence is achieved at the expense of liking. This is the recent work on minority influence where the initial minority, or deviant, disagrees with the majority view and attempts to persuade the majority to his/her position. Nearly every study in this area shows that the minority is disliked even when influential (Nemeth, Swedlund & Kanki, 1974; Nemeth, 1980). In fact, the theorists in this area argue that maintenance of the deviant position, a tactic that is likely to *invoke* dislike of the minority, is a necessary condition for minority influence (Moscovici & Faucheux, 1972; Moscovici & Nemeth, 1974; Nemeth, 1980). By being uncompromising and insisting on its own position the minority may well produce reactance (Brehm, 1966) in the form of intense dislike if not reactance in the form of resistance to influence. The minority influence literature, however, argues that such consistency and maintenance of position is the way that others see the position as a firm one, one in which the influencing agent believes. Such consistency then provides a stable anchor to which the others can move.

Empirical work has, by and large, substantiated this hypothesis. Moscovici, Lage & Naffrechoux (1969), for example, show that individuals can be made to judge blue stimuli as 'green' when the minority consistently takes the position of 'green'. When they are inconsistent (i.e. they respond 'blue' on some trials), they exert no influence. While this study demonstrates the importance of consistency in the sense of repetition, other work (e.g. Nemeth, Swedlund & Kanki, 1974) points out that the perception of consistency can be achieved more subtly than by simple repetition. Within a specific context a position needs to be maintained; when a property of the stimulus changes the judgments can change without affecting the perception of consistency or influence. Nonetheless, this and other studies have confirmed the importance of maintenance of position for minority influence. It appears to be the mechanism by which others see a stable and firmly believed position. This provides the mechanism by which they come to question their own judgment and to adopt the position being espoused (see Nemeth, 1980, for a review of related empirical work).

While the above perspective argues that consistency and non-compromise is the mechanism for influence, the literature on bargaining and negotiation offers a contradictory theory and evidence for it. Relying more on the implicit premise that liking is linked to influence or, perhaps more importantly, dislike is linked to resistance, reactance and no influence, the bargaining theorists argue for the efficacy of compromise. They, in fact, propose that compromise is *necessary* for reaching an agreement. From this perspective, compromise is a 'cooperative' gesture, one that promotes reciprocal concessions and, thus, ultimate agreement. Rather than detail the numerous studies on this issue, let me simply use the summary statements from an excellent review of the bargaining literature (Rubin & Brown, 1975) which the interested reader is encouraged to read. Based on an analysis of a number of studies, Rubin & Brown argue that:

1. Early initiation of cooperative behavior tends to promote the development of trust and a mutually beneficial, cooperative relationship; early competitive behavior, on the other hand, tends to induce mutual suspicion and competition. (1975: 263)
2. A bargainer who makes (positive) concessions is more likely to elicit cooperation the other than one who makes either negative concessions or no concessions at all. (1975: 272)

These propositions are based on studies primarily using the Prisoner's Dilemma game, or some variant thereof, which find that initially cooperative behaviour tends to induce cooperation in return more than initially competitive behaviour (Evans & Crumbaugh, 1966; Tedeschi, Lesnick & Gahagan, 1968).

While the bargaining literature makes it clear that compromise is necessary, it appears that *noncontingent* cooperation is not very effective. This strategy invites exploitation. The trick apparently is to be 'tough' and yet to be flexible and cooperative – contingently cooperative. Thus, we find support for the following:

3. Bargainers attain higher and more satisfactory outcomes when they begin their interaction with extreme rather than more moderate demands. (Rubin & Brown, 1975: 277)
4. Subjects tend to behave more cooperatively in the presence of another whose behavior is contingent upon, rather than independent of, their own behavior. A bargainer wants to believe he is capable of shaping the other's behavior, of causing the other to choose as he (the other) does (pp. 277–8).

These propositions are illustrated by studies (e.g. Komorita & Brenner, 1968) in which it is shown that an approach making extreme initial demands followed by gradual concessions is more effective than starting at a reasonable position and remaining there or starting extreme and remaining firm. The advice is to ask for more than you can reasonably expect but to make small and gradual concessions along the way.

In a similar vein, Morley & Stephenson's (1977) review of bargaining studies points to the usefulness of 'toughness' defined as larger initial demands, higher mean level of demand, fewer concessions, smaller concessions and higher level of minimum goals (pp. 86–8). The best strategy is to make concessions and yet appear strong (Pruitt & Johnson, 1970); it is to have high initial goals and bids followed by a series of small and conciliatory gestures (Kelley, 1966; Osgood, 1967).

Before attempting to address the reasons for such contradictory theories, let us first make some observations regarding the differential contexts in bargaining *versus* influence situations. In bargaining settings the individuals have a conflict of interests. The point of the interaction is to divide resources or resolve issues among the participants. The concentration is on the public agreement – the verdict, the 'resolution', the contract. In influence settings there are no resources to be divided. The participants may have a difference of opinion or judgment but they may or may not need to come to a public agreement. In fact, the researchers in the minority influence area have concentrated on private change rather than public agreement with the persistent minority. To some extent, the authors have assumed that there is little motive for public agreement with the minority unless it is accompanied by private change as well. And such an assumption appears to be corroborated. Most minority influence studies find private change on the part of the subjects. Moscovici, Lage & Naffrechoux (1969), for example, showed a change in categorisation of blue/green stimuli in the direction of calling more stimuli 'green' after exposure to the persistent minority.

Another study (Nemeth & Wachtler, 1974) provides still further evidence of latent change. In that study the authors used a 'personal injury' case (i.e. a legal case involving the injury of an individual who was suing a company for negligence), and had a 'confederate' argue for, and maintain a position of, much less compensation than the other individuals. He argued for $3,000 compensation whereas the others believed the person should be compensated by approximately $15,000. His maintenance of position and confident acts caused a lowering of compensation *not only* on the case under discussion but on related cases involving personal injury. Thus, minority influence in a decision-making setting was found to generalise to other judgments.

While such research points to the importance of private opinion change in minority influence studies, it should also be pointed out that there is a negotiation element to discussion settings, particularly when agreement is required. As in the example given earlier, individuals can negotiate a verdict (e.g. manslaughter) as a compromise between first degree murder and 'not guilty'. There are other expectations that differentiate the classical bargaining setting from that typically used in studying minority influence. In a bargaining situation one makes the assumption that each person wants to come to an agreement but that each one wants the agreement to be in his own best interests. If one is the buyer one wants to buy the product at the lowest possible price. If one is the seller one wants to sell the product at the highest possible price. While other considerations, e.g. equity or fairness, may be operative, the motive of self-interest and the justification for such a motive is quite clear. In a decision-making context, the motives and the definitions of self-interest are not so clear. In many settings, e.g. juries, one supposedly cannot gain or lose tangible rewards. Presumably it involves an honest interchange of beliefs in an attempt to find consensus. Thus, it may well be that the perception of the same behaviour may be viewed differently in these contexts.

Now we can return to the original contradictions between the findings of the bargaining studies and those in minority influence studies. In particular, the contradictions revolve around the role of compromise. Bargaining theorists argue that compromise is necessary for 'influence' in the sense of a successful agreement. Minority influence theorists argue that compromise is ineffective as a technique for influence; consistency and maintenance of position are the necessary ingredients for influence. Our assumption, in this paper, is that such theoretical and empirical contradictions are due to the inherent concentration on the public *versus* private aspect of influence. We propose that compromise is effective for achieving reciprocal concessions and ultimate public agreement but that such a technique is ineffective in fostering private opinion change. On the other hand, we argue that consistency and maintenance of position is the necessary ingredient for private opinion but that it may not be acknowledged in the public setting – thus appearing to be ineffective. It may even cause a reactance at the public level evidence by a polarisation of position.

If the foregoing is correct, it further suggests the possibility of a creative merging of the two strategies *depending on how the compromise is perceived*. If compromise is perceived as a *strategy*, one that does not indicate a change in position but one that is seen as a tactic aimed at reaching agreement, it may be effective at both the public and private level. The concession making should foster reciprocal concessions (and possibly agreement) at the public level. The perception of consistency should create private change as well.

Such thinking is rather loosely connected to some of our previous work on colour judgments (Nemeth, Swedlund & Kanki, 1974). In that study we argued that the *perception* of consistency was the necessary ingredient of minority influence, not repetition of response. Thus, we created a situation in which the minority changed their judgments from 'green' to 'green-blue', but where such changes were correlated with a physical property of the stimulus (in this case, brightness). Other conditions randomly paired the same responses to the stimuli or had repetition of response. Findings indicated that the minority was perceived as consistent and confident when their responses were correlated with the physical property of the stimulus and it was in those conditions that the minority was most effective. When the response change was random, no influence was exerted. Thus, changes in response may suggest an inconsistency of position or they may be attributed to something else. In this study it could be attributed to a property of the stimulus. In the decision-making setting discussed earlier it could be attributed to an attempt to reach agreement; it could be seen as strategy and tactic rather than a reflection of one's private opinion. In a bargaining setting one tends to assume that the private belief is the solution in one's own best interests and such interests are fairly obvious; thus, one sees behaviour primarily in tactical terms. In influence settings there is a blurring of perceptions. While the discussion is presumably a reflection of one's private beliefs, there can be a negotiation element as well, a desire to reach a public agreement in the direction of one's own position.

2. An experimental test

Quite recently we conducted a study investigating some of these premises (Nemeth & Brilmayer, 1982). Let us first summarise the basic hypotheses:

1. Compromise should be effective at inducing public change and in accomplishing agreement at the public level, i.e. a decision will be reached.
2. Consistency, however, will be more effective at inducing private or latent change. Individuals exposed to consistency will be more likely to have their private attitudes changed and such influence will be manifested in changes on related decisions.
3. Compromise that is seen as a *tactic* aimed at achieving agreement rather than seen as a change in position will accomplish both public and private change.

To test these hypotheses we used a jury deliberation setting and asked individuals to discuss, and to attempt to reach agreement on, a personal injury case. Consistency was operationalised in the form of maintenance of position. The individual 'voted' the exact same amount of compensation each time. Compromise was defined as a movement towards the majority position.

To accomplish our variable manipulations we designed a case in which the large percentage of subjects was in basic agreement on the amount of compensation that was appropriate. This particular case involved a ski accident arising from the collapse of a ski lift in mid-air. The ski corporation was found to be negligent by the Court but the 'jurors' were asked to determine the amount of compensation that should be given to the victim, Mr Turner (age 25, a white male), for the pain and suffering caused to him, past, present and future. The injuries amounted to the removal of a segment of the femur of his left leg, one inch of bone, which had created a limp as well as back pains. While the individual was asking for $500,000 in damages, most individuals felt that he should be given anywhere from $150,000 to $300,000. Only those individuals making such judgments were invited to participate in the experiment. Our confederate, the minority in this case, took the position of $50,000 compensation. Three 'naive' individuals who never differed more than $50,000 from each other then constituted the other 'jurors' in a jury of four people. The confederate was a white male university student in his early twenties, indistinguishable from the subjects.

For the deliberation we chose a variant on free discussion. Since it is very difficult for a confederate to be entirely consistent in his behaviour from one group to the next (e.g. other 'jurors' ask different questions, talk more or less, etc.), we decided to have a sequence of 'ballots'. We allowed the four people in a given group to 'discuss' the case, each one giving his opinion followed by one minute of argument, justification, etc. This was then followed by three minutes in which anyone else could speak. After one person finished, the second person gave his judgment, took one minute to defend it and there were then three minutes of general discussion. This same procedure was then followed for the third person and then the fourth person. The confederate was always person 'A', i.e. the first person. There were ten such rounds. If no agreement could be reached in ten rounds the jury was considered to be 'hung'. Jurors were apprised at the beginning of the deliberation of the rules of discourse and of the ten-round limit. The specific instructions were as follows:

Instructions: 'I am studying decision making in groups and I have asked you to come here to discuss the personal injury case in front of you as a group and come to an agreement on how much should be awarded to Mr Turner. I want you to act as though you were a real jury deciding this case that would affect the lives of real people who are involved.

Normally, in group discussion you would have a very free flowing sort of discussion. You would toss out your ideas, argue why your ideas were correct, why somebody else's were wrong, and interact with each other freely. For this experiment I want to change the rules a bit. Instead of interacting freely I would like you to take turns. Let us say we start with person A. Person A would state his position and defend it (that is, give his reasons for why he thinks that is a good amount of compensation) and then defend his position up to a minute. During this period persons B, C, and D should not interact with him in any way. They should not react to what he is saying, should not ask him any questions, or argue. After person A has stated his position, however, persons B, C, and D can – if they want – make comments about what they think about that position. In that case, they will be able to interact with each other freely. However, during this period person A should not respond. He should not ask questions or defend his position. He should sit and listen to what they are saying about his position. After that, person B will state his position and defend it for about a minute and persons A, C, and D should not interact with him. When he is through, persons A, C, and D can discuss person B's position, but he should not interact with them. After that, person C will state his position and defend it. The persons A, B, and D will have a chance to comment on person C's position. Then person D will state his position and persons A, B, and C will have a chance to discuss person D's position.

If you reach agreement after one round, I will assume the jury has come to a decision and end the discussion. If there is not agreement, however, we will go on to a second round of positions and comments. We will continue in this manner either until you have reached consensus – a unanimous opinion – or ten rounds have been completed.

For the purposes of this experiment it is essential that you act as though you were a real jury. In cases of this type, if a jury cannot reach a decision then it is considered to be hung and the case has to be retried at the great expense of all the participants. On the other hand, you should not compromise just to reach an agreement if you do not feel that agreement will be fair. So I am asking you to do a very difficult task. Try your best to reach an agreement, but do not compromise what you really believe to be fair.

Are there any questions?'

For the experimental conditions we attempted to operationalise consistency *versus* compromise. We then attempted to distinguish between a compromise that would be viewed as a tactic aimed at reaching an agreement *versus* one that would be viewed as a sign of inconsistency of position. With regard to the latter, our thinking was that concession making 'at the last minute' tends to be viewed as a tactic, a strategy for achieving an agreement. Thus, if one person maintains his position over the course of the discussion but during the last few minutes or on the last few rounds of votes makes a concession and moves to the position of the others – this is strategy rather than inconsistency. The most reasonable explanation for the movement is that it is his last chance to achieve an agreement. Thus, he should be viewed as making a tactical concession in the hopes of achieving a reciprocal concession and ultimate agreement. He should not be viewed as inconsistent or lacking in commitment to his position. Where compromise or concession making is not 'at the last minute', the reasons become less clear. Obviously, if they occur in response to another person's movement, they can be seen as strategy. This is undoubtedly what happens in the contingently cooperative conditions in studies using the Prisoner's Dilemma game (e.g. Evans & Crumbaugh, 1966). However, if they do not occur in response to other people's position changes, if they do not form a coherent pattern or if there is no clearly discernible strategy, one is more prone to see inconsistency or a lack of commitment on the part of the person.

Based on such an analysis, we utilised the fact that we had a ten-round limit on the discussion *and* that subjects were apprised of this fact prior to deliberation. Thus, subjects knew when time was running out. We assumed that compromise early in the deliberation would be seen as a sign of inconsistency. As such it might be effective in inducing reciprocal concession making at the public level. However, these subjects should not show preferences for lowered levels of compensation on the case under study, nor on related cases. This 'early compromise' was operationalised as a change from an initial position of $50,000 to $100,000 on round 2. For 'late compromise', or strategic compromise, we had the confederate move from his initial position of $50,000 to $100,000 on round 9.

To compare the efficacy of such compromise with simple maintenance of position, we also had a condition in which the confederate maintained the $50,000 position for all ten rounds. As a 'control', we had naive subjects deliberating the case; no confederate was present. For each condition we had six groups of three naive subjects, constituting 18 subjects in each condition, or a total of 72 subjects. All were male undergraduates at the University of California, Berkeley.

At the level of public change we were interested in whether or not these groups came to agreement as a function of the confederate's behaviour. We were also interested in the private or latent change induced by such behaviour. Thus, we asked individuals to return a day later to give judgments on the case under discussion as well as a number of other personal injury cases. One of the cases (the most similar case to the case under discussion) involved a Mr Brown, a white male 26-year-old architect who suffered from migraine headaches caused by leakage in a microwave oven that he had purchased. The headaches occurred about once a month, requiring rest for a couple of hours. The court had found the company negligent and again the 'jurors' were asked to decide on compensation for pain and suffering. In the other cases personal injury was again the issue, though an individual rather than a company was negligent. For example, one case involved medical malpractice; another involved reckless driving.

While the predicted results were stronger for the private change than the public change, the pattern was basically in support of our predictions. Let us consider the three types of results – public change, private change and perceptions of the confederate – in sequence. For public change, we kept an account of each person's public position on each of the ten rounds (remember, each person had to announce his position prior to defending it on each round). These positions were averaged for each round. Since subjects within a group are not independent of one another, the group mean was used as the datum. No differences in *average* compensation were found for rounds 1–4 among the conditions. However, the control groups had all reached agreement by round 4. None of the experimental groups had reached agreement by this time. The position on which the six control groups agreed averaged $242,500, a position very close to their starting position of $230,556. One control group reached agreement on round 1; two reached agreement on round 2; one reached it on round 3; and the remaining two groups reached agreement on round 4. Thus, the control groups quickly came to agreement by a process akin to normalisation (see Moscovici, 1974). By mutual exchange and compromise they converged 'in the middle'. In contrast, no experimental group reached agreement – even by round 10. To do so would have meant agreement around the confederate's position of $50,000 (or $100,000 in the compromise groups). No group did this.

There is some marginal evidence for our proposition that compromise would lead to more public influence than the consistent condition. While the differences at round 10 allow for such a conclusion, i.e. the late and early compromise conditions showed lower average compensation judgments than the consistent condition, the change from round 1 to round 10 does not allow for such a conclusion. While not significantly different, the early compromise condition started slightly lower than the late compromise condition which started slightly lower than the consistent condition. Thus, the change from this average judgment on round 1 to the average judgment on round 10 was not significantly different among the conditions. It is possible that, had there been more time for deliberation (e.g. 20 rounds), the compromise would have succeeded in achieving reciprocal concessions. It is also clear from observing the average judgments from one round to the next that subjects were less variable in the consistent condition than in either of the compromise conditions. In the compromise conditions, it appears that subjects were attempting compromise and then retracting it in the service of achieving favourable agreement. In contrast, they remained quite close to their starting

Table 1. *Mean position by round (awards in $)*

Round	Consistent	Late compromise	Early compromise	Control
1	251,389	246,111	237,500	243,130
2 (early compromise)	248,611	248,444	237,833	244,713
3	247,222	246,944	240,056	277,222
4	244,444	244,167	237,278	287,500
5	244,444	237,500	237,278	—
6	241,667	234,722	225,722	—
7	244,444	233,333	225,555	—
8	244,444	231,944	227,500	—
9 (late compromise)	250,000	226,388	226,944	—
10	259,000	230,555	228,055	—

point of $250,000 throughout the rounds when faced with the consistent confederate who repeatedly maintained a position of $50,000. (See table 1.)

Private change results were quite consistent with our predictions. Let us first describe how these data were collected. On Day 2, one day after the discussion, subjects were to return to the laboratory and give judgment on the original case that they had discussed a day earlier (the Turner case) as well as give judgments on six generalisation cases. As mentioned earlier, one of these involved a very similar case in which a corporation was negligent (i.e. the Brown case) whereas the others involved personal injury but were less generalisable, in that they involved individual negligence. Seventeen of the 18 subjects in each condition returned to the laboratory for the second day of testing. Again, the group mean was used as the datum and the subjects' judgments were analysed in terms of the specific predicted contrasts. With regard to private change, we had predicted that the late compromise and the consistent conditions would be more effective than the early compromise condition or the control. The results for the original Turner case on Day 2 showed no statistically significant differences between conditions. However, the predicted contrasts did appear on the generalisation cases. As can be seen in table 2, a test of this contrast proved to be highly significant ($p < 0.05$) for the most generalisable case (i.e. the Brown case) and marginally significant for the five other cases as well ($p < 0.08$).

The most influence (i.e. the lowest compensation judgments) was found for subjects exposed to the confederate who maintained his position on the original (the Turner) case or for subjects exposed to the confederate who compromised 'late', i.e. on the 9th round. The least influence (i.e. the highest compensation judgments) was found for subjects exposed to the confederate

Table 2. *Generalisation: judgments on other personal injury cases (awards in $)*

	Consistent	Late compromise	Early compromise	Control
Generalisation case: (corporation negligent, male victim) Brown	179,412	152,341	208,530	256,222
Other personal injury cases: 2 cases with male victim, 3 with female victim, individual negligent	226,924	240,906	268,059	267,543
Average over all cases	219,127	226,245	258,137	265,656

who compromised 'early', i.e. on the 2nd round, or who were not exposed to a confederate adopting a minority position.

As part of the questionnaire, subjects were also asked about their moods and their perceptions of the other individuals. Those who were exposed to the consistent confederate, i.e. the confederate who maintained the $50,000 position for all ten rounds, reported being most 'angry'. They also indicated that they had 'examined their feelings (more) about personal injury cases'. The late compromise confederate was seen as most 'flexible' and most 'influential'.

Thus, the results are generally in line with our predictions. There is some indication, though not convincing proof, that compromise may be more effective at inducing public change, at increasing the likelihood of agreement. However, it is clear that consistency of position is more effective at fostering private change. We found that subjects reported 're-examining their feelings towards personal injury cases'. Such re-examination appears to have led to a change in position on other, related, cases. Subjects exposed to consistent defence of very low levels of compensation gave lowered judgments on a highly generalisable case as well as four other personal injury cases.

It also appears that the 'late' compromise, i.e. a compromise that is a tactic aimed at reaching agreement, may have it 'both ways'. It has nearly the same impact as the consistent behaviour on private change; yet, it may well have some advantages in the public domain. Subjects report being much less 'angry' in the late compromise than in the consistent condition. Such lessened anger may, we presume, lessen the likelihood of reactance towards the position espoused by the minority. Reactance is a likely response to consistency, in that consistency involves a pattern of uncompromising behaviour and, as Moscovici (1976: 41) has pointed out, may 'signify the intention to maintain the conflict at its highest pitch, to block any attempt at communication or negotiation with the rest of the community'.

3. Some concluding remarks

Some previous research is similar in focus to that reported here, in that it concentrates on compromise by the minority. Kiesler & Pallack (1975), for example, asked subjects to read a case account of a juvenile delinquent named Johnny Politano (a case based on the Johnny Rocco case of Schachter, 1951). They were then asked to indicate 'the chances that Johnny's behaviour will improve greatly in the first three months'. Most subjects were unsympathetic to Johnny. However, they were given a bogus distribution of opinions in their particular group of six persons, such that there appeared to be a 4:2 split. All subjects believed themselves to be in the majority of four. A second distribution of opinion was then given, presumably because one page of the case account had not been given to the subjects. This allowed the researchers to make a number of experimental manipulations, for example, showing that one member of the majority defected, or became more reactionary, or that a minority member 'compromised'. It is the latter condition that is of interest to us here. Kiesler & Pallack recognised that compromise could have two different consequences. On the one hand, it could 'produce a cooperative spirit' on the part of the majority and hence increase the likelihood of mutual compromise. On the other hand, it could be seen as a sign of weakness and reduce the likelihood of compromise. Their basic findings were that compromise on the part of the minority did not induce attitude change. It didn't even increase their attractiveness to the majority.

The studies conducted by Mugny and his colleagues (Mugny, Pierrehumbert & Zubel, 1972–3; Mugny, 1982) are even more similar in approach but show different results from our study. In their studies a confederate either adhered to an exteme position on six different questions related to the military in Switzerland or was extreme on three questions and moderate on the other three questions. Their results indicated that the 'fair' confederate, the one who moderated his position on some items, was more effective than the 'rigid' confederate (i.e. the one who took an extreme position on all six items) on private or latent change. There were no differences between the two types of behaviour on manifest change, i.e. public change. Our findings, on the other hand, show such flexibility or compromise to be ineffective at the private or latent level.

While the studies cannot be fully compared, since they differ in so many details – e.g. the definitions of public *versus* private change, the degree of involvement in the issue, the nature of the confederate's arguments – some comments may be of use. When the confederate is responding to six different questions, even though all may be related to the topic of the Swiss military, extremism on some items and moderation on others may be viewed as a moderate position relative to extremism on all six questions. Though the person may go from extremism to moderation in sequence, it is not necessarily viewed as a concession or a compromise. It is not clear that the minority is reacting *to* the others. It is also a moderation on different issues rather than a compromise of position on the same issue. Thus, it appears more likely that individuals see this in terms of discrepancy of position. From the theory and empirical work of Asch (1956) and Sherif & Hovland (1961), such extremism should be less effective than moderation.

In our study the issue was not so much one of discrepancy of position as one of concession making. In the context of a decision-making setting, particularly if unanimity is desired or required, movement towards the position of the majority is a reaction to them as well as a signal to them. It occurs over time and offers the possibility of agreement through mutual concessions. It is this aspect that may allow the compromise to be effective in the public domain. The other side of this coin is that consistency or maintenance of position insists on its own position and refuses to compromise, thus accomplishing no public change. However, the fact of maintenance of position causes individuals to re-examine their own judgments and to show influence on related judgments, i.e. they show latent influence. The subtle variant on this is that concessions can be tactics rather than changes in position. The meaning of the concession changes with the context. And timing of the concession is one way to change its meaning. Compromise in the last few minutes of discussion is more clearly a signal of negotiation; it does not indicate a lack of commitment or a change in private beliefs as compromise at an earlier stage is likely to indicate. As such, one can show flexibility as well as consistency and thus be potentially influential in both the public and private domains.

As we reflect on these findings it becomes apparent that strategies for influence on the decision itself are quite different from those aimed at longer term, private belief change. One has to decide which type of influence one intends to exert. The power of consistency is again underscored for private change, but the usefulness of concessions, provided they come from strength (i.e. they are concessions and not changes in position), is still a possibility. This is particularly likely to be true in decision-making contexts. Previous work (e.g. Moscovici, Lage & Naffrechoux, 1969; Nemeth, Swedlund & Kanki, 1974; Nemeth, Wachtler & Endicott, 1977) has shown public influence for a consistent and persistent minority. Yet, persistence in sequential judgments of a stimulus (as illustrated in these studies) does not involve the restrictions of freedom that persistence (and prevention of consensus) does in a decision-making situation. In such settings, the ability to maintain a position while at the same time offering some acknowledgement of the positions of others may be the most effective mechanism for influence, both public and private. If public agreement is the goal to be achieved, compromise may be an effective mechanism. If private change is the goal, then consistency and sensitivity are the needed ingredients, a combination undoubtedly played out in more subtle terms than simple concession making. It is hoped that underscoring the public/private distinctions and pointing out the relative efficacy of seemingly contradictory strategies for each of these forms of influence have served to highlight important distinctions as well as to integrate seemingly disparate literatures.

4. Conflict and conversion

BERNARD PERSONNAZ and MICHEL GUILLON

1. Introduction

Social influence seldom proceeds without conflict and indeed without some suffering or discomfort, whether it entails the exercise of social control over the judgments and opinions of others or the recognition that one has, without being aware of it, adjusted one's own standards to incorporate an alien norm. One does not give in publicly to a group, or modify one's way of viewing the environment, without resistance and confrontations. When two points of view appear irreconcilable their respective sponsors are inclined to engage in conflict. They do not do so light-heartedly, since any questioning of the social consensus on this or that issue promises trouble and suffering for the future. What is more, as reality does not generally tolerate two definitions at once, this conflict will lead either to abandonment of the position and public conformity (during the interaction) to a norm not really accepted so as to reach agreement on the issue, or to the maintenance of the position (coming to terms only with oneself or one's own group), the other viewpoint being treated as the deviant or abnormal one.

Each of us has had occasion to wonder at such phenomena, observable in various areas of life, where populations modify their judgments, opinions or perceptions without being conscious of doing so; or else where they appear to be influenced on a social and verbal level whilst preserving beneath the appearance of consensus their original way of thinking about the world. In terms of influence, several questions come to mind. How does the behavioural style of an influence source produce a particular type of conflict? Does stronger conflict result in more extensive influence? How are types of conflict linked to levels of change in the influence exercised? Does the public response provided by individuals following social interaction correspond to a deeper change in attitudes or perceptions? Conversely, does an underlying change have any reflection at the verbal level? Do the dynamics of influence take a different form according to the type of conflict?

Upon further examination these questions turn on the central problem of the nature of conflict and its effects on the dynamics of influence. The problem is whether conflict with a social agent who provides a response which appears to be anomic is of the same nature and involves the same processes of influence as conflict with a social agent whose response is perceived as nomic or dominant. Hence, to summarise once again, we could say that it is a matter of determining whether the phenomena of minority and majority influence reflect fundamentally distinct processes or not.

The solution to this problem is not only theoretical but also methodological. The aim of this chapter is to identify the possible answers offered by the results of several empirical studies that have used new methodologies to capture more adequately the processes involved.

2. Styles of behaviour, types of conflict and private influence

2.1. Private and public conflict and influence. Although ignored by experimental social psychologists working on social influence up to the 1970s, the idea of a direct link between conflict and influence is not new. According to Tarde (1890), the duel of logic is one of the sources of imitation when two psychological orientations come to be confronted. Tarde makes of conflict a motive force in social change: 'The history of societies, like psychological development, *studied by the humble* is thus a continuation or simultaneity of logical duels' (p. 167; trans.). In his last sociological writings, Freud (1948, of 1939 work) described social conflict as a source of change:

The conflict of opinions continues over a period of time; from the beginning partisans and adversaries confront one another, the number and significance of the former never cease to grow and it is the adherents who in the end prevail. (1948: 91; trans.)

The reintroduction of the concept of conflict within the field of research on influence (Faucheux & Moscovici, 1967) has made it possible (as may be seen in the contributions on this subject) to envisage not just the study of normalisation and conformity but also that of innovation (Moscovici & Faucheux, 1972). It is by its *consistency* that the source of influence creates and sustains conflict and produces influence. These initial empirical studies emphasise, in effect, that the source's *repetition of verbal responses* has an influence on subjects at the level of their *overt and public responses*.

Starting with the study of the diffusion of new ideas and noting the fact that these may not be acknowledged while the innovator remains alive and present, Moscovici & Neve (1971) defined two types of conflict. When social agents are in one another's presence an interpersonal conflict develops. If one gives in to the other in public then self-esteem is at risk, and thus we find in their study a polarisation of subjects while the source is present. On the other hand, absence of the source of influence leads the subject into a cognitive conflict. He can then change his judgment in private without losing face. In our adaptation of this method, based on a presence/absence comparison of the source of influence, we have tried to show that different behavioural styles can accentuate or diminish either the public or the underlying aspect of the conflict and lead to its resolution in either inter-individual or strictly intra-individual terms.

2.2. Public and underlying conflicts. Influence of different behavioural styles: (a) negotiation, (b) repetitive consistency and (c) abjuration by the source upon the target's public and private responses. In an initial study, three types of behaviour on the part of the source of influence were compared (Personnaz, 1979): consistent negotiation, repetitive consistency and abjuration (M. Personnaz, 1976). This last behavioural style may be defined as the action of disowning one's own position publicly without changing it privately. Moscovici & Ricateau (1972) indicate that minorities can deny the consensus 'without it being possible to exclude them from the group, as is most often the case' (p. 160; trans.). Now numerous social situations show that this precisely is often the case. The theoretical problem is thus whether elimination of the novel response by conformity on the part of the source prevents diffusion of the innovation or actually accelerates it. If innovators often have an impact after their deaths, they are also often, during their lives, led to abjure their ideas (Namer, 1975; Gingerich, 1982). As Moscovici (1975) indicated, a behavioural style is a symbolic behaviour, signifying something for an individual or a group. Thus abjuration signifies that, in the face of pressures to conform and the violence of conflict, the innovator gives way at the overt or public level but in private rejects all compromise, entering into an, often long, process of resistance. One cannot analyse this phenomenon at the public level because this level only reflects the majority point of view. Besides, it suffices to note with what pains the majority monitors those innovators who have abjured their position to be persuaded that the entire process continues at another level. The conflict publicly set aside by the source becomes somehow clandestine, it underlies the interaction but no one is fooled.

The principal hypothesis in this study concerns the impact of the type of conflict (public, underlying) created by the three behavioural styles on public and private influence. The greater the conflict (abjuration, consistency), the more extensive will be the influence. The latter will be revealed only when the source is absent since:

real influence is not necessarily correlated with the *presence* and the control exercised by the influencing agent; on the contrary there are times when this influence can only manifest itself in his *absence*. (Moscovici & Neve, 1971)

The study was based on 54 subjects. The task consisted of describing the colour of a small luminous disc using a simple colour name. On the basis of a pre-test it was established that these were perceived by each subject as either blue or green. In each experimental condition the subject was alone with a confederate of the experimenter who gave the opposite response to that of the subject. Subjects gave responses in four phases of the experiment: phase 1, pre-interaction, written responses; phase 2, interaction in the three experimental conditions, oral responses; phase 3, post-interaction in the presence of the source, written responses; phase 4, identical to 3 except for the absence of the source, a plausible reason for which was given. In the negotiation condition, the subject and confederate discussed their divergence of responses for a few moments though the confederate displayed consistency in his judgments; there were a total of 20 trials if the subject did not conform earlier. In the consistent condition the confederate simply repeated his response over the 20 trials. In the abjuration condition, the confederate repeated his response for five trials and then conformed over the last five, after having said in a particularly non-convincing tone and with a wave of the hand, 'Okay, then it must be...[the response given by the subject]'. The results (table 1) indicate that negotiation produces the weakest influence (t-test for repeated measures significant at $p < 0.05$ between phases 1 and 4), while abjuration produces at least as much influence ($p < 0.005$, between phases 1 and 4), and particularly when the source is distant ($p < 0.0005$, between phases 3 and 4), as consistency based on repetition ($p < 0.01$, between phases 1 and 4; $p < 0.005$, between phases 3 and 4).

If public repetitive consistency is sufficient to produce influence in private (Moscovici & Neve, 1971; Brehm & Mann, 1975), abjuration, demonstrated by *public inconsistency* (Wolf, 1979) *and* symbolising a very strong *private consistency*, produces as much influence. However, a *public*, negotiative consistency leads to a very gradually increasing influence. The conflicts differ according to the conditions, and the influence they have at the two levels is a function of the phases. In the negotiation condition the conflict is less intense following the interaction; during interaction it is less focused on the stimulus object and rather more likely to involve the partners themselves, who can argue their points of view. In the consistency and abjuration conditions

Table 1. *Means of colour judgment scores*[a]

Experimental conditions	Phases		
Source behaviour	Phase 1 Pre-influence, source present	Phase 2 Post-influence, source present	Phase 3 Post-influence, source absent
Negotiative consistency (n = 18)	4.22	3.67	3.44
Repetitive consistency (n = 18)	4.11	4.33	3.11
Abjuration (n = 18)	4.28	4.33	2.83

[a] A lower score reflects greater influence. Responses were scored from 0 to 5. Each score corresponds to the number of responses identical to the dominant response provided by the subject in phase 1.

the conflict over the stimulus and the interpersonal conflict are more dissociated and, once the source has gone, the subject seeks to validate his response by examining the stimulus anew, since the conflict linked to this still poses a problem for him. This search for validity leads to change. This search is all the more necessary when the source has openly avoided public conflict in favour of an *underlying conflict with the subject* by rendering his own reference system more clandestine in the interaction context (B. Personnaz, 1976). The historian Favier emphasised (1979) that clandestinity was voluntary, constant, motivated withdrawal, and that assurances of clandestinity are only more specific versions of it; we could add that at the level of consistency they are only more symbolic (Moscovici & Neve, 1973). These results indicate that the level of effect of conflict determined by the behavioural style of the source of influence certainly plays a basic role in determining the extent of influence. In the case of negotiation, which is to say when the conflict is *explicit* and *external*, the exchange of information about responses diminishes the interpersonal and cognitive conflicts and thus results in weak private influence. In the cases of repetitive consistency and abjuration, the conflict after the interaction is *underlying*. Or indeed, when the source publicly disavows his response this allows the conflict to become more readily *internal* to the target who then has to come to terms with himself over the problem. This, certainly deeper, conflict has an influence which emerges quite forcefully when the source is absent; this phenomenon has parallels with that of the sleeper effect (Moscovici, 1980; Moscovici, Mugny & Papastamou, 1981).

2.3. Styles of disavowal by the source of his norm, creation of underlying conflicts and private influence. Let us consider for a moment the origins of the influence produced by a source who publicly disavows his response. The fact that the source conforms in the middle of a public conflict is interpreted differently according to whether the individual who conforms in this way permits this to be attributed to causes either external or internal to his own behaviour. If a confederate, after giving a consistent judgment about an object, then conforms to the subject's judgment, the latter may conclude that he has himself influenced the confederate. The subject therefore has no reason to change. If, on the other hand, the conformity of the source takes the form of an abjuration or, in other words, a purely public disclaimer, this behaviour will create dissonance between the target's public and private response, as we have already seen. This dissonance, made social by the source, will be internalised by the subject and produce change. It may be supposed that this dissonance will be even greater if the source makes explicit his actual underlying reference system and his decision to conform only verbally.

A second study was carried out, based on these hypotheses (Guillon, 1977). This research was in every respect identical to the preceding study as regards procedure. A total of 45 subjects was divided between three experimental conditions. The first (abjuration) condition was identical to the abjuration condition described above; the source conformed after five trials, saying, 'Okay, then it must be...[the response given by the subject in phase 1]'. In the second (disavowal) condition, the source's disavowal was explicitly and solely to reduce interpersonal conflict; this is the reason he gave for conforming publicly. He said 'Okay, I see...[response opposite to that of the subject], but it won't work if we stick to these positions, so it is...[response given by the subject in phase 1].' In the third (renunciation) condition, the confederate conformed without saying anything. Thus in each condition the confederate conformed after five trials. In contrast with our prediction, when the dissonance between public and private response was made explicit in the disavowal, less influence was produced than when it was left implicit (table 2; for differences between phases 1 and 3, and between 1 and 4, $p < 0.05$ in condition 1, and n.s. in condition 2). Simple conformity produced no influence. By comparing these conditions with the abjuration condition we obtain, for the source absent phase, a significant value for t ($p < 0.05$) between conditions 1 and 3 but not between conditions 2 and 3 (p n.s.).

A reinterpretation of the results in terms of underlying conflict provides us with a better understanding of the phenomena observed. In the case of simple conformity by the source, the conflict is resolved during the interaction. There is no underlying conflict when no *double language* is employed. In the case where the confederate explains his actions he can appear as anxious and as incapable of coping with the public conflict – as the post-experimental

Table 2. *Means of colour judgment scores*[a]

Experimental conditions	Phases		
Source behaviour	Phase 1 Pre-influence, source present	Phase 2 Post-influence, source present	Phase 3 Post-influence, source absent
1. Abjuration (n = 15)	4.73	3.26	3.66
2. Disavowal (n = 15)	4.46	4.26	3.86
3. Renunciation (n = 15)	4.66	4.60	4.60

[a] A lower score reflects greater influence. Responses were scored from 0 to 5.

interviews reveal: 'It was unnerving to say blue when the other said green; one of us had to give in.' Certainly the source is consistent in the sense that he claims to see the stimulus privately just as before, but his desire to reduce the interpersonal conflict prevents development of any underlying conflict. On the other hand, in the abjuration condition, which involves a purely public disavowal, this behaviour is perhaps interpreted in terms of concealing the source's true system of reference: 'His response has changed but not what he believes.' The subjects perceived the confederate as 'sure of himself', 'convinced' and 'stubborn'. As Smith (1936) emphasised, when an individual is sure of himself he does not feel threatened by a contrary opinion. By his behaviour, the source shifts the focus to the relation with the object and demonstrates that relations with the other are secondary. This creates a break in the dialogue which allows him to escape the social control inherent in the situation. This break causes the conflict to become subjacent to the interaction. The consequence of the source's double language is to prevent the subject from objectifying the conflict in the situation and to lead him to experience the conflict on an internal and imaginary level. The novel response is supported by the subject privately for, as Freud indicated, 'during the entire conflict, no one forgets what the question was about' (1948 edn: 92; trans.). Tarde studied a similar phenomenon when he described examples of 'peoples who, although they had been victorious in arms, bent under the "seductive" yoke of the vanquished and finally fell under its hold' (Milet, 1970: 222; trans.). He saw in imitation a kind of sleepwalking in which ideas are imitated before they are expressed. This set of results emphasises that increased conflict leads to more extensive influence.

3. Majority and minority influence and latent responses

Behind the idea of a deep influence and that of a distinction between public and private responses there lies a fundamental question which is always being put to social psychologists, namely, how 'genuine' is the change identified in judgments, opinions or perceptions in empirical studies following some given treatment? For example, Pecheux (1972) puts the problem in 'technical' terms as one of 'knowing if, in Asch's experiment, the overt disagreement has an effect exclusively at the level of descriptions and responses, or if it also affects the subjects' perceptions' (p. 103; trans.).

How can it be determined whether a change reflects simply a difference in the label applied to the object over which the conflict of responses occurs (a perceptual stimulus, an opinion, a belief, etc.) or whether it involves a true perceptual or cognitive modification? To answer this question several studies were carried out on perceptual influence and also on opinions, using latent measures with respect to the object that was the source of conflict.[1]

3.1. Latent responses and perceptual code. By introducing two levels of subject response, Moscovici, Lage & Naffrechoux (1969) were able to show that a minority which is consistent by virtue of repetition can produce change not only in the verbal judgments of members of the majority but also changes in responses based on the perceptual code. Following the experiment proper in which four subjects were confronted with two others, actually confederates of the experimenter, who invariably gave a green response to objectively blue stimuli ($\lambda = 483.5$ nm), a post-experimental phase was introduced. This used 16 discs the shades of which progressively changed from blue to green. This allowed comparison of the discrimination threshold of the experimental and control groups. Each disc was presented ten times on a table around which the subjects were seated. Each subject indicated in writing whether a disc was blue or green. The results indicate that in the minority influence condition there appeared a displacement of responses towards the green (which is significant for a discrimination threshold of 25 per cent green and 75 per cent blue).

Mugny (1975), using a Müller-Lyer illusion, measured minority and majority influence at the verbal and perceptual code levels. Mugny's results, like those of Moscovici & Lage (1976), revealed that a majority is more influential at the verbal level while the minority is more influential at the latent level.

In each of these initial studies, irrespective of the task involved, one of the objectives was to compare public agreement and personal opinion (Allen,

1965). Moreover, each characteristically involved measures of underlying influence which were (a) taken at the conscious level of the subjects and (b) used material directly linked to the original stimulus. Consequently we cannot be entirely certain that genuine cognitive or perceptual modifications were assessed.

It is possible, for example, that the changes found reflect a generalisation of public responses. As Moscovici & Lage (1976: 154) note, 'We cannot distinguish between what represents a verbal change and what involves a genuinely perceptual change, on the basis of these responses alone.'

3.2. Chromatic after-images as indirect measures of perceptual change. In an effort to solve this problem, Moscovici & Personnaz (1980) devised experimental procedures[2] in which the latent measure was replaced by one based on the chromatic after-image effect. This effect results from processes peripheral to the perceptual schema when the foveal area of the retina is saturated by a particular colour. If, after fixating on a colour for a few moments we look at a sheet of white paper or a projection screen, we perceive the complementary colour; this is because the visual system functions in such a manner as to eliminate the effects of the first fixation as rapidly as possible. Now, if subjects are presented with a slide that is blue in colour and if influence has occurred in the direction of a green response, the chromatic after-image should, in the case of perceptual influence, change from orange towards purple.

This method is indirect, since the after-image measure does not relate the perceptual change directly to the colour of the slide itself, but it does allow identification of possible agreement or disagreement between *public responses* concerning the colour of the slide and *perceptual responses* to its chromatic after-image. What is more, when subjects make a change in the latter type of response they are not conscious of having modified their perception of the stimulus, since they are unaware of this phenomenon of complementarity between the colour presented and the colour of the after-image.

Two related studies using this procedure were carried out with 46 and 28 subjects respectively. The task consisted of judging on each trial the colour of a blue slide ($\lambda = 486.6$ nm for tungsten light at $2854°$ K, and $\lambda = 481.5$ nm for artificial daylight) by giving a simple colour name, and judging the colour of the after-image on a nine-point scale from yellow to violet. Each study involved four phases (phase 1, private written responses; phase 2, public with conflict of influence; phase 3, private written; phase 4, private written with source absent). The experimental conditions were introduced following phase 1 when the experimenter provided fictitious

Table 3. *Means for the after-image scores[a] (first experiment)*

Experimental conditions	Phases		
	Phase 1 Pre-influence, source present	Phase 3 Post-influence, source present	Phase 4 Post-influence, source absent
Minority source (n = 18)	5.47	6.07	6.22
Majority source (n = 18)	5.90	5.56	5.54
Control group (n = 10)	5.70	5.45	5.40

[a] A higher score indicates a judgment closer to the complement of green (red-purple). Responses were scored on a nine-point scale from 1 (yellow) to 9 (violet).

Table 4. *Means for the after-image scores[a] (second experiment)*

Experimental conditions	Phases		
	Phase 1 Pre-influence, source present	Phase 3 Post-influence, source present	Phase 4 Post-influence, source absent
Minority source (n = 14)	5.10	6.35	6.59
Majority source (n = 14)	5.06	4.85	4.71

[a] A higher score indicates a judgment closer to the complement of green (red-purple). Responses were scored on a nine-point scale from 1 (yellow) to 9 (violet).

results regarding the colour of the slide. These were presented as derived from representative samples and the responses attributed to them were varied as follows:

Condition 1, minority source: 18.2% saw the colour green
81.2% saw the colour blue
Condition 2, majority source: 81.8% saw the colour green
18.2% saw the colour blue

In phase 2, which then followed, the confederate consistently gave a 'green' response on each trial in the two experimental conditions. In a control condition subjects were given no information and the phase 2 responses were given in writing. The results (tables 3 and 4) show that, in both studies, judgments of the colour of the after-image moved significantly towards the complementary of green when the source was a minority.

In the first study an analysis of variance with repeated measures on the latter factor (phases) indicated a 3(conditions) × 3(phases) interaction effect (p < 0.05). The means in the minority influence condition indicated that subjects' judgments shifted to the complementary of green (t-test *a priori* comparisons for first to third phase, $p < 0.05$; for third to fourth phase, $p < 0.02$). No such effects were obtained in the other conditions.

In the second study the repeated measures analysis of variance again yielded a significant 2(conditions) × 3(phases) interaction effect ($p < 0.05$). A series of comparisons revealed a shift in the judgments of subjects in the minority condition towards the colour complementary to green (from first to third phase, $p < 0.02$; from first to fourth phase, $p < 0.01$). When the source was absent the difference between minority and majority influence conditions was significant ($p < 0.05$).

In these two studies, subjects' change towards the complementary colour (purple) of the source public response (green) was only evident when the source was a minority one. What is more, this was a change only in the colour of the after-image (about which there was no externalised conflict during the interaction) and not in the colour of the slide (on which the interindividual conflict was based). In so far as subjects were unaware of the complementarity of the link between stimulus and after-image, the implication is that subjects in this condition genuinely modified their perception of the stimulus without realising it.

These results strongly suggest that public conflict with a minority leads to internalisation of the conflict and that the resulting perceptual change is manifested on the internal dimension (after-image) and not the interindividual dimension (slide), according to a process similar to that described above with respect to private change in subjects confronted with an innovating source.

Doms & Van Avermaet (1980) and also Sorrentino, King & Leo (1980) repeated the above two studies using the chromatic after-image method. In the first of these two replications the authors reported that compared to the control group a change towards the complementary of green was registered in the after-image colour with a majority as well as a minority source. Referring to work by Upmeyer (1971), they interpret their results in terms of an increase in attention when subjects find themselves confronted with contradictory and divergent information. This would lead to an improvement in perception independent of the source presenting this information. Conformity and innovation would thus reflect a single process in which the central mechanism would be essentially cognitive. Sorrentino, King & Leo (1980) found no difference between their minority experimental conditions and the control condition. However, if the subjects were reclassified in terms of their degree of suspicion with regard to the experiment, those who were more suspicious modified their responses in the direction of the colour complementary to green.

The differences between these results and interpretations and those reported by Moscovici & Personnaz (1980) pose a more general problem regarding similarity or difference in the nature of the processes involved in either minority or majority influence.

4. Is the nature of minority influence identical to that of majority influence?

As the reader will realise from the different contributions to this volume, this theoretical problem is not only raised by studies using a perceptual task. For his part, Moscovici (1976, 1980) reinterprets the phenomena of private or latent change in terms of conversion behaviours, and those of public conformity in terms of compliance behaviours.

4.1. Public conformity and private resistance. When one finds oneself confronted with a majority, its response appears as nomic; in the same way, when social pressure increases the individual finds himself dependent on others (Deutsch & Gerard, 1955; Thibaut & Strickland, 1956). Does this mean that an individual who conforms publicly adheres privately to the response he gives? Through a re-examination of Asch's (1951) post-experimental interviews, Bernard Personnaz (1976) attempted to study the post-consensual mechanisms of public and private resistance when an individual becomes dependent on a source in a perceptual task. If subjects conform to the source's judgments during the oral and written phases they nonetheless return to their own unchanged system of reference when the source departs, having remained in some sense secretive in the other's presence. In this case, it seems that the conflict is linked to the relationship with the other rather more than to the stimulus object itself.

4.2. Public resistance and conversion. When one finds oneself confronted with a minority, its response appears as anomic and individuals, as the studies described here indicate, have a tendency to reject this response publicly but may end up adhering to it privately or at the level of their latent responses. Here the conflict appears to be deeper and concerns the stimulus such that it may lead to a perceptual modification corresponding in this case to a response conversion. We understand by this an unconscious internal change followed by a consciousness of this change which may be registered at the level of overt responses.

This distinction has been familiar for a long time: 'imitation can be conscious or unconscious, studied or spontaneous, voluntary or involuntary'

(Tarde, 1890: 209; trans.). It has led us to a more painstaking attempt to determine whether there are two distinct types of conflict which underlie these two kinds of influence. The theoretical problem is clear. Is it the fact that confrontation with minority and majority responses creates in each case a conflict which unfolds in the same way, or is it that conflict in its internalised and/or externalised forms involves two quite distinct mechanisms, not just at any given moment *but in the course of the conflict itself?* It follows that, in order to be able to settle the problem in one direction or the other, the most defensible course of action would be to make as systematic an analysis as possible of the dynamics of the underlying processes involved in the course of a conflict of influence with a minority and with a majority.

4.3. Minority and majority conflict in terms of the dynamics of their representation. Following on from work by Guillon (1981), Guillon and Personnaz jointly carried out a study in Lille and Paris, the aim of which was to use a new procedure to analyse the dynamics of representations formed by subjects of (a) the source, and (b) the object of discussion, when they find themselves confronted with a minority or with a majority (Guillon & Personnaz, 1983). The subjects, all female, were invited to participate in a study of 'communication in small groups', in fact based on the theme of abortion. In a preliminary phase these subjects, who had all declared themselves in favour of abortion, were confronted with a confederate who defended the contrary position using predetermined arguments. The conditions varied as follows: minority source (one confederate, three subjects), majority source (three confederates, one subject). The procedure used was that of thinking out loud, or 'verbal protocol', as derived from American work in the area of artificial intelligence (Newell & Simon, 1972). The entire discussion was filmed, and at the end of the debate the recording was played back in two-and-a-half-minute sequences to each subject separately. The subjects were asked to verbalise aloud and as completely and as precisely as possible what they thought and felt during the experiment. These interviews were taped in their entirety. All assertions generated by the subject *relative to the source of influence* in the course of providing her verbal protocol were then coded in terms of two categories, X1 and X2.

X1 related to the 'content' aspect, to 'what is said' (by the confederate with respect to the object of discussion)

X2 referred to the 'relational' aspect, to 'the way it is said' by the confederate

Depending on whether it was negative, somewhat negative, somewhat positive or positive, each aspect (X1 and X2) of the subject's response was

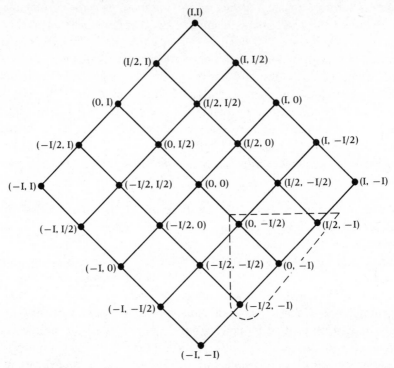

Figure 1. All the possible combinations of codes in the form of a vectorial lattice on which are indicated the codes corresponding to a negative interpersonal evaluation. Those enclosed within the dotted line correspond to (EI−).

given a value of -1, $-\frac{1}{2}$, $+\frac{1}{2}$ or $+1$. If an aspect was not evoked it was coded 0. Consider the following examples:

'What she [the confederate] says there is quite right.' 'She seems to have some quite interesting information...her arguments...well...were quite good, well...I don't know really...but one can see straight away that she has taken sides, that she wasn't open-minded.'

The first assertion refers to something said and affirms that this thing is true (positive); $(X1, X2) = (+1, 0)$. The second involves both aspects and is clearly negative on the relational aspect while somewhat positive on the content aspect; $(X1, X2) = (+\frac{1}{2}, -1)$. The set R of all assertions produced by a subject for a verbal protocol period T_i corresponds to the representation R_i that this subject had formed of the confederate's arguments during the course of the corresponding sequence of the discussion. As the verbal protocol was divided into twelve periods, the cognitive path of a naive subject is described by the succession of the 12 representations $R1$ to $R12$.

Table 5. *Mean values of relative compactness indices for the representational states across the 12 two-and-a-half minute sequences, comparing negative evaluations of the cognitive and interpersonal conflicts (EC− and EI−) as a function of minority versus majority source (the higher the index, the lower the corresponding representation given by subjects)*

Representations	Minority source		Majority source	
	Cognitive conflict	Interpersonal conflict	Cognitive conflict	Interpersonal conflict
R1	0.59	0.35	0.51	0.41
R2	0.51	0.39	0.57	0.37
R3	0.39	0.47	0.59	0.33
R4	0.47	0.37	0.51	0.39
R5	0.46	0.29	0.43	0.39
R6	0.62	0.33	0.36	0.43
R7	0.73	0.33	0.34	0.50
R8	0.73	0.35	0.33	0.58
R9	0.73	0.35	0.30	0.65
R10	0.77	0.23	0.30	0.70
R11	0.77	0.23	0.32	0.72
R12	0.73	0.19	0.34	0.82

The entire set of possible codes constitutes a structure of 25 elements in the form of a vectorial lattice (figure 1). On this structure we can distinguish four characteristic subsets, corresponding respectively to a negative *interpersonal* evaluation (EI−), a positive interpersonal evaluation (EI+), and a negative (EC−) or positive (EC+) *cognitive* evaluation. The mathematical theory of form recognition and automatic classification (Kaufmann, 1975) permits characterisation of the separations between a representation R_i and each of the subsets in terms of indices of 'relative compactness' (Guillon & Personnaz, 1983: 72; see also Guillon, 1982). Development in the representations of each subject in the minority and majority conditions can thus be translated into a series of indices. The indices of relative compactness for the positive evaluations (EC+ and EI+) remain constant across the 12 sequences, irrespective of condition.

The results for the negative evaluations (EC− and EI−) allow identification of two distinct phenomena (table 5). When subjects were confronted with a minority, they represented it increasingly in the cognitive domain, accentuating the conflict by negative evaluations of the content defended by the minority. When, on the other hand, they were exposed to the influence of a majority, representations linked to the interpersonal relations became increasingly salient; the argument essentially concerns the relationship with the other who

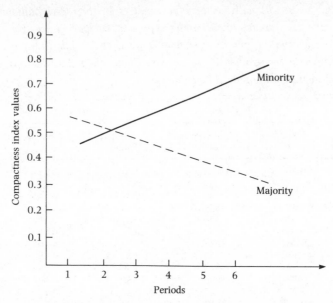

Figure 2. A comparison of trends in the relative compactness indices for interpersonal conflict (EI−) for the majority and minority source conditions. A lower score indicates higher conflict. Each period in this figure corresponds to two successive sequences of the verbal protocol.

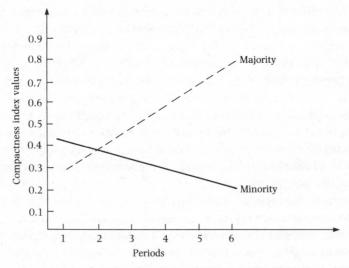

Figure 3. A comparison of trends in the relative compactness indices for cognitive conflict (EC−) for the majority and minority source conditions. A lower score indicates higher conflict. Each period in this figure corresponds to two successive sequences of the verbal protocol.

was perceived in increasingly negative terms as a function of time (trend analysis summarised in figures 2 and 3).

This study confirms the existence of two distinct representational dynamics with respect to influence on opinions. Minority influence leads to the accentuation of a conflictual process related to the object of discussion. Majority influence leads to a conflict in which subjects focus on the interpersonal relations. In the first process the subjects are led to focus on the object and to resolve the conflict relative to its definition, such that they may be led to perceive it in a new way. In the second process the object becomes blurred by the social relationship issue (Personnaz, 1979), confirming that dependence on others can only serve as an obstacle to perception of the object (B. Personnaz, 1976). As Moscovici (1980: 214) comments, 'The center of this conflict, its direction, will be different depending on whether it is aroused by the majority or the minority'. Confrontation with a minority induces subjects to examine the relation between their response and the object, to initiate a 'validation process'; while conflict with a majority leads them to engage in a 'comparison process'.

4.4. Analysis of the dynamics of the conversion process. Bearing in mind the methodological limitations of perceptual influence studies,[3] Personnaz (1981) has sought to analyse the processes involved in minority and majority influence using three measures of perception of the stimulus on each trial. The first measure is based on the overt judgment of the colour of a slide. The two others are recorded on a monochromatic type of spectrometer to determine more precisely (a) the wave-length corresponding to the slide colour, and (b) the wave-length corresponding to the subsequent image. The apparatus has an observation window and a button which allows the subject gradually to advance the chromatic spectrum and to halt this advance when the colour of the image corresponds to his perception of the colour of the slide or its after-image. A numerical indicator, giving values in ohms, then allows the experimenter to note from a distance the wave-length of the colour selected by the subject as corresponding to the colour of the slide and that of the after-image. Short of introducing large spreads into their estimations, subjects cannot take into account the changes in adjustments that they make from one trial to another. Furthermore, the two measures (a) and (b) use *the same metric scale*, and they correspond to *two underlying responses*. The first of these is implicitly linked to the conflict of responses over the colour of the slide, while for the second this relation is unrecognised by the subjects since they are unaware that if one sees the slide as more green the after-image will be perceived as more purple.

The procedure used thus permits determination of three types of possible change corresponding to three levels of consciousness of the conflict/response-type relationship (explicit, implicit and unknown) and observation of fluctuations in these changes across the different experimental phases. Within the framework of this new methodology theoretical problems regarding the nature of influence can be formulated in the following fashion.

(a) *In terms of the internal dynamics of the innovation process – either* this process corresponds to a cognitive mechanism reinforcing subjects' attention or a mechanism linked to suspiciousness, in which case we should find a *simultaneous* change in perception of the colour of the slide *and* that of its after-image; *or* this process corresponds to the internalisation of an external conflict of influence, the re-absorption of which derives from an unconscious modification in the subject's own perception. If this is the case then this process should first be apparent at an unconscious level, then at a more conscious level and finally should become apparent in the overt response. If there is to be consciousness of this perceptual modification, it must be revealed as a *lag* between change in perception of the colour of the after-image *and* change in perception of the colour of the slide, because the first change is not, *for the subjects*, linked to the conflict in responses, while the second is more directly linked.

(b) *In terms of innovation and conformity – either* minority and majority sources both lead to the same underlying process of change (or to closely related processes); *or* the dynamics of these two processes are qualitatively different.

The study was based on 30 subjects divided between three conditions, minority source, majority source and control group. The slide corresponded to a Kodak wratten filter ($\lambda = 486.6$ nm for tungsten light at $2854°$ K and $\lambda = 481.5$ nm for artificial daylight). The procedure was identical to that of the studies by Moscovici & Personnaz (1980; see above), except that on each trial the subject supplied, in addition to an overt judgment, spectral adjustments for his perception of the colour of the slide and for that of the after-image. In a post-experimental questionnaire subjects were asked to estimate the colour of the slide on a six-point scale ranging from extremely blue (1) to extremely green (6), and to state from memory the percentage of persons who saw the slide as blue and of those who saw it as green (representation of the ingroup–outgroup relation: majority–minority). The results indicate that the subjects exposed to majority influence made no modification in their spectral adjustments (see tables 6 and 7). Confronted with a minority source, subjects altered their adjustments significantly towards the response given by the source. With respect to the slide colour, there was a main effect for phases

Table 6. *Means for perceptions of slide colour*[a]

Experimental conditions	Phases		
	Phase 1 Pre-influence, source present	Phase 3 Post-influence, source present	Phase 4 Post-influence, source absent
Minority source (n = 10)	482.87	483.45	485.05
Majority source (n = 10)	482.18	481.33	481.98
Control group (n = 10)	482.19	482.30	482.43

[a] Values correspond to wave-lengths in nanometres. Each wave-length is the spectral measure of the adjustment of the slide colour by the subject. The higher the value, the greater the influence.

Table 7. *Means for perceptions of after-image colour*[a]

Experimental conditions	Phases		
	Phase 1 Pre-influence, source present	Phase 3 Post-influence, source present	Phase 4 Post-influence, source absent
Minority source (n = 10)	622.12	633.00	635.10
Majority source (n = 10)	624.11	625.63	619.47
Control group (n = 10)	622.24	621.95	621.24

[a] Values correspond to wave-lengths in nanometres. Each wave-length is the spectral measure of the adjustment of the after-image colour made by the subject. The higher the value the greater the influence.

($p < 0.01$) and a 3(conditions) × 3(phases) interaction effect ($p < 0.001$). With respect to the after-image, only the interaction effect was obtained ($p < 0.05$). *These alterations are thus not synchronised but out of phase*; by phase 3, subjects had significantly modified their adjustments with respect to the colour of the after-image (t-test between phases 1 and 3, $p < 0.01$; no significant difference between phases 3 and 4), while perceptual modifications relative to the colour of the slide itself occurred only in phase 4 (no significant difference between phases 1 and 3; between 3 and 4, $p < 0.01$). Results derived from the post-experimental questionnaire show that *these changes continue up to the overt level*; there is a significant difference between the minority source condition and the majority and control conditions in the direction of green in the former (between the minority condition and the two others, $p < 0.05$). This particular chronology indicates that there does indeed exist a specific minority effect which cannot be reduced to the effects of attention or perceptual intensity. It is, rather, a matter of a psychological process linked directly to internal conflict which leads to a modification in the perceptual schema. The direction of this modification is from an unconscious level (which has no direct link with the conflict) to a conscious level (one which is first implicitly and *then* explicitly linked to the conflict). This dynamic corresponds firstly to a process of internal conversion (phase 3) to the minority's anomic response, and subsequently to a true *process of conscious realisation of this conversion* (phase 4 and post-experimental questionnaire). Furthermore, when subjects were categorised as minority in being confronted with a majority source, they supplied incorrect estimates, underestimating the percentage of persons *in the minority of which they were a part* perceiving blue (a focus on the social relationship). In contrast, majority subjects confronted with a minority source gave a correct estimate of these percentages (cognitive mastery of the social relationship).

5. Conclusion

In attempting to provide a solution to the theoretical problem of the identical or differing nature of majority and minority influence processes, in terms of an analysis of the underlying conflict processes involved in innovation and conformity, a fruitful means seemed to be to devise new procedures capable of fulfilling needs across the entire social psychology of minorities, with the aim of understanding and describing the dynamics of the underlying processes which accompany and determine the observed phenomena of influence. Analysis of the dynamics of representations generated in the course of a conflict of opinions and analysis of the mechanisms of perceptual change thus supported the argument that there exist two qualitatively distinct processes of influence, differing in terms of whether or not the conflict arising in the interaction is internalised. In minority influence, subjects may be observed to achieve a cognitive mastery of the social relationship and to focus on the object which is the source of the dispute, this leading them to internalise the conflict relative to the stimulus. This psychological mechanism is accompanied by a process of *conversion* to the other's norm *without the subjects being conscious of it*, and is followed by a process corresponding to a *progressive conscious realisation* of these internal perceptual changes. In majority influence, subjects focus on the social relationship which they do not achieve cognitive mastery of, and this is accompanied by a blurring in their grasp of the object. It follows that the conflict remains on the surface and that following the interaction the minority subjects continue to perceive the world from their concealed frames of reference.

Notes

1. We will not consider here levels of response as examined in the work on thematic discussion by Zaleska & Chalot (1980), Mugny (1982) and Papastamou (1983).
2. With the assistance of Claude Bonnet (Laboratoire de Psychologie Expérimentale de l'Université Paris V. Associé au CNRS) and François Molnar (Institut d'Esthètique).
3. In studies using the chromatic after-image paradigm, perceptual change is deduced indirectly from the modifications recorded with respect to the after-image and is not measured directly with respect to the stimulus. This change is measured on a nine-point scale on which subjects can consciously compare their measures from one trial to the next.

5. Rigidity and minority influence: the influence of the social in social influence[1]

STAMOS PAPASTAMOU and GABRIEL MUGNY

A research programme may develop out of an apparently trivial and limited question. Such was the case with our research on the influence of minorities. The point of departure for our studies of minority influence was as follows. Moscovici and his co-workers (Faucheux & Moscovici, 1967; Moscovici, Lage & Naffrechoux, 1969) argued that the basis of minority influence is consistency; by behaving in a closed, stable and coherent fashion over time (diachronic consistency), and by behaving unanimously (synchronic consistency), a minority generates a social conflict whose resolution may entail some influence. These hypotheses were substantially supported by experimental evidence, principally involving perceptual tasks. In these, confederates of the experimenter representing a minority position (both in terms of numbers, since the naive subjects were in the majority, and in terms of the norm, e.g. pretending to see as green a stimulus that appeared obviously blue to the subjects) markedly modified the responses of the majority. They did so by closed and systematic repetition of the same unchanging response (see Moscovici & Faucheux, 1972), or by responses that were a little more variable but were systematically correlated with variations in the stimulus (Nemeth, Swedlund & Kanki, 1974), or by the unanimity of their responses (see Moscovici & Lage, 1976).

All would have been straightforward had there not been a few inconvenient and apparently contradictory findings, or observations that were, at the very least, difficult to interpret within the framework of the initially formulated theory of consistency. Thus, for example, in an experiment by Doise & Moscovici (1969–70), an extreme deviant had a negative influence although his behaviour was, in Moscovici's sense, undoubtedly consistent. Then again, how could one ignore the famous experiment by Schachter (1951) which showed that a stable (and therefore consistent) deviant was finally rejected? Without going on to provide an exhaustive listing of such counterexamples (of which there are several to be found scattered throughout what Moscovici has called the functionalist literature, particularly that on deviance), we can see that there is a problem. We are confronted with a theory which seems theoretically well founded, but which nonetheless requires adjustment to take account *also* of the – occasional though not frequent – failure of minority influence. Thus, to avoid throwing out the baby with the bathwater (which some people are inclined to do), we reasoned as follows.

1. Rigid versus flexible consistency

The consistency which characterises the organisation of minority behaviour induces effects on three separate levels. First of all, it provides the majority with information about the minority itself, confirming the stability and continuity of the stand it has taken and its capacity to resist the social pressures to which it is exposed. Then this consistency ensures that members of the majority clearly perceive the oppositional nature of the position the minority defends. One could say that consistency defines the boundaries of an alternative position within the social field. At this level, consistency appears to be an indispensable condition for minority influence. Finally, behavioural consistency also informs the majority with respect to the interactional dimension; it defines a social relationship marked by conflict, a conflict which the minority introduces through its blocking of all negotiation, through its refusal of all compromise or concession (expressed in the experimental studies by a repetition which, even when responses vary according to nuances in the stimuli, explicitly excludes any negotiation or any direct consideration of the responses given by members of the majority; here, minority independence really takes on the sense of an obstruction of negotiation).

In the research demonstrating a negative influence by the minority, it appeared to us that a kind of rigidity, of 'consistency carried to extremes', was displayed which went beyond the assertion of a specific and well-defined minority position and seemed to express a one-sided determination to influence, a clear and blatant refusal to piece together any negotiation of no matter what kind directed towards a possible compromise with the majority.[2] The actions of these minorities are therefore the extreme opposite of those stooges in Hollander's (1960) research whose strategy consisted of conforming before innovating. Our hypothesis, then, was that a minority could display different styles of negotiation in the interaction whilst remaining consistent in the expression of its position. As contrasted with a *rigid* style (refusal of all compromise, blocking of any negotiation), we defined as *flexible* a less unilateral style which, while not sacrificing any consistency, nonetheless expresses a desire to negotiate, a certain willingness to search for compromise. It was anticipated that a consistent *but* flexible minority would achieve a positive influence but a consistent *and* rigid minority would not.

An initial experiment (Mugny, Pierrehumbert & Zubel, 1972–3) thus attempted to separate out these two dimensions (consistency and style of negotiation) as orthogonal, so as to show that with consistency in the expression of a minority position held constant, and all other things being equal, a flexible minority would have more influence than a rigid minority. Let us now turn to the experimental manipulations on which our demonstration was based.

Subjects, drawn from people who frequented a leisure centre and who had been found, on the basis of a pre-test, to hold a position relatively opposed to the national army (the theme of this experiment), found themselves confronted with a pro-militarist stooge.[3] In the pre-test subjects responded to an eight-point scale from 'I am absolutely for' to 'I am absolutely against' the national army. They next answered six questions (such as 'Given the current balance of military and political forces on an international level, do you think that the Swiss national defence budget should be modified?') which then served as a theme for discussion. Finally, the principal dependent measure consisted of 40 adjectives relating to the army (20 positive and 20 negative); the subjects had to use these to evaluate 'the national army'. This provided us with an index of the pro- or anti-militarist attitude of the sample. These same questions were also presented in a post-test to allow us to evaluate attitude change.

In the experimental phase each subject had to discuss with another experimental subject and with the stooge each of the six pre-test themes for three minutes. Just prior to each discussion they gave a written response to the question and then expressed their choice orally. With the use of a magnetic chart it was possible to display to all the subjects the responses given by each member of their group. Consistency in the stooge's responses was held constant across the two experimental conditions, his responses following a pre-scripted pattern so as always to produce the same pro-militarist argument. In both the 'rigid' and the 'flexible' experimental conditions the stooge responded in an extreme manner (on the eight-point scale) to the first three questions. In the *rigid* condition, he continued to respond in the same extreme fashion to the last three questions, and this in the context of instructions from the experimenter inviting the participants in the discussion to arrive at an agreed position if possible. In the *flexible* condition, on the other hand, he 'agreed' to give less extreme responses to these last three questions (choosing the 6 or 3 instead of the 8 or 1 alternative, depending on the question), whilst asserting that his position remained exactly the same, that is, clearly pro-military. In so far as the stooge negotiated over the conflict, therefore, he did so in a purely formal manner, since his giving less extreme judgments was explicitly in an attempt to find a consensus (which would otherwise have been impossible, given the divergence of positions). The stooge was quite consistent with respect to the expression of his pro-militarist position, therefore, but modified those responses which had significance at the level of interindividual relations with members of the majority. The results were quite clear. Even though the stooge was judged consistent to the same degree in the two experimental conditions, he achieved more influence when he showed himself to be flexible in the negotiation than when he showed himself to be rigid. It appears that in this latter condition he was massively rejected; most of the subjects expressed an even more negative attitude to the army in the post-test, the very opposite of the pro-militarist stooge's position.

Why should this be, and what are the mechanisms involved? Our subsequent experiments have addressed this theoretical problem. They have also, however, addressed certain more significant questions, in so far as these are concerned with the very definition of what is minority or majority, questions dealing with the social nature of the mechanisms of minority influence.

(a) In this first experiment we defined as minority an ideological position opposite to that held by the population. In other words, the position is defined in terms of its statistically low frequency within our population. However, a pro-militarist attitude is also characteristic of the military establishment, which furthermore has enormous power at its disposal. Therefore, as a next step one might seek to represent more adequately the complexity of the social context of minority influence by locating it within a social system in which the part played by power relations can be acknowledged.

(b) We have defined minority rigidity by its actual behaviour, in fact by the extremity of some of the positions it adopts. However, it is evident that minority behaviour is not simply perceived; it is also interpreted. It is thus first a matter of finding means by which these perceptions can be identified and then of specifying their organisation and the dynamics which underlie and order them. It will thus be seen that minority influence really results from the modalities of perception of the minority by the subjects. It will also become apparent that rigidity does not constitute an entity in itself, that it does not exist in its own right, directly present in minority behaviour. It will be seen that the modality of perception itself will determine the degree of influence of a constant style of negotiation, particularly by virtue of the nature of the attributions upon which this perception is founded. This will provide the basis for a second development.

(c) The third aim will be to determine the degree to which there are socially rooted inclinations to perceive minorities in particular fashions, forms of ideological norm (which may futhermore make it sometimes seem a truism that a rigid minority will have less influence than a flexible minority). These inclinations we will try to vary experimentally.

(d) Moscovici, Lage & Naffrechoux (1969) have found that minority influence may not be direct and socially explicit but more often indirect and covert. Several chapters in this volume largely confirm this early intuition. Matters were no different in our own experiment, described above; during the discussions the subjects hardly ever modified their responses, and especially not in the direction of the stooge. This may indeed be due to a dynamic of social support (see, in this regard, the chapter by Doms & Van Avermaet), since both subjects found themselves opposed to the minority. Another interpretation of this difficulty that minorities have in achieving direct influence has emerged in the course of our research. It concerns forms of categorisation of the minority (and the self), and the social identification entailed in social influence behaviours, identification rendered more or less desirable according to the evaluative connotations rendered salient in influence situations (connotations indicated in the problems already identified). This is what has preoccupied us in our most recent research.

Let us now take these various problems in order, and first of all consider the nature of the social context of minority influence to see whether it is capable of defining the 'minority' or 'majority' nature of a social entity.

2. The social nature of minority influence

As the title of this chapter indicates, our theoretical and experimental approach is concerned with the social dimensions of the minority diffusion of an innovation. This has also, of course been a preoccupation of other research perspectives; all social psychological theory by definition constitutes a specific vision of social reality. However, it seemed to us (Mugny & Doise, 1979) that often in social psychology (and even more so in the treatment of social influence) the relation between social psychological mechanisms and the dimensions relevant to their operation in a more inclusive social system is obscured, if not ignored. Experimental situations are in effect often located in settings which exclude consideration of such dimensions, when it is not the theories that fail to include them within their terms. An indication of this is to be found in the fundamentally polysemic character of the concept of minority itself. On one occasion (and too often, in our terms) it may refer to numbers (a social entity is a minority in a situation if its numbers are less);

on another occasion it refers instead to the social position of a group or social category (men representing the majority in the Western cultural context because they are dominant, even though they are numerically in the minority; the opposite is the case for women); on yet another occasion it refers to the conservative or innovatory character of a social entity.

Certainly these various definitions do not, *a priori*, contradict one another and may often be complementary. The minority positions whose influence effects we have principally sought to study are innovatory; at the same time they are socially atypical from the numerical point of view and are therefore minorities from this latter point of view also.

What is the nature of the social relationships involved in minority influence? Let us first of all ask whether alternative methodological approaches have the same capacity to demonstrate these relationships. We can see that the use of perceptual tasks will not involve the same types of social relationships as will tasks involving social judgments. This point is not without importance because, as the preceding chapters indicate, reliance on perceptual problems has constituted a substantial part of the experimental support illustrating these approaches, and continues to do so.

Thus, when individuals have to provide judgments of perceptual stimuli (such as the colour of a slide or the length of three lines compared with a standard line) they almost automatically establish a unanimity in their responses to the degree that they have all acquired the social instruments of apprehending physical reality. Most of the time this uniformity is established independently of any ideological divergences or differences in the social positions these subjects occupy. Furthermore, not being divided initially by any interindividual conflicts, they constitute a majority in both the numerical and normative senses. If one, or indeed several confederates of the experimenter give responses contrary to this perceptual evidence they will thus be perceived as deviants in relation to a majority that is otherwise consensual. Therefore we have here two social entities, a majority and a minority (who are opposed in a single relation, the meaning of which is based in the search for 'objectivity').

Now, such a dichotomous division of the social context of influence (due to the nature of perceptual tasks which obscures other possible social relations, particularly those of power) is unlikely to generalise to situations involving social judgment. In particular it is unlikely because it would lead to an ideological conception according to which the majority is represented by the greater number, by what is more popular, or by what is essentially universal. However, things are not quite so simple. What determines the majority character of a social entity may be considered not as the numerical superiority of the members who make it up but the social position it represents in a power relationship. Thus the concept of *majority* itself is open to modification; if appearances sometimes suggest consensus, this majority is nevertheless deeply divided by relations of domination. To accept a dominant opinion within a given social system does not necessarily mean that one is integrally a part of the dominant group. Such acceptance can very well be the consequence of a relation of domination, expressed in ideological forms of domination when it does not flow from violent acts of repression.

Let us take an illustration from one of our paradigms (Mugny, 1975). Our subjects, young people who would soon be obliged to perform their military service, had to judge the degree to which positions relative to the national army were progressive or conservative. They were to some degree opposed to the army, if only moderately, regarding it as a symbol of violence with which they disagreed, though they also regarded the army as having some positive features (in shapes character, one should defend one's country, etc.). Thus they had a position which, although opposed to the dominant norms, was still relatively close to them. In this case can one talk of a *majority*? No, because relations of domination divided this superficial consensus; *via* various apparatuses of the state (the family, the school, work) our subjects had occasion to internalise to some degree the dominant ideology diffused by the powers that be. On the other hand, they were obliged to perform their military service, incurring the risk of repression if they resisted.

Under the general heading of majority one is thus led to distinguish two social entities between which very specific social relationships exist, on the one hand *power* (which is, moreover, most often in the minority numerically) and on the other *population* (analogous to the experimental population). By power we mean the dominant group that dictates the social norms and rules. Population refers to the social entity dominated by this power (though in reality it is a complex fabric made up of several groups and social categories capable of maintaining more or less narrow links with power), an entity alienated through its internalisation of the dominant ideology which partly shares in existing norms. It is only in appearance, therefore, that the population can be designated as the majority.

In such a social context, minority diffusion of an innovation takes on a different meaning since one can only consider as minorities those social entities whose norms entail a break with power and the ideology it supports.[4] Given the complexity of the social relationships implied by a context of innovation defined in this way, it becomes theoretically impossible to approach the processes of minority influence within the framework of a single, undifferentiated relationship (as has been the case in experiments based on perceptual tasks).

From this perspective, what meaning is assumed by the concepts of consistency and rigidity? Consistency may be regarded as defining the adversary relation the minority has with power. To have any chance of being recognised as an alternative within the social field, the minority effectively has no choice but to make a total break with power and it should therefore resist negotiation with it; the minority must be firm, coherent across time and situations and never concede anything in the conflict. Consistency can in this way define the boundaries of an alternative within an adversary relationship. In this consistency is necessary. But it is not sufficient to ensure the influence of the minority. Why should this be?

The fact is that the population which is the target of influence is, as we have seen, often subordinate to power in a relation of dependence or domination. Also the subjects, as members of this population, have internalised the dominant ideology. They have thus also adopted as their own, positions (opinions, behaviours, etc.) with respect to which the minority represents a clear break. Hence, by virtue of its consistency, the minority introduces a conflict not only in relation to power but also in relation to the population. To have any influence, the minority must negotiate over this conflict in a flexible, rather than a rigid, fashion.

Before examining the mechanisms, let us give an example of a more ideological type of negotiation. To this end, let us reconsider the example of the national army which we used to illustrate the distinction between power and population, and let us suppose that a minority wished to convince our experimental population that 'the capitalist national army is a danger to the working class; it is opposed to all forms of socialism and it is necessary to struggle within and against the army'. Let us suppose, in addition, that our population is to some extent in favour of conscientious objection as a means of struggling against the institution of violence. If, in its argument, the minority (in the form of one of its representatives) overtly declares that conscientious objection is an individualistic means of struggling against the army, it will exacerbate a conflict which already exists by virtue of a position which is violently opposed to the army (recalling that the subjects, although moderately opposed to the army, did not only see its defects and that they were soon to be active participants in it themselves). If in pursuing its argument the minority takes the offensive and accuses conscientious objectors of being 'petit bourgeois quasi-reactionaries', the conflict will be intensified. Its influence will be nil, moreover, when it is not opposed to minority expectations. This is what we found in the rigidity condition (Mugny, 1975). Let us now envisage what negotiation might be ideologically possible. In the flexible negotiation condition the minority representative continues to press his position, certainly, but in a way that modifies his preceding assertions.

He emphasises that conscientious objection may constitute a valid means of struggling against the army but does so above all in its most collective form, while he suggests that the essence of such struggle resides in active opposition within the army. Without abandoning any consistency (the argument takes the same form in the two experimental conditions, except for these two assertions), the minority concedes a compromise with the population and avoids exacerbating the conflict. By such negotiation, which is in fact ideological in form, the minority effectively achieves more influence and the subjects' judgments following the interaction are more critical of the army than they were on the pre-test.

Thus consistency defines the boundaries of a minority alternative and rigidity or flexibility defines the minority's negotiation with the population, rendered necessary by the subjugation of the latter to power. It will be seen in a later section how power may react against the consistent minority and lead the population to interpret it in terms which undermine the minority's credibility. But before reaching this point we must first consider how the population tends to perceive a flexible or rigid minority.

3. Perception of the minority

We have just seen how the complexity of the social context within which processes of minority influence are located requires identification of another feature of behavioural style, namely negotiation (flexible *versus* rigid), a feature displayed by the minority in its interaction with the population. We have also seen in the preceding experiment (Mugny, 1975) that the minority generally gains by displaying flexibility rather than rigidity, having a greater impact in the former case.

In this same experiment we studied not only the influence of the minority in these two experimental conditions but also the image that it generated in the population. To this end, subjects were asked to describe the influence source in terms of a list of 40 adjectives, ten of which corresponded to consistency, ten to inconsistency, ten to flexibility and ten to rigidity (Mugny, 1975). The results obtained confirm that negotiating styles are perceived as distinct: the rigid minority (which achieved less influence) was perceived by subjects as more rigid than the flexible minority. But this same rigid minority was also perceived as less consistent, although the consistent behavioural style was employed in absolutely identical fashion in the two conditions. This co-variation of perceived flexibility and consistency suggests that, at the very least, the rigidity the minority displays in its negotiation with the population contaminates, and may even determine, perception of consistency (a possibility supported, moreover, by the negative correlation between the perception of consistency and the perception of rigidity in the rigid condition).

But rigid or flexible styles of negotiation by active minorities do not exist as such; their differentiated impact on the opinions of the population is to a large degree determined by the image the latter forms of the source of influence. This may be illustrated by an experiment based on another paradigm concerning the problem of pollution (Mugny, 1982).[5] In this experiment subjects read a minority argument in its flexible version. They also received clear indications of the opinions held by others about the authors of the text. Thus, in an 'induced flexibility' condition they were given ten adjectives from our image measure which were in the direction corresponding to flexibility. In the 'induced rigidity' condition they were given the ten adjectives corresponding to rigidity. Now the results show that in the induced rigidity condition, and *in spite of the actual flexibility of the minority argument*, influence was significantly less than that produced by the minority in the induced flexibility condition.

However, it is not so much – or not only – the content of the representation of the minority which matters, but its organisation. It has been seen that, when rigidity is perceived, it produces a halo effect; the image is organised around a central dimension, that of rigidity, and this also colours the perception of consistency; even if consistency is perceived, it will be associated with the negative character of rigidity and will be understood by the population as a consequence of it. The cognitive field would thus be restricted to some degree, becoming organised around the dimension most salient to the relationship established between minority and population, that relating to the blocking of negotiation. This is revealed in an experiment carried out by Ricateau (1970–1). By inducing his subjects to use either more simplified forms of perception (involving fewer categories of judgment) or more multi-dimensional forms (involving a greater variety of judgment categories), he led them to apply these forms to their perceptions of a consistent and rigid minority source of influence. Thus, with respect to the same behavioural style, rigid blocking of negotiation becomes more salient in the condition of 'simplified' perception (rigidity thus being particularly clearly perceived) and strongly diminishes the influence of the minority.

These pieces of evidence give us a better appreciation of the generally negative effects of minority rigidity. This rigid resistance to negotiation on the part of the minority becomes the central dimension in the cognitive appraisal of the alternative advocated by the minority, the dimension around which all other dimensions become organised. It is therefore also within this dimension that the meaning of rigidity must be sought. But what is its meaning?

Table 1. *Mean change in opinion on*
a seven-point scale (+ denotes a
positive influence of the minority)

Text attribution	Flexibility	Rigidity
One minority	+0.55	+0.15
Two minorities	+0.44	+0.60

To settle this we must now take a further step in our theoretical analysis. It is a matter of recognising that rigidity, once it is rendered salient as an organising principle in the minority image, diminishes the minority's influence to the degree that a subjective link is established by the targets of influence between the image of the minority and the position it defends. In other words, rigidity is opposed to influence to the degree that the minority's behaviour is imputed to rigidity. It will be seen that it is not a simple matter of attribution but of a mechanism of an ideological form. But let us first examine an experimental illustration, based on the idea that various factors, but particularly the number of independent sources of influence, favour the establishment of such a link (see Wilder, 1977).

To this end we varied the number of those in the minority presenting positions which were otherwise identical (Mugny & Papastamou, 1980). Half the subjects in a flexible condition and half those in a rigid condition were presented with a complete text (concerned once again with pollution) which was attributed to a single minority. The other half were presented with the same text but this time divided into two parts. Two of the four paragraphs making up the text were attributed to a minority A (or B), the other two being attributed to another minority B (or A). Given that the different paragraphs were based on different areas in which the issue of pollution arises, the two minorities should indeed have been perceived as independent. (It was a matter of avoiding a single categorisation of the two sources, a tendency which Wilder, 1977, has shown can diminish the influence of the minority position.) Following their reading, the subjects responded a second time to the opinion questionnaire and then described the minority or minorities on the image-of-the-other questionnaire.

The results (table 1) are marked by a significant interaction between the two variables which confirms that effects of the minority do depend on a subjective link established by the subjects between their image of the source and the reasons for its behaviours or for its expression of an alternative position. First of all, when the text is attributed to the single minority the familiar difference related to styles of negotiation once again emerges; a rigid source is less influential than a flexible source. When, on the other hand, exactly the same position is defended by two independent minorities rather than one, the negative effects of rigidity disappear; the influence of two rigid minorities is equal to that of one or two flexible minorities. Why should this be? Is it that the rigidity of the minority is no longer perceived? No, because the entire image of the rigid source is less positive, whether of one or of two minorities, than the image of one or two flexible sources. The reasons for this differentiated influence thus reside elsewhere, in the link established between the perceived image and the attitude change conceded by the subjects. When the source is unified we find significant correlations (particularly in the rigidity condition) between influence and image. Since the image of the rigid source is less positive than that of the flexible source, influence would be expected to be less in this condition. When confronted with a source, its image would constitute an essential element in the interpretation of minority behaviour and consequently in the definition of new attitudes. Rigidity then is a pretext for rejecting influence. When there are, instead, two independent sources which are perceived as rigid, such a link disappears; even though the rigidity is perceived as such, it is no longer the element which determines modifications in attitude.

One could thus suppose that the normally negative effects of rigidity upon minority influence are due not simply to the forms of perception of the minority themselves (forms, we have seen, which are more likely to be 'simplified' with high salience of rigidity), but to the nature of the explanations of minority behaviour. Influence will be weak only when rigidity seems to account for the majority position. Why should positions be accepted which are defended in the name of a character trait? How can an alternative be acknowledged or accepted when what is expressed is not a true alternative at all but a characteristic of the minority itself, namely its 'dogmatism'?

We can now examine the way in which this form of attribution actually represents an ideological form of resistance to minority influence, and consequently to social change.

4. Ideological resistance to minority influence

We have just seen that the mode of apprehension of a minority that is induced to a large degree determines the impact it has on the population it seeks to influence. It can now be appreciated that minority influence will either be enhanced or counteracted according to the system of representation available to the population. By relocating processes of minority influence within the kind of social context defined above, it can be readily appreciated that power, in so far as it seeks to perpetuate itself and resist social change, will tend to generate immunity to minority influence, particularly by endowing the population with forms of interpretation likely to counteract any possible minority diffusion of an innovation. To this end it is necessary that the adversary relation between the minority and power (and consequently the relation of domination between population and power) be obscured by the latter. What could more easily achieve this effect than depriving minorities of the only weapon at their disposal, that of being a source of social conflict by appearing to be what they are, namely advocates of a coherent alternative to the dominant norms? There are good reasons to believe that it is the non-perception of minorities as alternatives in these terms that is the objective of the ideological apparatus activated by power when faced with efforts that threaten to undermine its hold upon the population. This, moreover, is one of the fundamental problems facing all active minorities. Thus, one of the basic functions of consistency is to evade this danger that threatens minorities. The consistent minority will ensure that the minority alternative is recognised by the population in so far as its arguments (or actions) are internally coherent and its confrontation with the dominant norms is characterised by firmness. But the rigid negotiation of the conflict that this tends to generate contains the same risk; in making its minority nature explicit (Papastamou, 1983) along with its claim to constitute an alternative, any rigidity will activate those modes of interpretation which power never fails to mobilise in the face of deviance; the result, generally, is that there is very little impact.

But what is the mechanism and how does it function? It will be recalled that minority behaviour is not only perceived, it is interpreted. We must therefore look for the mechanisms underlying ideological resistance to minority influence in this interpretation that the population makes of minority behaviour.

The experiments which we will now briefly describe reveal that this resistance is essentially expressed in a 'naturalisation'[6] of minority behaviour. It consists in interpreting their behaviour as deriving from the natural or intrinsic, idiosyncratic characteristics of the minority and its members, such as their psychological characteristics. This is what the experiment described above (Mugny & Papastamou, 1980) suggests: faced with a single (and rigid) minority, subjects were inclined to interpret the minority discourse in terms of the latter's idiosyncrasies (i.e. in terms of its perceived rigidity, which derives in particular from its style of negotiation). When faced with several

Table 2. *Mean change in opinion on a
seven-point scale (+ denotes a positive
influence of the minority)*

Experimental condition	Flexibility	Rigidity
Psychologisation	+0.40	+0.54
Non-psychologisation	+0.90	+0.57

minorities, however, this mode of mystification and 'psychologisation' was less likely to occur, and influence was substantial even when the minority behaviour was perceived as rigid.

In certain other experiments (Papastamou, Mugny & Kaiser, 1980), we have attempted to illustrate the functioning of 'psychologisation' as an ideological mechanism of resistance to minority influence. To this end we have sought to operationalise this functioning with respect to flexible *versus* rigid minority negotiation conditions, using once more the experimental paradigm organised around the pollution issue. To achieve this, the subjects were asked to read the minority text (which in all conditions was attributed to a single minority) very attentively, being led to expect that they would afterwards have to describe the author's personality (in terms of a list of adjectives) on the basis of a single reading of the text (psychologisation condition). Subjects in another (non-psychologisation) condition were led to expect that they would have to summarise the principal ideas contained in the text. It should be noted that in all conditions subjects were given the image measure and then summarised the minority text. If our hypothesis was correct, a clear diminution of influence should have been observed when subjects were invited to psychologise the minority source.

The results obtained (table 2) plainly confirm our predictions; psychologisation constitutes a very clear form of resistance to minority influence. The induction of a psychologising mode of interpretation did appear overall to have the effect of diminishing influence. Nevertheless, the interaction effect seems to indicate that matters are somewhat more complex. It appears that induction of psychologisation in fact, while it diminishes the impact of a flexible minority, affects a rigid minority only slightly. Why is it that inducing a psychologising form of interpretation does not counteract the influence of a rigid minority to the same degree as that of a flexible minority?

If the explicit induction of psychologisation does not affect the influence a rigid minority has in the absence of such induction, it is reasonable to suppose that this is because such psychologisation is already implicitly at work when the minority source is perceived as rigid; perception of rigidity alone would be sufficient to activate such an ideological process. It could, in other words, be a 'spontaneous' response to the strong conflict the population experiences. It is therefore not surprising to find that explicit induction of psychologisation adds nothing to the 'spontaneous' psychologisation activated by perception of rigidity alone.

When, on the contrary, the minority is perceived as flexible (and there is no additional induction) the less intense conflict experienced by the subjects fails to activate such a process 'spontaneously'. This is why the minority influence found in this condition is more substantial. Similarly, it is the reason why explicit induction of psychologisation significantly reduces the influence only of a flexible minority. The fact that explicit psychologisation of the flexible minority reduces its influence to the same level as that of the rigid minority also suggests that we have been successful in activating experimentally one of the ideological processes entailed in resistance to minority influence. And this, it is worth repeating, is a process which the rigid obstruction of a minority in the face of the population activates 'spontaneously' *via* the intense conflict it induces.

This effect, psychologisation as ideological resistance to minority influence, has emerged in several experiments using different paradigms. Thus, in an experiment on the national army theme, subjects were asked, after reading a minority text strongly opposed to the army, to give their impressions of the authors and of the text itself. In one condition they were provided with purely political terms, whilst in the other the terms were political but also psychological. As expected, in the condition involving both psychological and political characterisations the source had significantly less influence than on subjects in the condition involving solely political interpretations. This confirms that it is sufficient to lead the population to entertain the possibility of a description of minorities not solely in political terms but also in psychological terms (without specifying which) for the influence of the latter to be considerably diminished.

Finally, this diminution of minority influence by the induction of psychologisation has been found again in a recent experiment (Mugny, Kaiser & Papastamou, 1983). It concerned the issue of xenophobia in Switzerland, at the time of a referendum on the question. This time, however, to operationalise our non-psychologisation condition we sought to discourage subjects from focusing on the content of the minority text. This operationalisation, although effective, could pose several problems of alternative interpretation (even if inadequate in our terms). The most obvious alternative is in terms of 'distraction' (Allyn & Festinger, 1961; Festinger & Maccoby, 1964). Thus, we confined ourselves to inviting the subjects (in all experimental conditions) to describe the authors and the text, but we used a different method to do this. In the psychologisation condition, the subjects had to 'guess, from the content of the message, the personality characteristics of its author'. In the non-psychologisation condition, they had to 'analyse, on the basis of what you read, the characteristics of the content and the author of this text' (the various elements of the causal chain were therefore present but the causal link was not made explicit). Now, despite the fact that this operationalisation was clearly weaker than earlier ones, we found a substantial reduction in influence in the psychologisation condition. However, an additional effect may be noted. The minority text was attributed either to a Swiss minority (and thus the same nationality as the subjects), or to a foreign minority. The effect of psychologisation was more marked when the minority was of the same national identity as the subjects. Confronted with a minority categorised as an outgroup, the existence of a stereotype is sufficient to undermine minority influence. Psychologisation mitigates the unavailability of this alternative within one's own group. To psychologise is to exclude those who are not already excluded by virtue of their existing social characteristics. It is the social creation of stigma.

Another result confirms that the resistance to minority influence induced by psychologisation operates through the perception of rigidity. When the Swiss minority was psychologised it was perceived as far less tolerant than when it was not psychologised. What is more, consistency (which other measures indicate is clearly perceived) takes on a different meaning here when rigidity is involved in its interpretation. Let us note that this is, moreover, a characteristic specific to the perception of minorities. Riba & Mugny (1981) have proposed that consistency is associated with rigidity only when it characterises a minority source, and not when it characterises a majority source.

In a further experiment (Papastamou, Mugny & Kaiser, 1980), we wanted to see to what extent a minority, particularly when it is rigid (and thus 'by itself' induces a psychologisation of its argument), is able to counteract this resistance to the diffusion of its innovative norms. We attempted this using once more the pollution paradigm and creating three experimental conditions. In a condition without explicit psychologisation the subjects read the rigid minority argument with a view to forming a very general impression of the text and its authors. In a psychologisation condition subjects were instructed to guess the personality of the authors and to describe their principal characteristics. Finally, in a condition of counteracted psychologisation, the procedure was similar to that of the previous condition, with the exception that the minorities asserted that their position was based on scientific work in the area. They presented their argument as not deriving simply from their own psychological characteristics and thus demanded that they should be considered as presenting a genuine alternative to the dominant norms.

Without going into details, we can record that this third condition produced significantly more influence than the other two experimental conditions, and this in spite of the induction of a psychologising form of interpretation and in spite of the rigidity the minority displayed in its argument. It seems therefore that we have succeeded in counteracting the ideological resistance which is normally activated in the face of a rigid minority. The roughly equal impact obtained in the other two conditions also confirms that the failure generally found with rigid minorities does derive from the induction of such psychologising forms of interpretation, which serve to mystify the adversary relation of the minority to power and the ideology it supports. It confirms also that behavioural rigidity will increase the probability of such induction.

Of course, this experiment represents just one attempt to study the mechanisms by which the ideological processes stigmatising active minorities may be counteracted. We are aware, moreover, that the reference to science may be an option limited to the paradigm based on pollution. However, this experiment does shed some light on the actual mechanism involved in resisting psychological forms of interpretation, even if it does not yet identify the social conditions which either activate or de-activate it.

Although not directly concerned with the study of psychologising processes, two experiments described below provide further insights on this issue.

5. Minority influence, social categorisation and social identity

In the preceding sections we have considered the nature of the contents associated with a minority position (consistency, certainly, but also sometimes rigidity or dogmatism), and the nature of the mechanisms which regulate perception of the minority. When the minority is flexible it tends to be perceived in a multi-dimensional fashion, no special weight being given to any particular dimension. If, on the other hand, the minority is rigid, this gives rise to simplified perceptions, heavily saturated with the dimension relative to blocking negotiation. We have also seen how readily a minority, especially if it is rigid, gives rise to the internal and psychological attributions rooted in the dominant ideology and which destroy the minority's capacity for influence.

However, a complementary approach to minority influence is possible. It entails a consideration of the categorisation mechanisms (Tajfel, 1972) involved in conflict relations between groups. As we have seen, minority influence is indeed located within a complex social context of intergroup relations (or relations between social categories), specifically relations between minority, power and population.

Thus the social psychological mechanisms discussed above can be regarded as giving rise to evaluative contents or connotations assigned to minorities. However, these contents are applied to entities which may be more or less clearly categorised socially. When these connotations are particularly negative they also imply that the social field is therefore strongly categorised and that their social function is precisely to establish this categorisation. Somehow, they ensure that the scope of the ingroup (the population) will be clearly distinct from that of the outgroup (the minority). When they are less negative and more balanced they instead emphasise the existence of a certain commonality between these two categories, denying or attenuating a dichotomous categorisation of the social field.

Is it not possible that minority rigidity, by accentuating the social conflict between minority and population, in the same way accentuates the differences between them? Now, it is known that merely categorising individuals in terms of some random criterion is sufficient to induce discrimination, expressed in the search for a maximum differentiation between groups (Tajfel *et al.*, 1971). By its rigidity the minority may thus lead subjects to represent the social field as strongly dichotomised between population and minority (and from the latter subjects will then feel themselves to be totally excluded). By the influence they are willing to accept (which is often none), inter-category differentiation may be confirmed, though negative influence may actually serve to accentuate this differentiation (on this point, one might mention the experiment by Lemaine, Lasch & Ricateau (1971–2) on the dissimilation effect).

What about the effects of flexibility? A similar analysis can be made here in which the minority's attenuation of conflict may be regarded as discouraging such a clear categorisation of the social field. Crossed-category membership (Deschamps, 1977) may be mentioned here. If a minority induces a particular categorisation by its consistency (without which, as we have seen, it no longer constitutes an alternative), it may nonetheless attenuate this by its flexibility; it may focus attention on enough features in common to stimulate the perception also of various category similarities, thus encouraging convergence. Now Deschamps has shown that such crossed categories attenuate the differentiation and discrimination deriving from an initial simple categorisation; the accentuation of similarities on certain points compensates for the accentuation of differences resulting from the categorisation induced by consistency. Truly, this is a seductive interpretation of the effects of minority flexibility.

If our reasoning is correct, it should be possible to increase the influence of a rigid minority by inducing a mode of categorisation which, instead of emphasising the differences between groups, would stress the similarities. Thus influence should be greater if, all else being equal, one were able to convince subjects that they shared several category memberships with the minority, since this would counterbalance the categorisation implicit in the minority's rigid consistency. Furthermore, such an induction should not have the same effects on a flexible minority, since this latter's flexibility itself introduces this feeling of shared memberships. Let us now consider the details of an experiment which lends some credibility to this interpretation (Mugny & Papastamou, 1982).

Four experimental conditions were included. Half the subjects were presented with a flexible minority argument, the other half with a rigid argument (based on the pollution paradigm). In addition, half the subjects in each of these conditions were allotted to a condition of *one common membership*, the other half to a condition of *five common memberships*.

Thus in all the experimental conditions subjects were informed of the number of memberships in common. To do this it was explained that 'each individual can be defined by membership or non-membership of various very general social categories. Thus each is necessarily male or female, younger or older, intellectual or manual, student or worker'.

In the *one common membership* condition, it was then announced to subjects that a sociological analysis of their social origins and those of the authors of the argument they were going to read revealed that of eight categories (which were subsequently specified) only one ('or at the very most two') was common to themselves and these authors. In the *five common memberships* condition it was stressed instead that there were five ('and possibly six') categories that the subjects had in common with the source of influence.

Subjects were then asked to identify the single or the five categories in common. To do this they had to decide on either one or five propositions asserting 'we have in common that...' from the eight possibilities provided: we are intellectuals; we are the same sex; we are members of an ecology group; we have received a religious education; we are young; we are members of a political party; we come from a middle-class background; and, finally, we are students.

The categories were chosen to be plausible (the subjects being students at a private religious college), without however making any *a priori* judgments concerning the opinions they might imply with respect to the theme of

Table 3. *Mean change in opinion on an*
11-point scale (+ denotes a positive influence
of the minority)

Experimental condition	Flexibility	Rigidity
One common membership	+0.67	+0.39
Five common memberships	+0.80	+1.03

pollution. The only directly relevant memberships in this respect were ecology group and political party, and it should have been difficult for the subjects to choose these since they were very unlikely to have belonged to either. If the variable of one *versus* five memberships had an effect therefore, it should have been due to the act of categorisation itself.

The results are shown in table 3. First of all, it should be noted that, as predicted, the variable of one *versus* five category memberships had no significant effect on subjects who read a flexible text. On the other hand, the effects were particularly strong for the rigid text, as we expected and had generally predicted. In general, the number of memberships in common was decisive with respect to the amount of influence achieved; five common memberships were better than one.

These results support the idea that negotiation styles also make a difference because they induce specific forms of categorisation of the social field. Social influence is therefore quite clearly entailed in the category differentiation model (Doise, 1980). Differentiations induced (by rigidity in particular, or by psychologisation, etc.) at the representational level (mutually exclusive categorisations of the self and the other) lead to differentiations at the evaluative level (negative and saturated with one dimension, that of blocking of negotiation), and at the behavioural level (reduced influence of the minority source).

But for what reasons and through what mechanisms does this transposition of differentiations occur at various levels? One further hypothesis may be advanced. It is that by approaching or avoiding the minority position, or in other words by the degree of influence they accept, subjects in effect redefine their social identities. Let us see how.

The inspiration for this comes from the theory of referential informational influence, developed J. C. Turner (1981). According to Turner, the individual defines himself in terms of membership of a distinct social category. He will have established or learned the norms and attitudes stereotypic of this category. Certain modes of thinking, judging, acting, etc. are recognised as criteria that allow the assignment to an individual of this category membership. Certain appropriate, expected or desirable behaviours are used to define this category as distinct from other categories. The key claim of this theory, then, is that the individual attributes these norms and attitudes to himself in the same way that he makes self-attributions of the other characteristics that are stereotypic of this category, when this category membership is rendered psychologically salient.

By extension it is easy to grasp the difficulties one finds in minority influence. By a kind of reversal of Turner's proposition, one could propose that influence behaviour (consisting in accepting the minority response or at least moving closer to its position) entails the subject redefining his social identity. Rendering the identity of the source salient would then imply not only adoption of the response alternative it advocates but also, *via* a deductive process, self-attribution of all the attributes stereotypic of the source (or at least that portion rendered salient in the situation).

The reasons for the frequent failure of minority influence thus become clear. When the minority displays rigidity it is seen in these terms. And by a kind of halo effect other negative connotations emerge as when, for example, the perception of consistency becomes contaminated or when psychologisation makes certain attributes salient (such as abnormality, etc.). Being willing to approach the minority is thus to risk self-attribution of the entire set of negative connotations associated with the minority position and made salient in the situation. This entails a social cost (Larsen, 1974) that subjects will hesitate to pay. Here, then, is the fundamental factor which so strongly limits the explicit social expression or admission of minority influence, as discussed in the other chapters.

In one of the experiments undertaken to validate this hypothesis (Mugny, Rilliet & Papastamou, 1981), we manipulated the normative context surrounding the perception of the minority. In all the experimental conditions subjects were led to believe that the experiment was concerned with measuring either individual dispositions to social originality (defined as the tendency to accept new values and ideas in the direction of social progress) or individual dispositions to deviance (defined as a tendency to accept socially rejected values and ideas which question established norms). Thus the intention was to render salient either positive dimensions (originality) or dimensions with negative connotations (deviance) for the image of the minority. As predicted, the degree of explicit agreement with the minority was greater in the originality condition than in the deviance condition (thus confirming various findings reported by Moscovici & Lage, 1978).

Minority influence thus also depends quite substantially on the social context, as has already been seen, and particularly on the norms which are rendered salient within it. Viewing social influence as a redefinition of the target's social identity thus allows us to link those collective dynamics which have been shown to characterise the social context of minority innovation with dynamics involved at the individual level, particularly those of attitude change.

6. Conclusions

Such have been the major outlines of our experimental approach to minority influence. Our initial concern was to reconcile the apparent contradiction between consistency theory as advanced by Moscovici and various results which seemed to indicate at a practical level either no effect or, even, a negative effect of consistency. To this end we distinguished two dimensions of minority behaviour – and more particularly of the perception of minorities – one of consistency and the other of rigidity. The first defines the limits of a position (a coherent break with the dominant norms) while the other concerns the minority's negotiation within the influence relationship. Given equal degrees of behavioural consistency, a rigid negotiation style tends to allow less influence than a more flexible style. But these styles are not the only determinants of the image of the minority. This image has some degree of freedom and can in its turn accentuate the effects of rigidity (an induction at the level of the image may lead to effects similar to those of rigidity, even though the minority demonstrates flexibility). It may, instead, attenuate these effects, for example, when the subject is led to regard the minority position as derived from two independent sources; although rigidity is perceived it is no longer able to explain to the same degree the oppositional stand of the minority.

What is more, perception of the minority in terms of its actual behaviour is largely determined by the values and norms which regulate the interpretation of minority positions at the ideological level. It has been seen how psychologisation may constitute an obstacle to minority influence to the degree that minority positions are reduced to the expression of idiosyncratic characteristics – in effect, to personal biases. It has also been seen that a variety of social contexts (particularly if they encourage emergence of a norm with the positive connotations of social originality) can be unfavourable to the activation of such mechanisms.

Finally, we have suggested that minority difficulties in exercising direct, socially visible influence may be explained by the social cost of the identification entailed in accepting, or moving closer to, the minority position in a context which renders salient the evaluative connotations associated with minority positions (particularly by the bias to psychologisation); influence involves a negatively valued self-attribution which the subject will want to avoid.

The social context of minority influence thus appears to be decisive, confronting minority consistency with mechanisms of resistance whose effectiveness has largely been demonstrated.

Is this to say, then, that consistency and rigidity (or flexibility) as minority styles have only secondary importance, that the social determinants are the more significant? The answer is no, and for two reasons.

First of all, no social system can entirely control the innovatory strength of a minority entity. Conversion phenomena (Moscovici, 1980), those gradual processes of change, provide direct testament to this. It seems that minority influence is only rarely direct and socially explicit (it was to avoid introducing further complications into the presentation of our research programme that we intentionally ignored this issue). Minority influence seems instead to follow a subterranean, socially invisible path and appears only in an indirect fashion at levels of response which somehow escape social control. Moreover, minority rigidity accentuates this indirect effect. Rigid minorities principally fail in the exercise of direct influence. But at another level, where the responses are more indirectly linked to minority positions, a rigid minority's influence is substantial and sometimes even superior to the indirect influence of a flexible minority (Moscovici, Mugny & Papastamou, 1981; Mugny, 1982).

Secondly, precisely because of the strategy it chooses, a minority can itself activate or inhibit one mechanism or another. The social does not intervene in a mechanical manner. Rather, it is the behaviour and effects that are irreversible, to the extent that they frustrate this determinism. This is above all perhaps when minorities are, we might say, the convulsive expression of history in progress.

Notes

1. A major part of the research presented in this chapter was conducted as part of contract No. 1.681.0.78 with the Fonds National Suisse de la Recherche Scientifique, and also as part of a project involving the Laboratoire Européen de Psychologie Sociale and the D.G.R.S.T. (France).
2. This 'social attitude' is analogous to that of certain groups on the extreme left who make a political strategy of an unconditional break with power and the refusal of all negotiation.
3. It should be noted that two types of minorities can be distinguished as a function of their divergent normative orientations. Thus 'progressive' minorities may be defined as those who defend positions which imply a historical evolution of the

dominant norms in a social system, whilst those opposed to such evolution may be defined as 'reactionary'. Although, as will be seen, most of our experiments deal with progressive minorities, there are some such as this one which are concerned with the impact of a reactionary minority on the opinions of our population. In this experiment it remains to be seen whether the minority character of the source was further accentuated in the 'classic' manner by the comparative rarity of the opinion upheld by this minority within the population studied.

4. Note that in the experiment reported in our introduction, our stooge, although defined as a minority in purely numerical terms, could have been perceived as an agent, even if a particularly extreme and stereotyped one, of the power institution that a national army represents.

5. It will be helpful here to provide a succinct description of the paradigm around which were organised several of the experiments to which we will be referring (see Mugny & Papastamou, 1980; for a complete account of this paradigm, see Mugny, 1982). It follows the schema of pre-test, test, post-test. In the pre-test and post-test subjects respond to the same questionnaire about responsibilities for pollution. Some of the items attribute blame to industry while others do so to various categories of individual. The questionnaire thus contrasts social responsibility (the system of production) with individual responsibility (individual selfishness). In the experimental phase subjects read a minority argument which (consistently) questions the existing production system based on profitability and short-term profit maximisation, and at the same time strongly denounces explanations in terms of individual selfishness as obscuring the true nature of the pollution issue. The variable of flexible *versus* rigid negotiation is manipulated in terms of slogans which follow each of the four paragraphs constituting the body of the text (which is otherwise identical across conditions), and is based on the extremity of the concrete proposals advanced by the minority to control pollution. The rigid proposals push the reasoning to its most extreme conclusions (in effect, renouncing the current mode of production by arguing in particular that polluting industries be closed), thus inducing a particularly intense conflict. The flexible propositions do not accentuate the conflict already generated by minority consistency (as it is characterised by the body of the text), and only suggest, for example, that polluting industries be fined. Negotiation is thus implicit and in a sense anticipatory, and not direct as in the experiments cited earlier (Mugny, Pierrehumbert & Zubel, 1972–3; Mugny, 1975). This manipulation has, moreover, been shown to be capable of inducing a perception of the minority in terms of flexibility and rigidity (Mugny & Papastamou, 1975–6; Papastamou, Mugny & Kaiser, 1980).

6. Furthermore, such naturalisation is not only characteristic of a common form of interpretation of minority behaviour by the population. It can also take on an official form when certain regimes make a veritable institution of the 'psychiarisation' and indeed 'biologisation' of their dissidents or their 'minorities' (particularly the racial ones).

Part II
Minority influence in groups

Introduction

EDDY VAN AVERMAET

Whereas the first part of this book directly addresses fairly specific questions about the nature of minority influence processes, Part II is much broader in scope. It reflects the views of social psychologists who – at least until recently – were themselves not actively engaged in research in this area but who had the courage and the creativity to look at their own domain of interest through the perspective of minority influence. The products of their, at times speculative, endeavours constitute a worthwhile addition to the field because they force us back to very fundamental questions about the relationship between minority influence, group functioning and group processes in general. As such, the chapters of Part II truly put minority influence in perspective.

Observing that past research concerning small group processes has largely neglected the *mutual* influence groups and their members have on each other, and that it has not given sufficient attention to the temporal changes that occur in their relationship, John Levine and Richard Moreland present in chapter 6 a new model of group socialisation that does incorporate these two features. They view an individual's passage through a group as a series of phases, each characterised by a different relationship between the group and the individual. Within each phase the group and the individual evaluate one another in terms of their rewardingness. These evaluations lead to changes in commitment of the group to the individual and *vice versa*, which in turn lead to role (or phase) transitions. The recursive process can then start again. Against the background of this general model the question of innovation is raised both in general terms and in terms of the specific forms it can take at the various stages of the group socialisation process. Do individual members affect the group? What kinds of changes do they bring about? Do these effects vary with socialisation phases? What factors affect the direction and the intensity of the changes brought about by individual members? Both in asking and in answering these questions the authors use a very broad definition of innovation: it refers to the impact of *individuals* on the structure, dynamics, or performance of a group through their presence (or absence) and behaviour, intentional and unintentional. As the concept of evaluation plays a central role in their model, it should also come as no surprise that Levine and Moreland locate the major source of an individual's impact on the group in the latter's level of dependency on its members.

In chapter 7 Harold Gerard, a leading contributor to the field of small group processes in general and of conformity in particular, searches for the factors that would predispose a minority, more than a majority, to adopt a consistent behavioural style. This is an interesting and new question because it treats the behavioural style of the minority no longer as an independent variable but, instead, as a phenomenon to be explained in its own right. At first glance then, rather than focusing on the relationship between minority and majority or on the impact the former has on the latter, Gerard attends to the internal dynamics of minority subgroups. A rich blend of theorising, speculation, reinterpretation of old data and presentation of fresh evidence leads Gerard to the paradoxical conclusion that the very processes described in the American literature as relating to the larger group as a whole, and to the relationship between majorities and minorities, manifest themselves to a greater extent and with more force within the minority itself. Informational and normative influence, dependency and power, would operate more strongly within the minority and would constitute the basis for the development of within-minority cohesiveness and the resultant behavioural consistency and staunchness. Gerard's analysis is provocative, as it suggests that the factors long held responsible for the impact of the majority on the minority are also, and even more so, viewed as the indirect cause of the minority's impact on the majority.

Orthodox minorities and their relationship to the larger organisation of which they are a part constitute the topic of chapter 8 by Jean-Pierre Deconchy. Taking the Roman Catholic church as a prototypical example of a social system characterised by a tight ideological belief structure and a powerful social control system, the question is raised as to whether such systems allow for minority positions which at the same time may continue to be viewed as orthodox positions and what kind of role they play in the functioning of the system. Through a very incisive analysis Deconchy demonstrates that orthodox minorities play a vital role in the maintenance of the kinds of systems described because they are characterised by a compensatory relationship between their belief structure and their social control devices: weakening one pole leads to a strengthening of the other pole. Deconchy supports his arguments with data from a number of ingenious field experimental studies. His contribution is interesting for a variety of reasons.

Orthodox minorities of the kind he studies have not received much research attention in the past. He explicitly tries to establish the link between influence at the belief level and at the social control level. Finally, he makes a strong case for the view that influence processes cannot always be studied in a social vacuum, but instead derive much of their meaning from the institutional and ideological context within which they occur.

Observing that past research on conformity and innovation has failed to study simultaneous and reciprocal influence by both factions, Sharon Wolf and Bibb Latané consider in chapter 9 the application of social impact theory to social influence situations. The theory states that social influence can be viewed as the result of social forces which operate in a social force field and whose impact is governed by psychosocial laws (similar to psychophysical laws). In a situation of reciprocal influence the impact of each faction on the other and of each faction on its own members is both a function of the force emanating from each faction (determined by its strength, immediacy and size) and of the number of targets over which it is diffused. This elegant theory permits a relatively precise quantitative description of the functional relationship between source and target characteristics and influence. According to the authors, the theory has the additional advantage of treating influence as a unitary concept: minority influence is ruled by the same principles as majority influence, the difference being purely quantitative. Research evidence presented by them is consistent with this viewpoint. In line with other contributions to this book, Wolf and Latané treat minorities and majorities as active agents both of influence and change, but whereas they focus most on the similarities on the input side of the influence process, other authors focus more on the psychological mechanisms set in motion by this input and on the different response levels at which effects can be observed. As such, the two kinds of approaches nicely complement one another.

The final chapter, by Vernon Allen, is centred around the proposition that the phenomenal level at which an individual construes the social world will affect the perceived structure and the meaning of observed social behaviour and hence the individual's reaction to it. In essence, Allen makes a plea for the re-appraisal of the active role of the individual in his dealings with his social environment, and he then goes on to discuss the implications of this perspective for a better understanding of social influence in general and minority influence in particular. Observed actions can be construed cognitively at the infra-group, intra-group and intergroup levels. Applied to minority influence, he argues that it makes a major difference both in terms of the mechanisms of influence and in terms of the amount of influence whether the persons who advocate the minority point of view are construed as a mere aggregate of individuals, as members of one's own group or as a group with a separate identity. Allen's chapter is most stimulating because it contains a wealth of ideas that are easily amenable to experimental test. Our understanding of social influence processes will be greatly enhanced by taking his suggestions to heart. To Moscovici's argument that the mechanisms of influence depend partly on the minority or majority status of the source of influence he adds the important qualification that the mechanisms of influence also depend on the level at which these influence sources are construed cognitively.

In attempting to summarise the ideas set forth in Part II, and using Latané's notion of force fields, one could say that Latané and Wolf's attention is principally directed to the quasi-physical forces that operate on group members, whereas Allen deals principally with cognitively processed forces. Ideological forces constitute the prime interest of Deconchy, and Levine, Moreland and Gerard focus on social forces. This is, of course, an overstatement and a simplification, but at least it reveals that minority influence, and its relation to majority influence and social influence in general, can profitably be looked at from a wide variety of perspectives; it is to be hoped that together these chapters provide the basis for continued research along these same lines.

6. Innovation and socialisation in small groups[1]

JOHN M. LEVINE and RICHARD L. MORELAND

A number of social psychologists (e.g. Steiner, 1974; McGrath, 1978; Zander, 1979) have commented on the decline of interest in group processes since the 1950s. Rather than studying people as integral parts of a social system, social psychologists have tended to focus on the behaviour and cognition of individuals (Pepitone, 1981). It is heartening to note, however, that recently there has been a renewed interest in group processes. Much of the credit for this renewed interest belongs to our European colleagues. They have forced us to re-examine many of our basic assumptions about the relationship between the group and the individual and have offered provocative analyses of several neglected topics.

As we begin what promises to be a new era of small group research, it is important to keep in mind the factors that caused investigators to lose interest in group research in the past. Some of these factors are extra-disciplinary in origin, reflecting broad political and social forces of the sort described by Steiner (1974). Others, however, are intra-disciplinary, in the sense that they reflect how social psychologists conceptualise group processes and formulate research questions. One important intra-disciplinary factor has been a tendency to overlook the phenomenon of *reciprocal influence* in small groups. A good deal of research has focused on how groups influence individuals, but the impact of individuals on groups has been largely neglected.

Although Festinger's (1950) classic paper on communication in groups explicitly mentioned the possibility of reciprocal influence between groups and their members, and although sociologists (e.g. Coser, 1956) have discussed the positive consequences of conflict in groups, social psychologists have generally viewed influence as unidirectional (from group to individual) and conflict as maladaptive. Within the last several years, however, Moscovici and his colleagues have begun to redress this imbalance, arguing that influence is reciprocal and that conflict is adaptive. Specifically, Moscovici (1976, 1980) has sought to clarify the conditions under which minorities (including single individuals) exert influence on majorities.

Despite recent criticisms of Moscovici's work (e.g. Levine, 1980), it has led to a more balanced picture of social influence in groups. However, certain aspects of minority influence have not yet received sufficient attention. One important issue concerns how temporal changes in the relationship between the individual and the group influence the amount and type of innovation that occurs. Because previous research on innovation in small groups has utilised short-term *ad hoc* groups (Levine, 1980), temporal processes that may influence innovation have been neglected. Rather than existing for a short period of time, natural groups often endure for months or years. Members move in and out of the group at different times, rather than all entering and exiting together. The group seeks to ensure its continuity and viability by recruiting new members and by expelling old members who violate normative expectations. A group's expectations and behaviour regarding an individual, and an individual's expectations and behaviour regarding a group, often differ as a function of how long the individual has been a group member. These kinds of temporal changes can have important consequences for innovation in the group.

Temporal changes in the relationships between groups and their members have been largely overlooked by social psychologists. With the exception of several studies involving newcomers in groups (e.g. Merei, 1949; Ziller & Behringer, 1960; Nash & Heiss, 1967; Feldbaum, Christenson & O'Neal, 1980; Putallaz & Gottman, 1981), little attention has been given to the development of the relationship between a group and an individual (cf. Ziller, 1965, 1977). This lack of attention to temporal processes in small groups is somewhat surprising, given efforts to explicate such processes in dyadic relationships (e.g. Burgess & Huston, 1979; Levinger, 1980; Levinger & Huesmann, 1980; Altman, Vinsel & Brown, 1981; Duck & Gilmour, 1981) and in organisations (e.g. Schein, 1968, 1971; Feldman, 1976; Van Maanen, 1976; Van Maanen & Schein, 1979; Wanous, 1980). No one has yet investigated how temporal changes in the relationship between the group and the individual can influence innovation.

1. A model of group socialisation

To make significant progress in understanding innovation in small groups, we believe that it is necessary to frame research questions that reflect two critical aspects of group life: (1) that the group (or majority) and the individual (or minority) exert reciprocal influence on one another and (2) that over time important changes occur in the relationship between the group and the individual. A useful way to conceptualise this reciprocal influence and temporal change is to think in terms of 'group socialisation'. By group socialisation, we mean the affective, cognitive, and behavioural changes that groups and individuals produce in one another from the beginning to the end of their relationship. Stated somewhat differently, group socialisation involves the passage of individuals through groups.

Recently, we have developed a model of group socialisation that seeks to describe and explain the passage of individuals through groups. Our model adopts a reciprocal perspective, in that both the group and the individual are viewed as active social influence agents. In addition, the model is dynamic, in that the relationship between the group and the individual is assumed to change in systematic ways over time. The model is meant to apply primarily (but not exclusively) to small, autonomous, voluntary groups whose members interact on a regular basis, have affective ties with one another, share a common frame of reference, and are behaviourally interdependent. We will briefly describe the model and then discuss some of its implications for understanding innovation. A more complete description of the model can be found in Moreland & Levine (1982).

1.1. **Basic processes.** Our model of group socialisation incorporates three basic psychological processes: *evaluation, commitment* and *role transition*. These processes are reciprocal, in that they apply to both the group and the individual, and dynamic, in that they occur in a recursive sequence. Evaluation involves the way in which groups and individuals assess and attempt to maximise one another's rewardingness. Commitment, which depends on the outcome of evaluation, is based on the group's and the individual's beliefs about the rewardingness of their own and alternative relationships. Finally, role transitions, which occur when commitment reaches a decision criterion, involve re-labelling the individual's relationship to the group and thereby changing how the group and the individual evaluate one another.

Evaluation. Evaluation involves assessments of the rewardingness of relationships. Because every group has goals that it would like to accomplish, it evaluates the degree to which people contribute to goal attainment. In conducting these evaluations, the group decides which goals each person is expected to contribute to, determines the behavioural dimensions on which those contributions will be assessed, and develops normative expectations for each dimension.

Jackson's (1965, 1966) return potential model of norms provides a useful way to conceptualise behavioural expectations. Jackson suggests that for each behavioural dimension under consideration a return potential curve can be drawn specifying how much potential approval or disapproval ('return') an individual will receive from the group for various behaviours relevant to that norm. Jackson's model is applicable to any norm, regardless of the nature of the relationship (e.g. positive or negative, linear or curvilinear) between the individual's behaviour and the group's approval/disapproval. Moreover, the model specifies several important aspects of norms, including ideal behaviour, the range of tolerable behaviour and the intensity of the group's feelings about the behaviour. Ideal behaviour represents the group's preference for how the individual ideally ought to behave. The range of tolerable behaviour includes all of the behaviours for which the individual will receive approval from the group. Finally, the intensity of the group's feelings reflects the relative importance of the norm. Intensity is determined by the average level of absolute group approval/disapproval associated with all of the behaviours that the individual might exhibit.

Once a group has developed normative expectations for an individual, it can monitor his or her behaviour to determine the degree to which these expectations are being fulfilled. Monitoring involves assessing the individual's behaviour on each dimension and then comparing that behaviour with the group's expectation for the person on that dimension at that point in time. In so far as the individual fails to meet expectations, the group may take some form of corrective action. Such action might involve trying to alter the individual's behaviour, changing the group's expectations, or rejecting the individual.

As a result of all its evaluations, the group has a general sense of the rewardingness of its relationship with the individual at any time. Rewardingness is based on the rewards and costs associated with the individual's behaviour. Rewards are acts that fall within the range of tolerable behaviour, and costs are acts that fall outside that range. The magnitude of a particular reward or cost depends on the relevant return potential curve. Rewardingness is the algebraic sum of all the rewards and costs that the individual generates for the group.

The relationship between groups and individuals is reciprocal, so individuals also engage in evaluation of groups. Because every person has needs that he or she would like to satisfy through group membership, the person evaluates the degree to which different groups contribute to need satisfaction. In evaluating a group, the individual decides which needs the group is expected to satisfy, determines the behavioural dimensions on which that satisfaction will be assessed, and develops normative expectations for each dimension. Once again, behavioural expectations can be conceptualised in terms of Jackson's (1965, 1966) return potential model, except that here the individual evaluates the group's behaviour rather than *vice versa*.

Once an individual has developed normative expectations for a group, he or she can monitor the group's behaviour to determine the degree to which those expectations are being fulfilled. As before, monitoring involves assessing the group's behaviour on each dimension and then comparing that behaviour with the individual's expectations for the group on that dimension at that point in time. In so far as the group fails to meet expectations, the individual may take some form of corrective action, such as trying to alter the group's behaviour, changing his or her expectations for the group, or rejecting the group.

Individuals also have a general sense of the rewardingness of their relationship with the group at any particular time. Rewardingness is based on the rewards and costs associated with the group's behaviour. The relevant return potential curve determines both whether an act is classified as a reward or cost and the magnitude of that reward or cost. Rewardingness is again the algebraic sum of all the rewards and costs that the group generates for the individual.

Evaluations are usually focused on the present relationship between the group and the individual. However, evaluations may also be extended to the past or the future. Sometimes, the group and the individual think back to how rewarding their relationship was in the past, or think ahead to how rewarding it will be in the future. Evaluations also need not be restricted to the relationship that the group and the individual have with each other. Groups and individuals also evaluate the past, present, and future rewardingness of their available alternative relationships. Thus, groups evaluate other current members as well as people they might once have admitted or might someday ask to join. Similarly, individuals evaluate other groups to which they belong, as well as groups that they might once have joined or of which they might someday become members.

Commitment. Evaluation leads to feelings of commitment on the part of both the group and the individual. Groups and individuals evaluate their past (PR), present (R) and anticipated future (FR) relationships together, and as the perceived rewardingness of those relationships increases, the group and the individual become more committed to one another. Commitment also involves the rewardingness of other continuing and potential relationships. As the perceived rewardingness of past (PRa), present (Ra) and anticipated future (FRa) alternative relationships increases, the group and the individual become less committed to one another. Commitment is thus determined by six factors, which are hypothesised to combine in the following way:

$$\text{Commitment} = (\text{PR} - \text{PRa}) + (\text{R} - \text{Ra}) + (\text{FR} - \text{FRa})$$

As the formula indicates, commitment is the sum of three comparisons.[2] Commitment between the group and the individual will be high in so far as

(a) their past relationship is remembered as more rewarding than other previous alternative relationships; (b) their present relationship is regarded as more rewarding than other current alternative relationships; and (c) their future relationship is expected to be more rewarding than other future alternative relationships.

Commitment can have important consequences for the behaviour of both the group and the individual. Previous analyses (e.g. Kanter, 1968, 1972; Buchanan, 1974; Mowday, Steers & Porter, 1979; Gordon *et al.* 1980) have suggested that a committed individual will be likely to accept the group's goals and values, experience positive affective ties to other group members, exert effort on behalf of the group and attempt to meet the group's expectations, and try to gain or maintain membership in the group. These four consequences of commitment can be labelled, respectively, consensus, cohesion, control and continuance (Kanter, 1968, 1972). Commitment on the part of the group may have analogous consequences for its behaviour. That is, a committed group will be likely to accept the individual's needs and values, experience positive affective ties to the individual, exert effort on behalf of the individual and attempt to meet his or her expectations, and try to gain or retain the individual as a group member.

The levels of commitment that the group and the individual feel towards one another may or may not be highly correlated (Rosenblatt, 1977; Levinger, 1980; Duck, 1982). When commitment levels are not highly correlated, the party that feels less committed will probably have greater power in the relationship (Waller & Hill, 1951). It seems likely that the greater the commitment disequilibrium in a relationship, the less stable the relationship will be. Therefore, we assume a general pressure towards commitment equilibrium between groups and individuals.

Role transition. Group membership is not an all-or-none phenomenon. Instead, there is an ingroup–outgroup dimension along which all people associated with a group can be placed (Moreland, 1978). This dimension contains three major role regions: non-member, quasi-member and full member. Non-members include *prospective members* who have not yet joined the group and *ex-members* who have left the group. Quasi-members include *new members* who have not yet attained full member status and *marginal members* who have lost that status. Finally, *full members* are those individuals who are most closely identified with the group and who have all the privileges and responsibilities associated with group membership.

The levels of commitment that the group and the individual feel towards one another often change over time and, as a result, the nature of their relationship may change as well. Both groups and individuals formulate *decision criteria* to indicate important changes in their relationship, and these criteria can be conceptualised in terms of commitment. If the group's commitment to an individual rises or falls to a decision criterion, then the group will perceive the role of the individual differently and will try to impose a role transition on that person. Similarly, an individual whose level of commitment to a group rises or falls to a decision criterion will try to initiate a role transition, on the grounds that his or her role within the group has undergone a significant change.

Role transitions are important because they may produce alterations in the evaluation process. For example, groups often evaluate new members in a different way from full members, and new and full members may differ in how they evaluate a group. It is functional, therefore, if groups and individuals engage in *reciprocal* labelling of their relationship, so that any changes in the evaluation process can be mutually perceived and adhered to. Unfortunately, the potential for conflict regarding role transitions is often large because the group and the individual may be differentially committed to one another or may possess different decision criteria. As a result, disagreements may arise about whether a role transition should occur and/or whether a role transition has occurred. In order to minimise such disagreements, many groups formalise their decision criteria so that those criteria can be clearly and easily communicated to group members. Similarly, some individuals publicise their personal decision criteria in the hope that these criteria will be adopted by the group. Many groups also evolve elaborate rites of passage (Van Gennep, 1908/1969) to provide a public demonstration that a role transition has taken place. Similarly, some individuals stage personal rites of passage (e.g. having a party, getting drunk) in order to prove that their role within the group has changed.

1.2. Passage through the group. An individual's passage through a group can be viewed in terms of a series of phases, each representing a different relationship between the group and the individual. These phases are separated by role transitions. Each role transition represents a significant change in group and individual commitment levels, which are themselves determined by changes in evaluation. The model thus involves a temporal process that is basically recursive in nature. Within each phase, evaluations produce changes in commitment, which in turn lead to a role transition whenever a decision criterion has been reached. Once a role transition has occurred, a new phase is entered and evaluations begin again. In this way the individual moves through different phases of group membership.

Figure 1 illustrates how the relationship between a group and an individual

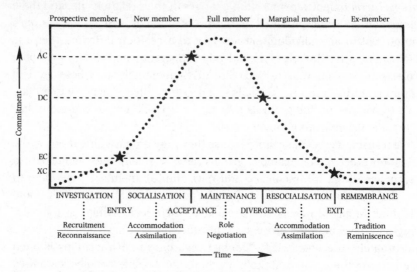

Figure 1. A model of group socialisation. (From Moreland & Levine, 1982.)

might change over time. The diagram, which relates changes in commitment to specific kinds of role transitions, can be viewed (at least potentially) from the perspective of either the group or the individual, since the same basic psychological processes (evaluation, commitment, role transition) are assumed to operate in each case. The dotted line in figure 1 represents the personal 'history' of a hypothetical person who has passed through all the phases of group membership. It should be noted, however, that many different dotted lines could be drawn, each reflecting a unique passage through the group.

To begin with, both the group and the individual go through an *investigation* phase. During this phase, the group engages in *recruitment*, looking for people who seem likely to contribute to the attainment of group goals. Similarly, the individual engages in *reconnaissance*, looking for groups that seem likely to contribute to the satisfaction of personal needs. As time passes, the group and the individual may become increasingly committed to one another. If the group's commitment to the individual rises to its *entry criterion* (EC), then an offer of membership will be made. Similarly, the individual will try to join the group when his or her level of commitment has passed a personal entry criterion. Once the group and the individual agree to begin their relationship together, entry occurs and the person is jointly re-labelled as a new member.

After a new member enters the group, both the group and the individual go through a *socialisation* phase. During socialisation, the group attempts to change the individual in ways that will increase his or her contributions to the attainment of group goals. In so far as the group is successful, the individual undergoes *assimilation*. At the same time, the individual attempts to change the group in ways that will increase its contributions to the satisfaction of personal needs. In so far as the individual succeeds, the group undergoes *accommodation*. The socialisation phase ends when the group's and individual's commitment to one another rise to their respective *acceptance criteria* (AC) and the individual is jointly re-labelled as a full member.

During the *maintenance* phase, the group and the individual engage in *role negotiation*. The group attempts to define a specialised role for each full member that maximises his or her contributions to the attainment of group goals and minimises the group's obligations to the person. In contrast, each full member attempts to define his or her own role so as to maximise the satisfaction of personal needs and minimise obligations to the group. If the group feels that a particular person is not meeting its expectations, then pressure will be exerted on the individual. Similarly, a person who feels that the group is not meeting his or her expectations will exert pressure on the group. In so far as these tactics fail and the group and the individual regard their relationship as unrewarding, both will feel reduced commitment to one another. If the group's and the individual's levels of commitment fall to their respective *divergence criteria* (DC), then the person will be jointly re-labelled as a marginal member.

During the *resocialisation* phase, the group tries to restore the individual's contributions to the attainment of group goals, and the individual tries to restore the group's contributions to the satisfaction of personal needs. To the extent that the group and the individual are successful, *assimilation* and *accommodation* will again occur. If the group's and the individual's commitment to one another rise to their respective divergence criteria, then a special role transition (convergence) will occur and the individual will be returned to full membership. However, if the group's and the individual's levels of commitment to each other fall to their respective *exit criteria* (XC), then a joint re-labelling of the individual as an ex-member of the group will take place. (This second outcome of resocialisation is shown in figure 1.)

Finally, after the individual has left the group, a period of *remembrance* occurs. The group develops a consensus about the individual's previous contributions to the attainment of group goals, and this consensus becomes part of the group's *tradition*. In an analogous fashion, the individual engages in *reminiscence* about the degree to which the group contributed to the satisfaction of his or her personal needs. In both cases, commitment eventually stabilises at some level.

It should be noted that the sequence of events shown in figure 1 is an idealised example that masks several complex issues regarding group socialisation. For example, group and individual commitment levels may sometimes undergo sudden and dramatic shifts rather than changing smoothly and gradually as the diagram suggests. In addition, group and individual decision criteria may not be stable over time, and changes in decision criteria may influence how long individuals spend in membership phases. Some phases may be shortened until they disappear altogether, while others may be lengthened until they last almost indefinitely. Finally, with some constraints, decision criteria may vary in their positions relative to one another, and there may be variability in the number of role transitions that an individual experiences and the order in which these transitions occur. For example, exit can occur in the investigation or socialisation phase under certain circumstances. Despite these potential variations, the pattern of events shown in figure 1 is probably fairly representative.

2. The role of socialisation in innovation

Our model of group socialisation raises many interesting issues regarding social influence in small groups. Some of these issues involve social control, or the ability of the group to influence individuals. However, because social psychologists have devoted so much attention to this type of influence (see Moscovici, 1976), we will focus our attention on innovation, or the ability of individuals to influence the group. Innovation, from our point of view, occurs whenever an individual produces some significant change in the structure, dynamics, or performance of a group. Such changes are often intentional, resulting from deliberate attempts by the individual to influence the group, but they need not be so. On a general level, the three basic psychological processes (evaluation, commitment, role transition) embodied in our model of group socialisation all suggest ways in which an individual might influence a group throughout their relationship with one another.

2.1. General forms of innovation. Several forms of innovation involve changes in how the group conducts evaluations. For example, an individual whose behaviour seriously violates the group's expectations may cause the group to (a) develop a more restrictive return potential curve for the behavioural dimension under consideration, (b) increase the number of behavioural dimensions that are evaluated, (c) engage in more frequent and regular monitoring of behaviour, and (d) become more punitive in reacting to behavioural deviation. In contrast, an individual who exhibits ideal behaviour may cause the group to (a) develop a less restrictive return potential curve for the behavioural dimension under consideration, (b) decrease the number of behavioural dimensions that are evaluated, (c) engage in less frequent and regular monitoring of behaviour, and (d) become less punitive in reacting to behavioural deviation. These changes in the group's evaluations may apply only to the person who caused them to arise, or they may be generalised to other people the group evaluates. The probability of generalisation will increase in so far as those other people are seen as similar to the individual who produced the original changes in evaluation.

Innovation is also influenced by feelings of commitment between the group and the individual. In general, the ability of a particular person to influence the group will be positively related to the level of commitment that he or she elicits from the group.[3] Full members are thus capable of producing more innovation than are quasi-members, and non-members produce the least innovation of all. Among the quasi-members of a group, newcomers are probably more influential than marginal members because newcomers are more likely to make future contributions to the attainment of group goals. Among the non-members of a group, prospective members are probably more influential than ex-members for the same reason. Innovation may also be related to the degree of commitment disequilibrium between the group and the individual during any phase of their relationship. In so far as the group feels more commitment towards an individual than he or she feels towards the group, the group is more likely to allow innovation to occur. Finally, the group's commitment towards any one individual may affect its commitment towards other people, because commitment is based on comparisons between relationships. Thus, increased commitment towards one person often produces decreased commitment towards other people, and *vice versa*. Such changes in commitment can alter the probability that those other people will be successful innovators.

Another way in which commitment can influence innovation is by altering the probability that an individual will make an innovation attempt. Innovation attempts are more likely to occur when the individual wants to change the group and believes that his or her attempts will be successful. In general, people who are less committed to the group are more likely to want to change it so that it will better satisfy their personal needs. However, these same people are also less likely to believe that their innovation attempts will be successful. Because levels of commitment between the group and the individual are typically correlated, people who lack commitment to the group are likely to perceive that the group lacks commitment to them and that it will therefore be unreceptive to their innovation attempts. In contrast, people who are more committed to the group are less likely to want to change it, but more confident that their innovation attempts will succeed. Regardless of the individual's absolute level of commitment to the group, innovation attempts are more likely to occur in so far as the group's commitment to the individual is higher than his or her commitment to it. This kind of commitment disequilibrium strengthens the individual's belief that any attempted innovations will be successful.

Finally, role transitions can also affect innovation within the group. An approaching role transition, for example, can have a significant impact on the probability that an individual will attempt to produce innovation. Few innovation attempts are likely to be made by the individual when he or she wants to make a role transition and believes that innovation makes that transition less probable, or wants to avoid a role transition and believes that innovation makes that transition more probable. Attempts at innovation in either case become less likely as the role transition approaches (Schein, 1971). In contrast, many innovation attempts are likely to be made by the individual when he or she wants to make a role transition and believes that innovation makes that transition more probable, or wants to avoid a role transition and believes that innovation makes that transition less probable. In these cases, attempts at innovation become more likely as the role transition approaches.

The success of innovation attempts by the individual may also be influenced by approaching role transitions. The group is more likely to allow innovation to take place when it wants a role transition to occur and believes that innovation makes that transition more probable, or wants to avoid a role transition and believes that innovation makes that transition less probable. Innovation becomes more likely in either case as the role transition approaches. In contrast, the group is less likely to allow innovation to take place when it wants a role transition to occur and believes that innovation makes that transition less probable, or wants to avoid a role transition and believes that innovation makes that transition more probable. In these cases, innovation becomes less likely as the role transition approaches.

When a role transition occurs it may produce conflict between the group and the individual and thereby lead to a variety of innovations. The group may, for example, decide to formalise the relevant decision criterion and publicise it more widely in the hopes of easing future role transitions. A more elaborate rite of passage marking the relevant role transition might also be devised and carried out for the same purpose. These changes in decision criteria and rites of passage may also be generalised to other role transitions. Such changes necessarily involve the other members of the group and may also influence how the group is perceived by non-members. Thus, the ability of the group to gain or retain members may be affected.

After a role transition has occurred, the individual continues to be evaluated by the group, often on different behavioural dimensions than before. To the extent that the individual violates the group's new expectations, the group may decide that the decision criterion associated with the recent role transition was too lenient. As a result, the decision criterion may be adjusted to inhibit future role transitions by other people. To the extent that the individual completely fulfils the group's new expectations, the group may decide that the relevant decision criterion was too harsh and adjust it to facilitate future role transitions by other people. These changes in decision criteria represent yet another form of innovation, because they can alter the length of the various membership phases and thereby influence the passage of people through the group.

2.2. Specific forms of innovation. As the above discussion suggests, several general forms of innovation related to evaluation, commitment, and role transition can arise throughout the relationship between a group and an individual. There are also, however, many specific forms of innovation that arise primarily during particular phases of group membership. Each membership phase (investigation, socialisation, maintenance, resocialisation, remembrance) provides special opportunities for innovation.

Investigation. During the investigation phase the group and the individual assess the potential rewardingness of their relationship with one another. It is interesting that even before an individual actually enters the group as a new member, he or she can produce at least some forms of innovation. Several factors can affect the ability of a prospective member to influence a group. One such factor is the number of prospective members who are being considered for group membership. The lower the number of prospective members relative to the number of 'open positions' available for new members, the higher the commitment each of those prospective members will elicit from the group (Arnold & Greenberg, 1980). Individuals who elicit relatively high commitment are likely to succeed in producing innovation. The number of prospective members that a group attracts can also affect how current members are treated. For example, groups that have many prospective members may raise their divergence and exit criteria, on the grounds that current members who violate expectations can be easily replaced. In contrast, groups that have few prospective members may lower their divergence and exit criteria, because deviating members cannot be replaced and therefore must be tolerated.

The characteristics of prospective members can also influence how successful they are in producing innovation. One important factor is the perceived relevance of the individual's characteristics to the group's goals. In many groups members disagree about what the group's goals should be and/or how these goals should be attained. Such disagreements may be latent, in the sense that they are not salient to group members and therefore are rarely (or never) discussed; or they may be manifest, in the sense that group members have aligned themselves into factions that disagree about the goals. The characteristics of a particular prospective member, or the distribution of characteristics within the total pool of prospective members, can either increase or decrease the salience of goal-related issues and the corresponding probability of conflict within the group. Thus, the mere presence of a prospective member with certain 'sensitive' characteristics can produce important changes in the relationships among current members.

Even if group members agree about goals and methods of attaining them, the characteristics of prospective members can still influence innovation. In particular, the 'quality' of prospective members, based on their perceived ability to contribute to group goal attainment, is often a critical factor. When its prospective members are of high quality, the group may feel a sense of pride and the average level of commitment among current members may increase. People outside the group may also view it more favourably. As a result, internal and external pressures may arise to keep the group as it is, thereby decreasing the probability that innovation will occur. In contrast, when the quality of the group's prospective members is low the average level of commitment among current members may decrease and the group may be viewed less favourably by outsiders. As a result, internal and external pressures may arise to improve the group, thereby increasing the probability that some form of innovation will occur.

The perceived quality of a particular prospective member will also determine whether he or she produces innovation in the group. Individuals who seem more likely to contribute to the attainment of group goals will elicit higher levels of commitment from the group. Such prospective members are more likely to be successful innovators. Successful innovation is especially common in situations involving commitment disequilibrium, when the group's commitment to a prospective member is higher than his or her commitment to the group.

One type of commitment disequilibrium during investigation is particularly important. This occurs when one party's commitment exceeds its entry criterion, but the other party's commitment does not. The party with higher commitment will try to convince the party with lower commitment to allow entry to take place. In contrast, the party with lower commitment will try to convince the party with higher commitment that entry is not a good idea.

Thus, reciprocal influence directed towards quite different ends will occur between the group and the individual.

When a group's commitment to a prospective member is higher than the individual's commitment to the group, the person will be in a relatively powerful position. The group will try to convince the individual that membership in the group will serve his or her interests and may offer the individual direct inducements, such as power or money, to join. Some of these inducements may reflect *anticipatory accommodation*, in which the group changes itself so as to better fulfil the individual's needs. Anticipatory accommodation can involve current alterations in the group and/or promises that alterations will occur once the individual has become a member. The degree to which promised alterations are believed will depend on the explicitness and publicness of the promises, as well as the prospective member's perceptions of the group's ability to make the promised changes and its record of fulfilling promises to other new members in the past.

It is important to note that anticipatory accommodation can have important consequences above and beyond attracting new members. In some cases, anticipatory accommodation can weaken the group's power to retain a new member once he or she has joined. For example, a group that exaggerates its attractive qualities and minimises its negative ones in order to attract new members may discover that those individuals become disenchanted with the realities of group life and leave the group as a result (Wanous, 1977, 1980). An overly eager group may also discover that the resources it used to induce new members to join are not available when needed to encourage those new members to stay. There are also cases in which anticipatory accommodation to one prospective member causes a decrease in the group's flexibility in accommodating to other prospective members. Finally, anticipatory accommodation can weaken the group by (a) producing envy in oldtimers who compare themselves to the newcomers and feel relatively deprived and (b) depleting resources that are needed for the attainment of group goals.

When a prospective member's commitment to a group is higher than the group's commitment to the individual, the group will be in a more powerful position. Nevertheless, innovation can still occur. The individual will try to convince the group that his or her membership will be beneficial to it and may offer the group direct inducements, such as information or service, to promote entry. These inducements often represent real and/or potential resources that can help the group to attain its present goals and allow the group to set higher goals for the future. In either case, the individual has changed the group, regardless of whether he or she is later admitted as a new member. A group that feels relatively low commitment to an individual will not, of course, engage in anticipatory accommodation. Instead, the reluctant group will try to convince the individual to abandon his or her attempts to join. In some cases, the group may suggest that membership will be harmful to the individual and may even engage in *anticipatory anti-accommodation*. This latter tactic involves purposely violating the individual's expectations so that he or she will be less eager to join. Anticipatory anti-accommodation may do more than drive the individual away temporarily. It may also make it impossible to recruit the person in the future if the need should arise, and it may alienate other prospective members who hold similar expectations for the group.

Socialisation. During the socialisation phase the group accommodates itself to the individual, and he or she in turn is assimilated into the group. As in other phases of group membership, innovation can take a variety of forms during socialisation. Innovation can arise from active efforts on the part of individuals to alter the group, as well as from the group's responses to individuals who have no specific intent to produce change.

Many forms of innovation that occur during socialisation are based on individuals' efforts to alter the group. Newcomers are often anxious about being accepted by the group and are therefore fearful of appearing too assertive. This anxiety typically dampens newcomers' efforts to produce innovation (Nash & Wolfe, 1957; Heiss & Nash, 1967). However, under certain circumstances newcomers' anxiety may be dispelled (or overridden) by other factors that can cause newcomers to exert strong efforts to change the group. One factor that may dispel anxiety about the group's reaction to attempted innovations is the 'grace period' often accorded to newcomers. In many groups there is an initial period during which newcomers are exempted from the usual sanctions for deviance (Ziller, 1965; Van Maanen, 1976). A second factor is the perceived safety that newcomers feel when they confront the group collectively rather than as isolated individuals. Innovation attempts are more likely to occur and to succeed if newcomers are socialised as part of a collectivity than if they are socialised alone (Becker, 1964; Wheeler, 1966; Van Maanen, 1978). Collective socialisation of newcomers often builds a sense of ingroup solidarity and causes newcomers to develop their own norms, which may be inconsistent with those of oldtimers (Becker *et al.*, 1961; Evans, 1963). In other cases newcomers' anxiety is not dispelled, but rather overridden in the sense that newcomers are so motivated to change the group that they give little thought to sanctions for deviance. This may occur, for example, when a newcomer's expectations about the rewards of group membership are so grossly violated that the deprived individual angrily attempts to change the group with little concern about the consequences of his or her actions.

Newcomers may also experience anxiety because of a fear of de-individuation (Ziller, 1964; Snyder & Fromkin, 1980). When a person first joins a group, he or she may feel a weakening of personal identity. This is particularly common in groups that use degradation ceremonies to mark entry or engage in the collective socialisation of new members. In order to strengthen their sense of personal identity newcomers may choose to identify with the group as a whole (Tajfel, 1978). Such identification, which is most likely to occur when the individual is highly attracted to the group, usually produces conformity to group norms. Other newcomers may choose to deviate from group norms as a way of increasing their feelings of distinctiveness and thereby strengthening their sense of personal identity (Lemaine, 1974; Lemaine, Kastersztein & Personnaz, 1979). Such deviation can produce innovations in the group.

Besides the innovation that stems from newcomers' efforts to alter the group, innovation can also occur when newcomers have no specific intent to produce change. The simple presence of newcomers can sometimes cause a variety of changes in the group's structure, dynamics and performance. As Platt (1974) suggests, both the criteria that the group uses to define the pool of acceptable prospective members and the procedures that it uses to select new members from this pool determine the distribution of individual characteristics in the group. These characteristics include demographic variables (e.g. age, race, sex), skills and abilities, and personality traits. By changing the distribution of group members' characteristics, newcomers can affect various aspects of group life, including power and status relations among group members, group cohesiveness and conflict, and the group's ability to attain its goals. These effects may occur immediately, or they may emerge at some later time, long after the individuals involved have ceased to be new members.

Newcomers can also produce innovation by influencing the manner in which other group members engage in socialisation. The higher the number of newcomers relative to oldtimers and the lower the similarity of those newcomers to the oldtimers, the more effort the group will devote to socialisation. Thus, a large number of dissimilar newcomers will force the group to invest a good deal of time, energy and material resources in socialisation. This expenditure of effort will distract the group from other tasks and may reduce the rewards of group membership for oldtimers, thereby decreasing their commitment to the group.

A third way in which newcomers can produce innovation without specifically intending to change the group is by altering the relationships among oldtimers. For example, when a salient newcomer is perceived as threatening, other group members may become more cohesive and may resist any efforts by the individual to change the group (Merei, 1949). When the newcomer is viewed as a potentially valuable addition to the group, however, other group members may adjust their relationships in ways that facilitate the person's ability to innovate (Ziller & Behringer, 1960; Fine, 1976).

Finally, Ziller (1965) suggests two additional ways in which newcomers can alter group processes without intending to do so. First, if the newcomer has had experience in other groups, then the newcomer can make intergroup comparisons that reflect positively or negatively on the group that he or she has just joined. A similar point is made by Schuetz (1944), who emphasises a newcomer's 'objectivity' in evaluating groups. To the extent that oldtimers perceive that the newcomer is evaluating their group, they themselves may evaluate the group more often and on new dimensions. Thus, the newcomer may produce 'objective group awareness' on the part of oldtimers (Wicklund, 1975). When the newcomer focuses members' attention on positive aspects of the group, oldtimers may feel more commitment to the group and more attraction to one another. In contrast, oldtimers may feel less commitment to the group and less attraction to one another when the newcomer focuses their attention on negative aspects of the group. Second, competing factions within the group may vie with one another for the newcomer's allegiance (Snyder, 1958). To the extent that this occurs, intra-group conflicts may be exacerbated, and oldtimers' commitment to the group as a whole may be reduced. In addition, because of a desire to recruit the newcomer into a particular faction, oldtimers may lower their acceptance criterion and offer the newcomer valuable resources. These tactics can substantially reduce the group's future viability.

Maintenance. During the maintenance phase of group membership, feelings of commitment between the group and the individual are at their highest levels. As a result, full members are more likely to be successful innovators than are prospective, new, marginal, or ex-members. As in the other phases of group membership, an individual's ability to produce innovation during maintenance depends on the amount of commitment that he or she elicits from the group and the amount of commitment disequilibrium that exists between the group and the individual. In general, full members will be successful innovators in so far as they elicit high levels of commitment from the group and are less committed to the group than it is to them.

Because they tend to occupy positions of high status within the group, full members enjoy special opportunities for innovation that are not available to other people. In order to produce innovation an individual often must act in ways that might be regarded as deviant by the group. Full members, if they have high status within the group, may find it relatively easy to deviate from group norms and thereby produce innovation.[4] Deviance on the part of high-status persons is sometimes overlooked, because it seems inconsistent with their public image or suggests that the group has bestowed its status unwisely (Hollander & Willis, 1967; Wahrman, 1970). There is also evidence that high-status persons are punished less harshly than others when they deviate, so long as their deviance occurs on relatively unimportant behavioural dimensions (Wiggins, Dill & Schwartz, 1965; Alvarez, 1968). When high-status persons deviate on relatively important dimensions, the reactions of the group depend on how the deviance affects the group's goal attainment. Thus, Suchner & Jackson (1976) found that a high-status member who facilitated group goal attainment by deviating received more approval than a high-status member who achieved the same result by conforming. In contrast, when a high-status member inhibited goal attainment, deviation produced less approval than conformity.

Full members are often invited or thrust into positions of leadership within the group, and leadership also provides many special opportunities for innovation. Innovation by leaders is not unusual and indeed may be expected by group members, especially when the group has been unsuccessful in attaining its goals (Hollander, 1958, 1964; Coser, 1962; Homans, 1974). Clearly, the primary objective of a responsible leader is to change the group in ways that will enhance its level of goal attainment. A selfish leader, however, may introduce innovations that will also enhance the degree to which the group satisfies his or her personal needs. A particular act of innovation may thus serve two purposes, one public and the other private. Whether the rest of the group recognises the more selfish aspects of a leader's innovations probably depends on such factors as (a) how familiar the group is with the leader's personal needs, (b) the clarity of the group's goals and the degree of consensus among group members about how those goals should be attained, and (c) the degree to which the leader's needs and the group's goals are compatible. Even if group members realise that the leader has changed the group for his or her own purposes, they may decide not to object if the leader's previous innovations have helped the group to attain its goals.

An individual who is especially powerful can sometimes force innovations on the rest of the group. More commonly, however, a full member will require the cooperation or consent of others in order to produce change. A variety of social influence techniques (Kelman, 1958; Raven & Kruglanski, 1970) may be used by full members as they seek to build coalitions that support their innovations. For example, a full member often has control over important group resources, such as money, information, or status, that can be dispensed or withheld as a way of eliciting compliance on the part of other group members. A charismatic and attractive person may acquire a band of devoted followers within the group who identify with the individual and therefore support his or her innovation attempts. Finally, a full member who is perceived as credible and trustworthy may be able to persuade other group members that his or her plans for the group should be adopted. Not all social influence techniques are equally effective, however. For example, as Raven & Kruglanski (1970) suggest, the use of coercive power will alter overt behaviour in the direction desired, but will alter private beliefs in the opposite direction. In contrast, the exercise of informational power will change both behaviour and beliefs in the direction desired.

In building coalitions to support their innovation attempts, full members have to consider several important factors. First, other group members differ both in their vulnerability to social influence pressures and in the kinds of pressures to which they are most susceptible. In general, a full member will find it hardest to gain the support of other full members, because those persons have the ability to ward off many types of attempted influence. Quasi-members are probably more vulnerable to social influence pressures because of their lower status within the group. A full member may recruit newcomers to his or her cause by promising to make their period of socialisation shorter or more pleasant. Marginal members may be recruited by promises that they can converge back to the status of a full member or that their exit from the group will be delayed or made less traumatic. Prospective members are probably most vulnerable to social influence pressures, because they tend to have the least status within the group. A full member may recruit prospective members by promising to hasten their entry into the group or to minimise unpleasant experiences (e.g. initiation ceremonies) associated with entry. Ex-members may or may not be susceptible to influence, depending on the degree to which full members can reward or punish them. Ex-members who continue to be dependent on the group (for financial, social, or other reasons) may be quite susceptible to influence from full members. In contrast, ex-members who no longer need the group may be very difficult to influence.

Another factor that full members have to consider in building coalitions is how much support other group members can provide for the attempted innovation. Obviously, some members are more powerful than others and are therefore more valuable coalition participants. One determinant of power is the level of commitment that the individual elicits from the group. Full members generally strengthen a coalition more than do quasi-members, who in turn are more valuable than non-members. Among quasi-members, new members strengthen a coalition more than do marginal members. Among non-members, prospective members generally strengthen a coalition more than do ex-members, although both kinds of persons may be useful. Thus, a full member may try to recruit prospective members favourable to his or her cause and may also invoke the names of respected ex-members, or arrange for such persons to lobby within the group, as a means of legitimising his or her plans for innovation. A second determinant of power, of course, is the degree of commitment disequilibrium between the group and the individual. People who are less committed to the group than it is to them will tend to be more powerful and thus will be more valuable coalition participants. Such persons also may be more open to suggested innovations since they are relatively dissatisfied with their group membership.

Finally, full members who are seeking support for their innovations also have to consider the potential costs of including other group members in their coalition. Some individuals may demand so many resources for their cooperation that the full member later is unable to carry out the planned innovation. Coalition participants also may require that the planned innovation be altered in significant ways or may introduce new innovation ideas of their own. In general, full members will probably be more demanding coalition participants than quasi-members, who in turn will be more demanding than non-members. In building a coalition, therefore, a wise full member will seek out persons who are relatively undemanding but who yet possess enough collective power to produce the desired innovation (Gamson, 1961, 1964).

Resocialisation. The resocialisation phase follows the role transition of divergence. Although divergence sometimes signals the beginning of a planned and natural separation from the group (e.g. graduation, retirement), divergence may also indicate an unplanned and premature break in the relationship between the group and the individual. We will restrict our attention to the latter situation, in which resocialisation involves attempts to return to maintenance. Here, both the group and the individual try to provide one another with the knowledge, ability and motivation necessary to make their relationship satisfactory once again.

One important type of change caused by marginal members involves the alterations in group structure and dynamics that arise from the group's resocialisation efforts. These changes, which are typically unintentional on the part of marginal members, can have significant implications for the group. If the group must devote time and energy to resocialisation, then it will have fewer resources to expend in trying to attain its goals. Failure to attain these goals will cause the group to be less rewarding, thereby reducing members' commitment to it. The need to engage in resocialisation may also produce conflict among group members. This conflict may centre on (a) how much effort should be devoted to resocialisation, (b) which resocialisation techniques should be employed, and (c) which individuals should play a dominant role in resocialisation activities. To the extent that resocialisation efforts succeed, those members responsible for the success may gain status and power. In so far as resocialisation efforts fail, responsible members will lose status and power.

Marginal members may also produce unintentional changes that are beneficial to the group (Dentler & Erikson, 1959). For example, the presence of marginal members clarifies group norms and increases the probability that other members will conform to these norms. Deviation by marginal members can even lead to constructive normative change under certain circumstances. Finally, the criteria that the group uses in defining marginal members and its overt reactions towards them communicate important information about the group's goals. This information contributes to boundary maintenance by increasing the group's perceived distinctiveness to both ingroup and outgroup members.

Sometimes marginal members intend to produce innovation in order to increase the group's rewardingness. In so far as group rewardingness increases, the marginal member's commitment to the group will rise and he or she will attempt to become a full member again. In contemplating innovation a marginal member faces a difficult situation. Marginal members want to produce innovation because they find the group relatively un-rewarding. However, since the group feels low commitment to them, marginal members anticipate difficulties in changing the group. Marginal members are unlikely to attempt innovation, therefore, unless they can devise special strategies that seem likely to increase the group's commitment to them. One such strategy is to 'call in favours' previously extended to specific persons during earlier phases of group membership. A related strategy is to remind other members of one's previous contributions to the welfare of the group as a whole. Both these strategies involve increasing the salience of past rewards that the individual has generated for group members. Alternatively, a marginal member may attempt to decrease the salience of past costs that he or she has generated for individual members or for the group as a whole. This might be achieved through convincing other members that those costs are unimportant or through publicising similar costs generated by full members who have not been labelled as marginal.

To the extent that these strategies are successful and the group becomes more committed to the marginal member, he or she is more likely to be a successful innovator. Many other factors, however, can also affect a marginal member's ability to influence the group. First, the higher the commitment that the marginal member elicited as a full member, the more likely the person is to gain a hearing for his or her suggested innovations during resocialisation. Second, the harder the group has tried to prevent divergence during the maintenance phase, the less likely the marginal member is to produce innovation later on. This occurs because a marginal member who resists strong group pressure is perceived as deviating for internal, or dispositional, reasons. A dispositional attribution for deviance, in turn, lowers the marginal member's perceived expertise and/or trustworthiness. Finally, of course, the number of marginal members relative to other group members can influence innovation. Just as newcomers can band together to alter group norms, so marginal members can join forces to exert pressure for change.

A more subtle, but nevertheless important, factor that can influence marginal members' success in producing innovation involves their potential ability to leave the group (Ziller, 1965). A potential egressor's effectiveness as an innovator derives from several sources, including the individual's ability to (a) flout group expectations with impunity, (b) deny the group the benefits of his or her skills and knowledge, (c) threaten the group's self-image by signalling that he or she does not value group membership, and (d) reveal negative aspects of the group to outsiders. These actions by a marginal member who expects (or at least threatens) to depart can have a variety of consequences for the group. Other members who might have to take over the marginal members' responsibilities may dread the time and energy demanded by those tasks. The group's authority may be called into question by the marginal member's deviance, thereby encouraging other members to express their latent dissatisfactions. The possibility of leaving the group may become more salient to other members, whose contributions to group goal attainment may decrease as they explore the rewardingness of alternative relationships. Finally, prospective members may be less attracted to the group because of its apparent inability to elicit high levels of commitment from all its members. As Ziller (1965) suggests, however, the power of a potential egressor over the group is not absolute. Such factors as the length of time before the egressor departs, the likelihood that the egressor will be replaced, and the attractiveness of the group that the egressor intends to join will all constrain his or her ability to produce innovation.

Remembrance. The fifth and final phase of group membership is remembrance. Although the individual is no longer an active member, both the person and the group continue to evaluate one another and experience feelings of commitment as a result. Because of this commitment, even ex-members may be motivated to change the group and may be successful innovators.

Innovation is sometimes related to the group's memories of how an ex-member behaved before he or she left the group. Such memories can affect the group's relations with its current members in a variety of ways. If an ex-member evokes especially positive memories, then the group may use that person as a model in developing normative expectations for current members. Individuals whose behaviour most closely matches that of the ex-member when he or she passed through the same stage of group membership will be evaluated more positively and therefore will elicit higher levels of group commitment. The group may also change its decision criteria in the hope of obtaining or retaining more people who will generate the same rewards that the ex-member did when he or she belonged to the group. Analogous forms of innovation can occur when an ex-member evokes especially negative memories. Once again, the group may use that person as a model in developing normative expectations for current members, but now individuals whose behaviour most closely matches that of the ex-member will tend to be evaluated more negatively and therefore will elicit lower levels of group commitment. Similarly, the group may change its decision criteria in the hope of obtaining or retaining fewer people who will generate the same costs that the ex-member did when he or she belonged to the group.

Innovations during remembrance do not arise solely from the group's memories of how an ex-member behaved before he or she departed. Innovations may also be influenced by the individual's exit from the group. One important factor is simply that the person is no longer a group member. As Staw (1980) suggests, the mere departure of an individual can produce both positive and negative changes in the group. Positive changes include: (a) higher average levels of group performance, (b) reductions in intra-group conflicts associated with the presence of the ex-member, (c) expectations of increased upward mobility within the group and (d) improved adaptation of the group to its environment. Negative changes include: (a) costs associated with selecting, recruiting and training replacements for the ex-member, (b) disruptions in the group's activities and (c) demoralisation of remaining group members. To these negative changes can be added the unfavourable public image of a group that is unable to retain its members.

Innovation can also be influenced by the conditions surrounding the individual's exit and the degree to which the group and the individual have been successful since exit occurred. Under certain circumstances groups attempt to strengthen their relationships with ex-members. This is most likely to occur when (a) the ex-member 'graduated' from the group (in the sense that exit was expected and occurred under favourable conditions) rather than left prematurely or was expelled; (b) the ex-member has been successful since exit; and (c) the group has been unsuccessful since exit. Sometimes ex-members may be invited back into the group as full members. More coi imonly, the group will attempt to increase the informal involvement of thf se individuals in group activities. Ex-members who possess skills related to group maintenance may be asked to counsel dissatisfied members, arbitrate intra-group conflicts, or rehabilitate marginal members. Similarly, ex-members who possess skills related to group achievement may be asked to train new members, advise the group about how to attain its goals, or aid in the acquisition of new resources. In so far as ex-members actually become re-involved in group activities, their behaviour can change the group in many ways. Of course, ex-members may not always be willing or able to participate in the group. In such cases, the group may simply use such persons (with or without their permission) as models for appropriate behaviour. The group may also emphasise its prior relationships with the ex-member. When done within the group, this tactic increases current members' morale and commitment. When done outside the group, this tactic allows the group to 'bask in reflected glory' (Cialdini & Richardson, 1980), which makes the group more attractive to non-members and therefore may facilitate the acquisition of new members and other resources.

Naturally, groups do not always want to strengthen their relationships with ex-members. The group will be most likely to avoid contact with an ex-member and to minimise the salience of his or her prior relationship with the group when (a) the ex-member graduated from the group; (b) the ex-member has since been unsuccessful; and (c) the group has since been successful. Under these conditions, the individual will not be allowed to produce innovations in the group, should he or she desire to do so. However, in its efforts to avoid contact with the ex-member, the group may nonetheless experience changes. These changes include abandoning policies identified with the ex-member, imposing sanctions on current members who seek to maintain contact with the ex-member, and so on.

The ex-member's desire to approach or avoid the group can also be influenced by the conditions surrounding the individual's exit and the degree to which the group and the individual have been successful since exit occurred. The ex-member is most likely to attempt to strengthen his or her relationship with the group when (a) the ex-member graduated from the group; (b) the ex-member has been unsuccessful since exit; and (c) the group has been successful since exit. In this case, an ex-member may attempt to publicise his or her prior relationship with the group (Cialdini & Richardson, 1980), rejoin the group as a full member or participate informally in group activities, and establish or renew close relationships with powerful group members. As suggested earlier, however, the group is likely to discourage all of these activities. Therefore, the ex-member is unlikely to produce any intentional innovations in the group.

There are two sets of conditions under which an ex-member is likely to attempt to weaken his or her relationship with the group or to alter it in fundamental ways. First, an ex-member may feel ashamed of the group when (a) he or she graduated from the group; (b) he or she has been successful since exit; and (c) the group has been unsuccessful since exit. This feeling of shame may lead the ex-member to deny his or her prior relationship with the group and to avoid all contact with it. Such behaviour can lead to negative changes in the group, including an unfavourable public image that limits the group's ability to recruit new members, restricted access to resources controlled by the ex-member, and so on. Alternatively, an ex-member who is ashamed of the group may actively seek to improve it. Such a person will attempt to produce many innovations and is likely to be successful, as noted earlier. Second, an ex-member may feel angry towards the group when (a) he or she was expelled from the group; (b) he or she has since been unsuccessful; and (c) the group has since been successful. This feeling of anger may lead the ex-member to denounce the group publicly, restrict its access to resources, persuade current members to leave the group or prospective members to avoid it, and so on. In extreme cases, an angry ex-member may even try to destroy the group, either alone or by joining forces with others (Birenbaum & Sagarin, 1976).

3. Concluding comments

In this paper we have argued that researchers concerned with small group processes in general and innovation in particular should keep in mind that (a) groups and individuals exert reciprocal influence on one another and (b) important temporal changes occur in the relationship between groups and individuals. The notion of group socialisation provides a useful way of thinking about reciprocal influence and temporal change. We have outlined a model of group socialisation based on three psychological processes (evaluation, commitment, role transition). The model encompasses five consecutive phases (investigation, socialisation, maintenance, resocialisation, remembrance), separated by four role transitions (entry, acceptance, divergence, exit). We have used the model as a springboard for speculating about various forms of innovation in small groups.

Clearly, many of our ideas are speculative, and the hypotheses that we have offered need to be empirically tested. Longitudinal studies on natural groups are essential for adequately testing many of our ideas. In addition, important information can also be obtained from cross-sectional studies on natural groups and even from laboratory experiments. It is possible, for example, to create laboratory situations in which individuals perceive that they are newcomers to an existing group (e.g. Moreland, 1978). Such situations allow one to investigate a variety of issues about how newcomers perceive the group and attempt to change it.

Because of the focus of this book, we have emphasised the implications of our model for innovation, or the ability of individuals to influence the group. However, it should be noted that the group socialisation perspective also has important implications for understanding social control, or the ability of groups to influence individuals. Temporal changes in the relationship between the group and the individual can affect the group's efforts to exert social control, the kinds of control techniques that are used, and the degree to which attempts at social control succeed. Our model of group socialisation suggests a number of specific ways in which temporal processes can influence social control (see Moreland & Levine, 1982).

Finally, regardless of whether specific hypotheses about innovation and social control prove to be correct, we hope that our approach will at least stimulate interest in how group processes change over time. From our perspective, the neglect of temporal phenomena has been a serious weakness of 'group dynamics' research. We believe that, in order to make real progress in studying groups, social psychologists must accept the dictum that the one constant in group life is change.

Notes

1. Preparation of this chapter was supported by Grant BNS-8104961 from the National Science Foundation. We have contributed equally to the chapter and the order of authorship was therefore determined arbitrarily.
2. A more detailed discussion of the commitment formula is provided in Moreland & Levine (1982).
3. We are *not* suggesting that people who elicit low commitment cannot produce innovation (see Moscovici, 1976). Rather, we are suggesting that innovation is more difficult for such people than for those who elicit high commitment.
4. Although high status is likely to facilitate an individual's ability to innovate, recent evidence does not support Hollander's (1960) assumption that initial conformity to group norms is a necessary precondition for status and influence (Wahrman & Pugh, 1972, 1974; Ridgeway, 1978, 1981).

7. When and how the minority prevails

HAROLD B. GERARD

In the past decade or so the study of social influence has shifted its focus somewhat from a concern with the determinants of the person's conformity to a majority to an examination of factors that enable a lone dissident individual or a small dissident minority to successfully influence the majority. This work has been spearheaded by Moscovici and his colleagues (see Moscovici, 1976 for an overview of that work) who correctly argue that if the majority always prevailed, society would never change. Change must somehow be instigated initially by those who are out of step with prevailing norms. Supported by research evidence, Moscovici maintains that a key factor in minority success is a consistent, resolute behavioural style which serves to gain the attention of majority members, who are then likely to attribute high confidence and conviction to the members of the dissident group. On the basis of the evidence, there is little doubt that such a minority, even of one, can be a potent force. According to Moscovici, the minority's effect on majority members tends to be internalised as a true information change and is therefore long-lasting. On the other hand, change by a minority member towards the majority is often mere overt compliance, which is typically superficial and fleeting. Such conformity avoids potential group sanctions implicated in normative pressure (Deutsch & Gerard, 1955).

Will a dissident minority always be successful or are certain moderating conditions necessary? In addition to this question, I also want to consider the special endowments that enable a minority to project a resolute image. The typical minority experiment paradigm utilises confederates of the experimenter to espouse a dissident minority position which they would not have adopted had they been expressing their true beliefs. In life, on the other hand, members of dissident minorities express positions they actually hold, usually with considerable passion. The research thus far has, for the most part, taken the dissident, unswerving minority as a given, having created it through experimental manipulation. The question as to how such minorities emerge naturally (and they do) in the real world has not been studied. My attempt to answer the first question concerning factors other than consistency that are necessary in order for the minority to be successful will be brief and entirely speculative. How a staunch minority develops is a multi-faceted question which requires considerable discussion. Also, fortunately, there is some research evidence that provides hints as to the dynamics underlying what appears to the majority as a consistent behavioural style.

1. The necessary condition for minority success

It seems intuitively obvious that consistency alone by the minority is not enough to win converts; the minority must also be seen as credible. Moscovici acknowledges that, but it deserves additional emphasis. History is littered with fervent political factions and religious sects that persisted, spluttered and then faded out. Initially they may have drawn a small following but they failed to make the grade because their philosophy or preachings were just too far removed from prevailing norms.

In order to be successful the minority must strike a resonant chord, however faint, in the majority. In the programme put forth, they must somehow engage needs of the majority or appeal to the ambivalence the majority may feel towards current social norms. Consistency alone will not convince potential converts that their interests will be served by throwing in their lot with the minority. The early Christian zealots became a potent minority because they provided answers and solace to the chaotic lives of first- and second-century Romans. Similarly, Hitler's small band of fanatics provided a programme for solving the problems Germans faced in the wake of the collapsed Weimar Republic. The more recent success in the United States of the women's liberation movement has traded on the improved status of women represented by the earlier gains in voting rights after World War I and in job status during and after World War II, in spite of a strong reaction against women's rights in the 1950s. The women's movement also caught the coat-tails of the Black Power movement of the early 60s. Moscovici, in discussing the constraints accepted social norms often place on the majority, suggests that certain forbidden behaviour, which a dissident individual or group freely engages in, may appeal to majority members who secretly would like to give vent to suppressed impulses. Also, as he points out, members of the majority may feel some guilt about repressing or excluding certain individuals from participation in the political process. A majority may be able to appeal in its programme to those misgivings.

The majority must somehow be primed by circumstances to resonate at some level to the minority's appeal. The minority, on the other hand, must, in their programme, represent what Durkheim (1895) called 'currents of opinion', the incipient precursors of social change. The majority establishment, which typically has a stake in maintaining the *status quo*, tends to be deaf to currents of opinion that might undermine their vested interests, whereas the marginal minority, with no such stake, can afford to be open to such information. The closed, confirming, biased stance of the majority, which reflects the post-decisional side of the basic decision 'antinomy' (Jones & Gerard, 1967), is the seed of the majority's eventual undoing. The minority, by virtue of being in touch with the reality of social facts which the majority is not able or willing to countenance directly, in a sense has right, if not might, on its side. Having some modicum of a reality base, however small, is the necessary condition, and the persistent, consistent behavioural style described by Moscovici the sufficient condition for the eventual success of the minority in converting sufficient numbers of the majority to its position. Rather than eliciting attributions of credibility by the majority, persistence by the minority without supporting facts and argument which the majority can understand and appreciate will result in scorn, derision and rejection. Such discrediting of fervent minorities is more the rule than the exception. In arguing that the minority must appear flexible and fair, Moscovici recognises that, at some level, the minority must appear credible if it is to be successful.

The more open information posture of the minority may also be related to the objectivity conferred upon groups that are marginal to the society at large. Both Simmel (1950) and Veblen (1934) analysed the position of the Jew in the history of Europe. According to Simmel, the stranger, i.e. the marginal person, is 'not committed to the unique ingredients and peculiar tendencies of the group and therefore approaches them with the specific attitude of objectivity' (p. 404). In medieval Europe the itinerant Jew, because he was seen as not having a stake in the matter, was often called upon to adjudicate disputes between Gentiles. Veblen attributes the prominence of Jews in science, especially the social sciences, to the detachment and objectivity they are able to maintain. Many minority groups, by virtue of their marginality, are able to enjoy similar objectivity, making them more sensitive to the winds of change.

2. Minority internal dynamics

Moscovici argues that a consistent behavioural style by the minority affords the minority 'figure' status against the majority 'ground', thus drawing attention to itself. It is behavioural style, he further argues, that 'is *specifically* related to influence phenomena' (p. 110) and is crucial to it. What factors predispose the minority to adopt a consistent style? Are there certain minority endowments that are lacking in the majority and that provide a foundation for consistency and staunchness? I have isolated what I believe to be a number of such factors that mostly characterise political-type minorities. In discussing the factors I have in mind a minority consisting of a number of people who, in some sense, are a critical opposition mass to be reckoned with. I am not considering the lone dissident individual, although some of the factors would apply to him or her as well. My purpose is to remove the question one step. It is Moscovici's thesis that a consistent behavioural style by the minority induces dependency upon it by the minority. My inquiry will focus on factors that enable the minority, in the first place, to take such a stance towards the majority.

2.1. External threat and intergroup competition. The typical dissident minority is under threat by virtue of its unpopular stand. The belief by the minority members that they face a common threat serves as a binder to bring them into a close cohesive relationship with one another.

In my doctoral dissertation (Gerard, 1953) I was able to study the attitudes and social influence behaviour of minority and majority subgroups that formed within a larger group context containing anywhere from 8 to 14 members. The basis for the division into the two subgroups had to do with which of two issues the members considered more important. Most groups split into majority and minority subgroups. Within each subgroup there was a spread of opinion on the chosen issue. The subject could choose to influence a member of his own or the other subgroup. The data clearly showed a tendency for influence to be more intense within the minority than within the majority. Furthermore, influence within the minority was more successful as evidenced by a greater convergence of opinion within the minority than within the majority. Unfortunately no direct evidence was collected on the relative cohesiveness of the minority as compared with the majority.

We are just assuming that since the minority members probably felt somewhat overwhelmed by the majority presence, they developed stronger ingroup bonds and *esprit* than did the majority members. The greater cohesiveness, in turn, led to more intense efforts at reaching a consensus which, in the end, was relatively successful.

It seems to me, from what we know about dissident political or religious minorities, that these findings have a strong ring of what happens in actuality. A minority that is under the gun, so to speak, does not easily brook disagreement among its members. Since strong normative pressures to adhere to the group's position tend to develop within a minority, we would expect overt conformity in order to avoid potential sanctions. Under such pressure alone the minority member is not likely to internalise the group's position. We must remember, however, that informational influence is occurring simultaneously. The others' opinions are the most ready reference points available to the ingroup member. It is paradoxical that while each minority group member may overtly espouse the group's position, he or she may not initially agree privately with that view. Yet, over time, overt agreement may, through informational influence, lead to covert acceptance. Unfortunately, no direct evidence exists either of the effect of threat on minority inter-dependence or on pluralistic overt compliance within the ingroup leading to covert acceptance.

The minority is in competition with the majority both in espousing opposing views and in the attempt by the minority to win converts from the majority. Such intergroup competition tends to increase group cohesiveness and heighten the self-esteem and lower the anxiety of its members (Meyers, 1962; Julian, Bishop & Fiedler, 1966). This *esprit* building leads to interpersonal acceptance, mutual trust, and a sense of security among the group members. An experiment by Pepitone and Reichling (1955) demonstrated the increased sense of security among members of a highly cohesive group in the face of threat. Either a high or low level of group cohesiveness was established experimentally in laboratory groups followed by an attack from an outsider. Members of the high cohesive groups freely engaged in retaliation against the outsider, whereas those in the low cohesive groups tended to sit quietly and discuss matters unrelated to the threat. These results are consistent with the notion that high cohesiveness induced a greater sense of security in the members of the high, as compared with those in the low, cohesive groups.

The feeling of being potentially overwhelmed by the majority induces the minority to take counter-measures in order to withstand the real or imagined threat to their position. Such counter-measures manifest as a consolidation and convergence of opinion within the minority which, when the minority is greater than one, is mediated by increased ingroup dependence. Such a Newtonian 'equal and opposite' reaction, in effect, counterbalances and makes up for the relative numerical superiority of the majority. The larger the relative numerical superiority of the majority, the more will the minority converge in their opinions as a counteractive measure. Although there is no direct evidence bearing on this speculation, it can easily be put to experimental test.

The processes described in the American influence literature as they pertain to the larger group as a whole manifest to a greater extent within the minority than within the majority. It is as though the amount of dependency and power that might occur on a group-wide basis becomes redistributed between the majority and the minority, with the minority assuming a larger share. It is not that the American literature has been wrong, rather it has missed this essential point.

2.2. Commitment and self-bolstering. Joining a minority may, under certain circumstances, mean that the person has, so to speak, burned bridges behind him or her. Ties may have been irrevocably cut with others in the 'establishment'. To the extent that the person has limited his options for group membership, others in the present group will have power over the person and he or she will, in turn, be dependent on the group. Group standards can thus be enforced *via* normative pressure. In recent years certain religious cults in the United States that attract teenagers and young adults have received considerable press coverage. These cults invariably attempt to sever ties the new recruit may have with family and friends. In severing such ties, the new member becomes totally committed to the cult. Membership in one of these cults represents an extreme form of such commitment. Minorities of all kinds engender some degree of commitment by virtue of the cost of leaving the group. This degree of commitment is typically greater than it is for members of the majority.

Another process engendered by commitment to minority group membership is self-justification, a tendency which will be greater, the greater the commitment. Although there are no studies that offer direct evidence for increasing self-justification with increasing commitment to a group, two early dissonance studies (Festinger, 1957; Cohen, Brehm & Latané, 1959) offer relevant, if tangential, evidence. Those studies, using a playing card paradigm, asked the subject to play one or the other side of the game. At any point during the 30 'hands' of the game, he or she could switch to the other side if he or she forfeited $1.00 which represented a considerable cost relative to the amount of money the subject could win or lose. After 12 'hands', the subject was shown a fictitious graph of what was purported to be the cumulative probability of his or her chances for winning and losing money. Regardless of which side he or she had chosen, the graph showed, if properly interpreted, that the subject had chosen the losing side. The results of the experiments are somewhat complicated but they do show indirect evidence of self-bolstering for the subject who was losing moderately as evidenced by his or her apparent unwillingness to examine the graph, which represented dissonant information. It is a long inferential leap from the results of these two studies to arguing that greater self-bolstering is likely to occur for minority, as compared with majority, group members. If, however, we equate the dissonant information represented by the graph to the very fact of being in a minority, which is inherently dissonant with establishment norms, it would follow that a minority member would engage in more self-bolstering. This hypothesis can be easily tested experimentally.

An internal analysis of data from an early Asch-type conformity experiment (Gerard, 1964) revealed that if the subject was initially steadfast in maintaining his independence of the majority he tended to remain independent on subsequent trials, whereas if he or she yielded early on, he or she continued to yield on subsequent trials. In that study the subject's task on a sequence of trials was to match a single comparison line with one of three comparison lines. On two-thirds of the trials the three other subjects, who were actually confederates of the experimenter, were unanimous in making clearly incorrect judgments. On those trials the subject was thus in a conflict between making the physically correct judgment or going along with the group. If early on the subject resolved the conflict by committing himself or herself to an independent stand, he or she continued to remain independent. In supporting this adamance, the subject engaged in cognitive bolstering (Gerard & Rotter, 1961; Gerard, 1965). In a more recent study, Santee & Maslach (1982) found that dissenters in a modified Asch paradigm were more confident than conformers. It is likely that the conformity pressure felt by the subject built up with successive trials which necessitated the 'equal and opposite' reaction of strengthened self-bolstering. With continued disagreement by the confederates and steadfastness on the part of the subject it is likely that at some point the subject, after sufficient self-bolstering, would no longer attribute much weight to the others' judgments. His or her minority opinion would be consolidated, as it were. Discounting the others' ability is part of the self-bolstering process (Gerard, 1965). Although there appears to be increased cognitive consolidation over time (Gerard, 1965), we have not examined evidence of a commensurate diminution of conflict with increasing consolidation. We would assume, however, that over time the dissident minority member does develop a sense of equanimity. It would be relatively easy, utilising a variant of the Asch paradigm, to determine if such equanimity does increase over time. Collecting self and other ability estimates periodically during a sequence of trials, along with data reflecting degree of conflict (e.g. skin conductance), would provide the basis for inferring whether or not consolidation and conflict reduction both occur. Further, structural equations statistics would enable us to make a good guess as to whether consolidation leads to conflict reduction or *vice versa*.

A recent experiment conducted in our laboratory by Orive (1982) found evidence of what appears to be self-bolstering by a minority member. Each experimental group consisted of four men and one woman or four women and one man. Each group thus had a sex-linked majority of four and a minority of one. The subjects, in each others' presence, were asked on a questionnaire to indicate their opinion on two issues that were male-relevant, two that were female-relevant, and two that were gender-neutral. Gender relevance was determined on a pre-test using a large number of issues. The subjects had no way of knowing the opinions each of the others had indicated on the questionnaire.

The data show that subjects who were in the minority were more extreme on all opinions than were those in the majority. In addition, extremity for minority members was more pronounced for gender-relevant, than for gender-neutral or gender-opposite, issues. This effect was due simply to the *mere presence* of a majority of opposite-sex others since subjects were prevented from communicating with each other. A simple social facilitation effect would predict that the minority subject would be equally extreme on all three types of issues. Greater extremity for the gender-relevant, rather than for the other two types of issue is strongly suggestive of self-bolstering.

An interesting question remains concerning the effect of possible repudiation. Suppose the subject knew that he or she could at any time, and with little or no cost, desert the minority position and join the majority; how would the process of consolidation be affected as compared with a situation where considerable cost would be incurred? On the one hand we could argue that when the cost is high the subject should consolidate rapidly since he or she has little choice but to accommodate to minority status. On the other hand, if joining the majority is a continuing viable alternative and the subject *chooses* to remain a minority member, considerable self-bolstering would be likely to ensue. It is probably the case that voluntarily taking a minority position results in self-bolstering *via* dissonance reduction (Brehm & Cohen, 1962). To the extent that the person is able to repudiate his or her stand, self-bolstering will presumably continue until the person is comfortable with his or her position. At that point it may be costly to undo the cognitive accommodation in spite of the fact that repudiation is still theoretically possible. Free choice, according to this line of reasoning, creates its own built-in costs of undoing the accommodation.

From the above argument it would follow that holding minority status with no easy 'out' would lead to rapid acceptance of the status by the person with relatively little cognitive accommodation, whereas with an easy way out acceptance would be slower but accommodation would be greater. Under both conditions the person may appear staunch, but under the free choice situation he or she would be less vulnerable to subsequent persuasion from the majority position.

As a final sidelight here, we would also expect the minority member with an easy 'out' available to be a more fervent recruiter of new members than one without the easy 'out'. This would follow if we assume that recruiting consensus is one possible avenue of self-bolstering. There is evidence from an epidemiological study by De Alarcon (1969) of heroin use in England, and one in the United States by Hughes & Crawford (1972), that new heroin users are much more active in recruiting others into using the drug than are old users. Recruiting virtually ceases after a user has been on the drug for a year. While there are other possible interpretations of this finding, it is consistent with the hypothesis that recruitment occurring during the early phase of drug use is an attempt by the novice user to provide cognitive consolidation *via* consensus for his or her minority position. Recruitment of one's friends, who are presumably co-oriented with the person, is especially useful as consensus bolstering. In the early phase of drug use the person is typically in conflict about his or her new habit and the possibility of an easy 'out' still exists. A hardened user, on the other hand, has resolved the conflict and also knows that it would be extremely difficult to repudiate the behaviour. Proselytising as an index of staunchness by the minority group member may reflect his or her attempt to 'work through' certain misgivings about his or her minority status as well as the conflict posed by the possibility of an easy way out.

2.3. Minority distinctiveness. The work initiated by Tajfel (1970) on social categorisation has demonstrated clearly the development of positive feeling among individuals who simply find themselves categorised together. This work has revealed what is probably the bedrock of ingroup *versus* outgroup feeling.

Building upon that work, Gerard & Hoyt (1974) have shown that the smaller the ingroup (down to two members) relative to the outgroup, the greater will be the positive ingroup feeling engendered. Additional evidence from a study of school desegregation (Gerard, Jackson & Conolley, 1975) showed that minority subgroup members within a predominantly white classroom chose to associate almost exclusively with other minority subgroup members. Although there are alternative explanations for these data, they are consistent with the hypothesis that the smaller the ingroup relative to the outgroup, the greater is the we-feeling that develops within it.

Greater we-feeling within the minority will lead to greater dependency and, therefore, to greater uniformity of opinion by virtue of the normative pressures that arise in such groups. Categorisation in a relatively small ingroup may thus lead to greater opinion staunchness.

2.4. Less diversity of opinion-relevant background within the minority. Individuals who hold the same or similar opinions on an issue to begin with are probably more similar in relevant background characteristic than are individuals who do not hold similar opinions. Typically, the range of opinion within the minority is much smaller than it is within the majority. We have already discussed certain bases for the likelihood of greater opinion convergence within the minority. It is, however, also likely that individuals who are attracted into the minority fold initially agree with the unpopular view espoused by the minority even before being exposed to minority social pressures. They would therefore tend to be similar in opinion-relevant background.

There is by now an extensive body of evidence that individuals who share the same or similar backgrounds are attracted to one another (Byrne & Rhamey, 1965; Byrne, Ervin & Tamberth, 1970; Griffitt & Veitsch, 1974). We would therefore expect that minority members, by virtue of their similar backgrounds, would form a more cohesive group than would members of the majority whose backgrounds are likely to be heterogenous.

Since minority members are likely to have more in common with each other than are members of the majority, we would expect them to spend more time together. The more time they spend together, the more likely are they to influence each other and become more uniform in opinion. Furthermore, as a result of the more intense association within the minority, the members will come to know each other in a more personal way and form deep bonds of affection and loyalty. Minority members would also, on the basis of their greater commitment to the issue, be expected to spend more time than majority members discussing issues with fellow ingroup members.

2.5. Opinion importance. Whatever the issue or issues about which the minority and majority disagree, the minority will almost invariably take its position more seriously than will the majority. The minority will have sounded the clarion call for social change and its position will typically assume great importance for its members. The majority, on the other hand, has tradition on its side, so that the position it endorses will be taken more or less for granted. The issue, therefore, will not assume the significance that it does for the minority.

The importance of an opinion for the person will determine the intensity with which he or she holds it. Opinions prepare the person for forthcoming transaction; the more important the transaction or the more imminent it is, the more prepared does the person have to be for the transaction. Well prepared opinions are typically more intense than less well prepared ones. The importance of the transaction as well as its immediacy will determine the importance of the opinion or opinions upon which the transaction is predicated. The importance of the opinion establishes a required level of opinion preparedness which the person attempts to reach through various avenues of support seeking. This 'requiredness threshold' is that level of opinion preparedness that will enable the person to maintain an unequivocal behavioural orientation (UBO) (Jones & Gerard, 1967) in his or her transaction with or about the issue or object of the opinion. To the extent that the person is below the requiredness threshold, he or she will experience uncertainty which can be reduced by generating information in support of the opinion. This supportive information can be in the form of self-bolstering, as described earlier, or social support. Whatever avenues of information generation are utilised, it is likely that a minority member will increase opinion preparedness (intensity) up to a higher level than will a majority member. Thus, the mere fact of greater issue importance for the minority will make its members more staunch.

2.6. Social projection. There is a pervasive tendency for the person to project judgments and opinions on to others who share his or her vantage point. Thus, if I am crossing the street with a friend I assume he or she also sees the oncoming cars. The power of the Asch line judgment conformity paradigm derives from the tendency for the subject to assume that the other subjects see the lines the way he or she does; they presumably share the same perspective. Disagreement with the others is tantamount to a distressing disconfirmed projection to which the subject attempts to accommodate. In the subject's past history such projection on to others of judgments of length or distance were typically confirmed. This tendency to project on to similar others is at the basis of informational social comparison.

Minority members are more likely than those in the majority to project their opinions on to fellow subgroup members since, as compared with majority members, they are more likely, as we discussed above, to share a common opinion-relevant background. Disagreement within the minority would tend therefore to be more rapidly equilibrated than would disagreement within the majority. This hypothesis is tantamount to asserting that those within the minority, because they tend to be co-oriented, are more likely to use each other as informational referents than are those within the majority. To the extent that members of a group utilise each other as informational referents they are likely to equilibrate opinion differences that arise. Since the members of a minority are more likely than majority members to utilise each other in that way, a minority is more likely than a majority to reach and maintain opinion consensus, a prerequisite for staunchness.

One consequence of social projection is the person's tendency to create a consensus for his or her opinions. Although his description of the process was incomplete, F. H. Allport (1924) was the first, at least in modern times, to describe fabricated consensus through social projection in the service of intensifying opinions. He identified four steps: self-awareness on the part of the person that he or she has an opinion; projecting the opinion on to others, thus fabricating a consensus; the reciprocal effect of this consensus as information supporting the opinion; and finally, the intensification of the opinion as a result of this informational support. Allport failed, however, to note the necessary and sufficient conditions for the intensifying effect to occur. The necessary condition is that the person was initially uncertain about the opinion, i.e. that he or she was below his or her requiredness threshold. The sufficient condition is that the others, that is, the projection targets, be perceived by the person as sharing his or her opinion-relevant background, otherwise projection will not occur. Projection occurs regardless of opinion uncertainty, but it will increase intensity only if the person was initially below the intensity level required by whatever situational imperatives were operating on him or her.

I would now like to briefly describe several recent experimental studies of social projection that bear on minority staunchness. The first study by Wolfgang Wagner and myself (Gerard & Wagner, 1984) examined the effects of the similarity of potential projection targets and opinion importance on the degree to which the experimental subject polarised his or her opinion. The opinion concerned what was to be done about a youth who had committed a serious crime. The four subjects in each group initially filled out a value profile that consisted of 16 values that were related to the case material about the delinquent youth they were subsequently going to be judging. The experimenter then provided bogus value similarity information which indicated to the subject either that the others were similar or dissimilar in value background. A no similarity information condition was also run, which we expected would be mid-way in attributed similarity. Opinion importance was manipulated by informing the subjects that they would participate in a jury deliberation with other subjects not in their present group either immediately after the present session, or in a session next week, or probably not (since scheduling difficulties made such a session unlikely). The design was thus a

3 (similar, dissimilar, no information) by 3 (immediate, next week, not likely) factorial. Our prediction was that polarisation would be greatest in the similar and least in the dissimilar treatment, with that effect being accentuated by opinion importance (degree of immediacy).

The data pretty well substantiated the predictions. Similarity produced a linear effect on polarisation under the 'no-wait' treatment, a near linear effect under 'next week' with no effect under the 'deliberation not likely' treatment.

As compared with someone in the majority, a minority member is in a group with others who are more value co-oriented and is likely to attach greater importance to group-relevant issues. These experimental data therefore suggest that minority opinions are likely to be more polarised than opinions in the majority.

A second experiment was run by Stefan Folster and myself (Gerard & Folster, 1982), utilising a similar format to the above experiment, in which subjects anticipated discussing two issues, the restriction of Japanese imports by the US government and US military spending. The background similarity of the others was manipulated by a procedure similar to the one used in the previous experiment. Three conditions were established, a 'similar', 'dissimilar' and an 'alone' condition in which subjects were run individually instead of in groups of four.

Tesser (1978) reports a number of experiments in which delayed measurement of an opinion in a context similar to the one we used resulted in more polarised opinions than did immediate measurement. Similar results were reported earlier by Bateson (1966) and Flanders & Thistlethwaite (1967). In Tesser's studies, several subjects were run simultaneously which is a situation ripe for social projection and reciprocal consensus to occur, especially since the subjects were all college students similar to each other. In our study we delayed the measurement for one of the opinions by 90 seconds (the delay used by Tesser) and measured the other one immediately, counterbalanced, of course, for the two issues. The results showed that only under the 'similar others' treatment did delayed measurement cause greater polarisation than immediate measurement. The 'alone' and 'dissimilar others' treatments showed virtually no effect of delay. Again, the implication for minority opinion polarisation is clear.

In a third experiment run by Wagner and myself (Wagner & Gerard, 1983) value-laden *versus* factual issues were compared regarding the degree to which background similarity is likely to induce opinion polarisation. The format was similar to the above two experiments. Groups of 11 subjects at a time were run under a similar, dissimilar or no similarity information treatment using three value-laden and three non-value-laden opinions. The data were clear; polarisation effects as a function of similarity were found for value-laden, but not for factual, opinions.

A study by Orive (1982) examined the effect of minority status on opinion polarisation, utilising black and white students on the UCLA campus. The subject, who was run individually, was asked if he or she agreed or disagreed with each of four statements, two race-related and two non-race-related. The subject was then informed either that 80 per cent or 29 per cent of students of his or her race agreed him or her. Following this instruction, the subject filled out a questionnaire asking for more detailed opinion information.

For blacks, being told that they were in the opinion minority intensified their opinions on race-relevant, but not on race-irrelevant, issues. Whites, on the other hand, were less extreme on race-relevant issues when told they were in a minority as compared with when they believed they were in the majority. Overall, blacks considered the racial issues but not the non-racial issues much more important than did whites. The results suggest, in line with much of our previous discussion, that when an issue is important (the racial issues for blacks), the person will project his or her opinion on to similar others. Finding disconfirmation, i.e. being in the minority statistically, the person will bolster his or her opinion, which will result in greater opinion intensity. In this experiment the 20 per cent minority black was a minority within a minority. Whites who found themselves within a statistical minority lowered their opinion intensity on the racial issues. Their confidence was lowered by the disconfirmed projection but they did not proceed to bolster their opinions because the issue was relatively unimportant.

2.7. The personality function of minority membership. Being in a minority may be an assertion of the member's individuality and distinctiveness. Group membership is a public statement about a side of the person that demands expression. It is a badge of identity, defining an aspect of the self the person considers important. In his analysis of the protests of the late 1960s Turner (1969) maintains that the phenomenon cannot be fully understood unless the value-expressive function of protest is taken into account.

Smith, Bruner & White (1956), in their analysis of the attitudes of ten men towards the Soviet Union, argue that personality is the context in which opinions exist and that opinions serve various adaptive functions for the personality. Seen in this light, it is reasonable to assume that membership in a group that embodies certain opinions may serve an expressive function (see also Katz, 1960).

Smith, Bruner & White also maintain that an opinion may serve a social adjustment function, providing the person with either access to, or continuing membership in, social groups. A particular opinion may be the ticket of admission, as it were, to some group, thus affording the person social contact. Once having established membership in the group, continuing to espouse that opinion will enable the person to remain in the good graces of the other members and thus protect his membership status.

Minority group membership can confer upon the member the status of being 'chosen'. Membership may carry the sense of exclusivity, that there is something special attached to minority status. I remember vividly a terribly frustrating discussion I had in the early fifties with a member of the American Communist Party in which he maintained that being a communist is evidence of superiority as a human being. Years later, after he had left the party, as so many did in the aftermath of the crushed 1956 Hungarian uprising, he was excruciatingly embarrassed when I reminded him of that earlier conversation.

2.8. Confrontation leads to polarisation. An intriguing study by Cialdini *et al.* (1976), which examined the effects of anticipated confrontation on opinion polarisation, showed that polarisation occurred for an important opinion whereas moderation occurred for an unimportant one. Although the experiment was not run within a majority–minority context, the implications for such a context are clear. The minority is typically more committed and more serious about its stand than is the majority, and since the two are in a confrontation, minority opinion should polarise to a greater extent than majority opinion. Opinion moderation for the unimportant issue occurred presumably because the subject's priority for the anticipated confrontation was self-presentational rather than having a correct opinion. Similar effects of confrontation on polarisation have been reported by Paicheler (1976, 1977, 1979).

Results from my dissertation referred to earlier (Gerard, 1953) nicely complement these results. In that experiment, the groups in one treatment anticipated a confrontation in the form of a debate with a group of experts who were likely to take an opposing view, whereas the other groups did not expect such a confrontation. In that context, where social influence was possible, there was greater social influence and greater movement towards uniformity for the groups that anticipated a confrontation than for those that did not. As you will recall from our discussion earlier, most of the groups split into majority and minority subgroups. The effect of anticipated confrontation was more intense within the minority than within the majority.

Whereas in the Cialdini *et al.* study anticipated confrontation regarding an important opinion resulted in polarisation and in my study it led to convergence of opinion, both responses can be interpreted as a response to a high requiredness threshold relative to the non-confrontation condition. If the subject were going to be able to defend his or her opinion adequately, high opinion preparedness would be necessary. We can expect that the high informational concerns of dissident minority group members, who see themselves in a struggle with the establishment, will lead to intense social comparison with fellow minority members, resulting in opinion convergence. Earlier we discussed additional convergence tendencies as a result of high normative pressures in the minority in the face of a threat, which is what a confrontation represents.

3. Conclusion

There is no doubt that Moscovici is basically correct about the potency of staunch minorities, but he has overlooked some of the forces that make them potent in the first place, forces which have been the focus of study of American social psychologists. Potency and persistence must be based on a high level of commitment and unanimity on the part of the dedicated minority. I have examined some of the factors that produce unanimity and commitment, the glue that holds the minority together. If we are able to understand fully the way in which dissident minorities succeed in recruiting consensus for their programmes, we must study the methods by which individual opinions are polarised and maintained within a social context.

In many of the minority influence experiments the minority is represented by one or two dissidents, confederates of the experimenter, whose pre-programmed behaviour is designed to give the impression of certainty and resoluteness. Someone who stands up to the crowd must have conviction behind him or her. Those in the majority may come to believe that this conviction bespeaks correctness of opinion. The stalwart minority in real life, who are under pressure from the majority, would tend, in the face of such pressure, to harbour some doubts. In allaying those doubts, they are likely to engage in self-bolstering in the process of digging their heels in. Individual opinion dynamics can maintain opinion preparedness at or above the requiredness threshold, the greater the pressure from the majority, the higher the threshold and the greater the self-bolstering effort that must be expended. Since the social comparison avenue is not available to the lone dissident, he or she must rely on self-generated information to reach and sustain opinion preparedness at or above the requiredness threshold. With a minority of two or more, information generation can occur *via* informational social comparison and normative influence. It is then that dependency and power, emphasised in the American literature, come into play.

8. The paradox of 'orthodox minorities': when orthodoxy infallibly fails

JEAN-PIERRE DECONCHY

Amongst the forms of 'active minority' whose typology he has so convincingly established, Moscovici (1979) locates the category of 'orthodox minorities'. Compared to traditional social psychology's frequently demonstrated taste for excessively simple concepts, Moscovici introduces a dialectical and paradoxical notion here. The term 'minority' contains a flavour of deviance, untimely initiative, and indeed anomy; the term 'orthodox' conjures up social functioning characterised by absolute conformity.

I have been led to operationalise the concept of 'orthodoxy' and to attempt to relate it to empirically demonstrable social functions, using experimentation in a natural social milieu. I have thus embarked upon a study of ideological processes from the very opposite direction to that taken by Moscovici, and in taking this path I have been able to consider the issue of the existence of 'minority' phenomena that are internal to orthodoxy systems themselves (Deconchy, 1971, 1980). Approaching from this direction we uncover social strategies as paradoxical and dialectical as those that initiated the quest, that is, those relating to the concept of an 'orthodox minority'. We are therefore concerned here with a scientific journey in an opposite direction from that made by Moscovici but finally converging with it.

Our principal interest has been in the study of complex social systems which are, in institutional terms, highly organised and strongly oriented ideologically and whose models of functioning are inherently dependent on the conditions of their historical development. For a variety of reasons (which we have justified elsewhere) we decided that it would be both meaningful and informative to make a particular study of individuals and groups belonging to the Roman Catholic church. This choice of social objects, a choice relatively seldom made in experimental social psychology, has forced us to acknowledge that, despite the convergences noted above, the theoretical and methodological tools introduced in research on the minority paradigm do require some reassessment. There are several reasons for this.

Firstly, in the type of social system that we have studied, processes of influence between individuals and/or subgroups occur within the framework of institutional and ideological 'givens' which structure these influences at this level. If such processes were to be examined independently of these 'givens', then the processes themselves would probably be denuded of precisely those features that constitute them as influence processes. Secondly, in this type of system, 'agreement' between individuals and/or subgroups is not based on some objective stimulus the empirical perception of which can be rendered more or less ambiguous. Finally, this agreement does not resolve around claims derived from an ideological framework which is only in the process of being created. Hence, these claims are not susceptible to flexibility. Neither is this agreement related to a social context in which the terms can be negotiated from one individual to another independently of the position that each occupies in the overall system, or of the power or status each has in this system.

Given these considerations, I shall, within the framework of this chapter, confine the concept of 'orthodox minority' to that of minorities internal to an orthodox system, although Moscovici's typology undoubtedly attributes to it a much wider conceptual and operational status. Before considering the experimental work, the extraordinary explicit ambiguity of a 'minority' status within an orthodox system must be recognised. And before trying to appreciate how minority disputation might function with regard to this or that particular content or claim, we need to establish what social epistemology forms the background to this dispute. We will try to identify the functions of dispute in relation to an epistemology shared by the protagonists, rather than in relation to conflicts between claims considered in themselves.

We have used the concept of *orthodoxy* on the basis of some preliminary definitions. We say that a *subject* is orthodox in so far as he accepts and even requests that his thoughts, his language and his behaviour will be regulated by the ideological group of which he is a part and particularly by the power structures in this group. We say that a *group* is orthodox to the degree that this type of regulation is well established and its technological and axiomatic merits themselves form part of the 'doctrine' upheld by the group. Finally, we mean by an orthodox *system* the entire set of these social and psychosocial mechanisms which regulate the activity of the orthodox subject within the orthodox group.

At first sight this game of definitions seems to bring us back to a hyper-centralised and hyper-unified social field and to strictly conformist types of social interactions. The weight of research evidence, however, shows that the situation is rather more complex.

Within the framework of our thinking and research it seems possible to conclude that minority positions within an orthodox system are at the same time, and according to models of functioning which are particularly difficult to isolate:

1. doctrinally unthinkable and functionally impossible,
2. often advantageous and sometimes even indispensable to the adequate functioning of the system,
3. programmed and ultimately created by the latter for its own protection.

Given that they are based on the analysis of a few studies of limited scope (Deconchy, 1971, 1980), the reflections that follow cannot hope to deal in an exhaustive fashion with the problems raised, and can really only begin to define their outlines.

1. In an ideologically orthodox system everything is arranged so as to render minority positions doctrinally unthinkable and functionally impossible

(a) The claims around which the consensus of an orthodox ideological group is established and in relation to which minority positions, should the occasion arise, may *negotiate, dispute* or *dissent,* possess at least three characteristics.

First, in an orthodox system as elsewhere, for those who take them to be true, these claims diverge most in relation to norms of 'rationality'. This fact is evident with respect to the beliefs characterising the orthodox 'religious' group with which our own work has been most concerned. It is rather more subtle with respect to ideological systems as a whole. Before going further, it should be noted that this characteristic which is intrinsic to 'basic' claims does give rise to extremely complex cognitive and argumentative strategies. In Catholic orthodoxy, for example, it involves the adherent in resorting to 'meta'-rational argument while asserting as an article of faith that human reason can prove the truth of one of the central elements in this system of beliefs, namely the existence of God. It would be anathema for him to do otherwise. Certainly, this is an unusual cognitive strategy, and it is given here only by way of example. But compared to this, the *description* of a concrete position that an orthodox minority might possibly take would obviously necessitate extensive preliminary investigation on its experimental operationalisation.

Secondly, in an orthodox system agreement with a particular claim tends to regulate group membership in an implicit fashion. When an orthodox subject asserts a belief he is not only giving expression to his own agreement.

This agreement is implicitly combined with an evaluative judgment about the legitimacy or importance of using this belief as a criterion regulating membership of the group. Similar to the notion of 'opinionation' introduced by Rokeach (1960) in his theory of dogmatism, this characteristic of any proposition asserted in orthodox systems intensifies the proposition in that it establishes the social control function of this evaluation. Again, at this level one is confronted with particularly complex socio-cognitive strategies in orthodox systems. In the Catholic church, for example, the absolute liberty of the subject is asserted (including cognitive liberty) and at the same time an entire social machinery, hierarchically and centrally organised, exists with the aim of controlling the subject and preserving him from the 'error' to which he would succumb were he left to his own devices. Compared to a social dialectic of this type, here again the *description* of a concrete position that a minority might possibly take would obviously necessitate extensive preliminary investigation on its experimental operationalisation.

Finally, in an orthodox system, any proposition that is asserted will not be an isolated entity. It will form an integral part of a body of doctrine which will, furthermore, by its very weight lend credence to a particular interpretation. Conversely, a proposition with religious content will be rejected by an orthodox subject if it does not form an integral part of the body of doctrine controlled by the orthodox group and which serves to control the functioning of this orthodox group. Within the Catholic church, for example, the interpretation of this doctrinal corpus is based on extremely sophisticated hermeneutic models. It appeals to and encourages theological forms of *inquiry* but simultaneously asserts that the set of meanings and beliefs is already established and to some degree understood (particularly by the agents of social control), and that because of this nothing of any significance can either be added or subtracted.

At this point in the analysis it may already be seen that the possible adoption of a minority position that is internal to a socio-cognitive field of this type will be linked to an almost infinite variety of functions, since in a way, at the level of what might be called the *social epistemology* of the beliefs around which the group consensus is established, every position and counter-position has already been defined.

(b) Though every position and counter-position has been defined, the whole possesses a high degree of coherence. Indeed, this coherence seems to subsist with a greater degree of solidity, stability and serenity than that displayed by apparently less contradictory social systems. But the basis of this coherence is an organic structure of beliefs, theological rationality and social regulation. The dialectic and variegated meanings of this structure give rise to such an abundance of social situations that one might suppose their analysis could only be achieved through historiographic, sociographic, ethnographic or clinical description.

However, we have taken a different view, regarding this set of functions as deriving from certain relatively simple models. Specifically, and following theoretical speculations which it would be too difficult to describe in detail here, we have advanced the hypothesis that in such systems 'the rational weakness of ideas is compensated by the strength of social regulation'. We have sought to verify this hypothesis in a series of experimental studies. If the rational weakness of a belief appears to increase (either as a result of historical change, or through the effects of minority influence, or as a result of an experimental manipulation), the system of control with which the group is equipped should become stricter. If the system of control becomes more relaxed (either through historical development in the system as a whole, or in the course of disputes with minority elements which still remain to be identified as 'internal' or 'external', or as a result of an experimental manipulation), the rational weakness of a belief should become more apparent, with all the risks of attrition to the system that the pluralism of these two changes brings about. A number of experimental studies have lent support to this hypothesis and we will refer to them below. But once again it is necessary to remark how much the concept of a minority position on the inside of such a system depends at the level of the social epistemology accredited by the system on quite paradoxical processes.

(c) Before trying to appreciate these paradoxes more clearly, however, we should attempt to be more precise about the material content on which a genuinely minority position could be based and still remain truly orthodox. The evidence suggests that such minority positions, if they are internal to the system, cannot be adopted in relation to the entire body of doctrine. But the particular claims on which these minority positions could be based do contain within themselves a view of the paradoxical nature of the functioning which characterises the corpus of which they form a part, a corpus which is regarded as possessing a perfect internal coherence.

The representation an orthodox subject has of this absolute internal coherence of the doctrinal corpus is not, however, a simple social object. This representation is constructed at the intersection of two distinct psychosocial functions whose effects are normally multiple and which it has been necessary at the experimental level to attempt to isolate.

Firstly, if the orthodox subject contains within himself a representation of a unified and coherent body of doctrine in which each doxeme[1] has an identified or identifiable position, then this subject has every 'objective reason', so to speak, to perceive it in this way. To take only the Catholic church as an example, it has, in the course of time and in response to circumstances and disagreements, come to construct a body of doctrine that possesses a surprising ingenuity of form. Though this may be for the researcher no more than an object of curiosity, the theological corpus that the Catholic church has erected on the foundation of a set of propositions which cannot themselves be derived on the basis of hypothetico-deductive or experimental reasoning, displays a prodigious logical inventiveness. What we cannot do here is retrace the history of an enterprise that has provided logical credibility to a set of non-rational claims by means of a rhetoric and a system of argumentation which itself contains virtually no flaws. All the more remarkable is that the logical achievement of this type of erudite theology has become absorbed into widely disseminated vulgarised cultural objects. We have in mind, for example, the catechisms for children. The moment one puts certain unverifiable propositions beyond the reach of rational critique, it becomes almost impossible to find any genuine flaws in the logical structure within which they are organised. Thus, when the orthodox subject (in this case a Catholic) considers either implicitly or explicitly that a doxeme which is true has an identifiable place within the corpus and that for it to be true it has to have an identified or identifiable place, he is simply appealing to an obvious empirical proof and a kind of objective perception. He is appealing, in other words, to the extraordinary logical coherence of the corpus of his church. From this perspective it may be said that when the orthodox subject represents the internal coherence of his body of doctrine as being without flaws, he is appealing to a representation which in certain respects refers to a 'rational' order. But this is not a rationality that can be considered as such in itself. Rather, it is in the form we have identified as occurring within the framework of the hypothesis of 'rational weakness compensated by the strength of social regulation'.

Secondly, besides this 'perception' of the qualities of the logical structure which articulates the corpus, there are other psychosocial functions which lend weight and necessity to the representation of the corpus as having 'absolute coherence'. Within the logic of the orthodox system, and in a sense independently of this established fact, it would be illegitimate to perceive the doctrinal corpus otherwise than as having a total coherence. This corpus can only be a single, indivisible entity because, on the one hand, truth cannot be anything but indivisible and, on the other, because the apparatus of orthodox power and the social control which it exercises can know no error in representing it to adherents. *A priori*, the corpus controlled by the orthodox group will thus be incapable of presenting any internal flaw. The doctrinal corpus groups together in a quite systematic fashion a whole series of unverifiable dogmas, to the point of rendering the entire set internally coherent. But beyond this the 'dogmatic' mechanism is applied to itself so as to base the outcome of this grouping and systematisation on dogmatic necessity. As a result we have the representation of an indivisible corpus without flaws which can truly resist analysis or candour; the idea that any cognitive domain divided against itself runs a risk because this very fact demonstrates its inadequacy with respect to truth; the representation of a system of socio-cognitive power perfectly adapted to its role as guarantor of true belief. All this is based, without always being explicit, on the overall functioning of the orthodox system, on its teachings, on its institutional settings, on its programme of rituals, on its disciplinary apparatus and on an entire affective and cognitive climate which at every point gives credence to this representation of the 'absolute coherence of the doctrinal corpus'. From this perspective it is possible to say that when the orthodox subject refers to the absence of flaws in the internal coherence of this body of doctrine, he is appealing to a representation which in certain respects also refers to the dimension of social control, at least in so far as we have identified it within the framework of our hypothesis.

This representation of the 'absolute doctrinal coherence of the orthodox corpus', if it is relocated within the conceptual framework of our basic hypothesis (that the rational weakness of ideas within an orthodox system is compensated by the strength of social control), and if it is considered in relation to the two elements of this hypothesis (rationality and social regulation), is therefore clearly mixed in form. For example, dissent by a minority from any element of the corpus will thus be based on particularly ambiguous cognitive and social strategies. The content of what one professes is ultimately of less significance than the formal characteristics of the socio-cognitive domain to which this profession refers. In certain respects and within limits, one can in some situations say, and say one believes, 'the same things' and be deviant, or say, and say one believes, 'different things' and remain conformist.

(d) In these conditions, and at the content level, the idea of a genuine minority which not only regards itself as within the orthodox system but is acknowledged to be so by the socially organised majority is obviously rendered impossible and indeed unthinkable. On the one hand, adoption of a minority position obviously cannot be based on the group's central and basic beliefs without such a minority ceasing to perceive itself, and be perceived, as orthodox. But on the other hand, the most peripheral belief apparently benefits on its own level from the aura of truth that the unity of the orthodox corpus creates, and thus abandoning it or disputing it would never be completely devoid of significance. Moreover, some of these peripheral beliefs are concerned with explicitly socio-regulatory functions; they involve various rites, morals, ethics and codes. Others, possibly emptied of the meaning that they were once accorded by the system in response to particular historical circumstances, nonetheless retain something of the social obligation which had originally been associated with their inclusion within the doctrinal corpus. To question the truth of these two kinds of belief is, in effect, to strike at the strength of social regulation, if only in a discrete fashion. Within the framework of our hypothesis, and on the basis of some of the results we have obtained, it does lead in the same way to what also appears to be the rational weakness of the beliefs in terms of which the group thinks.

What is true of a belief or a particular claim is also true at the level of the individual. He is a reflection of the group as a whole ('where there is a Christian there is also the Church'). But his own knowledge is strictly limited by the place he occupies within the system of power, to the degree that this is hierarchically distributed. All isolated knowledge, all relatively idiosyncratic cognitive procedures (personal experience, mysticism, intuition...) are suspect.

From this perspective it may be said that in the type of system we have tried to explore everything is so arranged that any inclination to take up internal minority positions is rendered doctrinally unthinkable and functionally impossible. But matters cannot be left at this because it would be an over-simplification. It is necessary to recognise that in practice, in the functioning of this type of social group, minority positions, although 'doctrinally unthinkable and functionally impossible', are constantly emerging and taking form. Indeed, it seems almost to constitute an activity essential to the vitality of the system.

2. Minority positions play a useful and occasionally indispensable role in the adequate functioning and survival of the orthodox system

(a) Within an orthodox system, everything is so arranged, if one may put it this way, that internal disputes are never based on the group's central beliefs; thus, at the worst, dispute is pushed towards the peripheral zone of the belief system, and moreover any dissent remains socially unorganised. In practice, however, the orthodox system is buffeted by challenges which sometimes involve basic issues and it contains many often unruly organisms or small groups whose interactions with the overall system take on an astonishing variety of forms. To the eyes of an observer this cognitive and institutional agitation is so forcefully and conspicuously apparent that it is difficult to regard it as merely the free play of the type that even the most centralised systems often find desirable or politic to tolerate on their fringes. This perpetual internal agitation could be interpreted in terms of negotiations, stratagems and tactics. Alternatively, it could be viewed as a phase in the personal development of individuals whose dissidence is being expressed from within the group before, perhaps, being pursued on the outside of a system which has failed to respond to their expectations. Or again it could be interpreted as a kind of transitory disorder precipitated by historical changes. From this perspective, internal challenges to an orthodox system can form an object of research in terms of a relatively classical methodology. Nevertheless, it seems to us that, independent of these possible models of functioning, disputes that are internal to an orthodox system, when considered carefully, do play an essential role here, and that this role is played within the socio-cognitive field that this system creates.

(b) To account for some of the mechanisms that are internal to this field we have introduced the hypothesis that the rational weakness of ideas here is compensated for by the strength of social control. It has been possible, on the basis of this hypothesis, to create a series of experiments within a well-established institutional milieu, the Catholic church. It has thus been shown that the damage which occurs, as a result of minority challenges, to the system of social control on which the orthodox structure is based is the only kind not to be repaired, at least in the first analysis. By leading subjects to think that some of the beliefs they held in reality defined the regulation of membership less adequately than they first thought, we also led them to perceive to a greater degree on the one hand that these beliefs were not susceptible to rational or empirical verification ($N = 17$) and, on the other, that the theological corpus of which they were a part did possess some internal flaws ($N = 23$) (Deconchy, 1971). Furthermore, by making some of these flaws in the corpus clearer we also led orthodox subjects to perceive to a greater degree the distortion these beliefs create in the norms of what is normally called 'rationality' ($N = 28$).

But not all the assaults that may be made upon the integrity of the orthodox system, from within or from without, have such a distressing effect. Thus by an experimental induction into the functioning of orthodox groups of polemics demonstrating the non-rationality of the beliefs around which these groups organise their consensus, we led most of the subjects in these groups on the one hand to reinforce their representations of the perfect internal coherence of the doctrinal corpus ($N = 25$) and, on the other, to render the regulation of membership even more demanding and rigorous ($N = 27$). This reinforcement of their beliefs that in fact and by right they formed a powerfully organised and rigorously defined group was also achieved by demonstrating in this or that situation in which orthodoxy was threatened the flaws and contradictions that are present within a body of doctrine that is nevertheless strongly unified (N = 35). In other words, damage to some of the elements that constitute the orthodox consensus may have a beneficial effect on some aspect or other of the system. And this is not least because it concerns elements that are dependent on social control.

Thus, in terms of our study, minority positions based on the elements just described can have functionally beneficial effects independently of any of the tactical, calculated or political games that we have briefly referred to. In a way, through its exposure to minority positions, the system changes nothing on which its consensus is based and there is no alteration in its functioning. In allowing itself to be 'influenced' by the minority, the system only reinforces its own functioning at the same time as it, paradoxically, increases the rigour of the mechanisms which, should the occasion arise, will be capable of expelling the minority when the system judges that the time has come to protect itself from an influence that is now considered perverse.

(c) From this perspective some minority challenges can thus have favourable effects on the functioning of the orthodox system. The analysis of another series of processes may cause us to ask whether in some cases this challenge is not practically indispensable to the effective functioning and survival of the system.

Up to now we have presented the affirmation of orthodox belief as a kind of system in balance between several poles. More graphically, one could say that these poles, which depend on social regulation, are constantly activated to prevent any perception of the non-rationality of belief, while the rational appetite searches for any lapse in social control that could reveal the weakness of this belief. Various other experimental studies have been aimed at unravelling this system of balance, and in these experiments we have again found various paradoxical processes at work. By discretely reinforcing an idea that orthodox subjects habitually held, namely that the religious propositions which they asserted were more rationally based than the religious propositions they rejected, they were quite quickly led to accept more readily the idea that there nonetheless existed flaws in the doctrinal corpus (N = 23) and that the criteria for group membership were less rigid than they previously believed (N = 27). By discretely reinforcing the idea that their beliefs were not claims which supported the liberty of thought of each person but that they more or less adequately regulated group membership, these same subjects were quite rapidly led to a more ready acceptance of the idea that flaws did exist within the doctrinal corpus (N = 32) and that these beliefs were not dependent on rationality alone (N = 29). By discretely reinforcing the idea that the beliefs they held were not isolated and more or less free-floating objects, but formed part of a highly unified corpus, these subjects accepted the idea more readily that these beliefs were not dependent on a strict rationality (N = 29) and perhaps that their regulative role with respect to membership was less strict than they had previously believed (N = 23).

In these situations, therefore, in which orthodoxy is 'pacified', in which belief is assumed to pose no problems, belief faces structural risks either from a cognitive perspective or from the perspective of social regulation. These are the same risks as those faced in certain of the situations in which orthodoxy is threatened when damage occurs to the system of social control. In these situations rational weakness tends to be perceived more clearly while the internal coherence of the doctrinal corpus declines and regulation of membership becomes less important. 'Half-heartedness', the dangers of which orthodox systems never cease to denounce, will not simply take affective, mystical or ethical forms. There will be a cognitive half-heartedness whose centrifugal and destructive effects orthodox systems are inherently inclined to oppose. In these situations, and as long as they do not bear directly on the system's social control, minority challenges, whether internal or external, are treated in such a way that one is inclined to wonder whether, apart from straightforward tactical issues, it might not be necessary functionally for an orthodox system to induce them itself, and to do so by introducing into its functioning the image of dangers to belief and the system. And this could be parallel to the taking-in-hand of a direct reinforcement of social control.

Thus one may appreciate the grounds on which we have been able to conclude that the adoption of minority positions can play a useful and occasionally indispensable part in the functioning and survival of an orthodox system.

3. In some cases majority positions may be created around positions that are minority in form and inspiration, so that the system may survive

(a) Within an orthodox system a whole complex of social mechanisms immunises the system against attempts to fragment it. These include institutional mechanisms which are strongly hierarchical and centralised and which are constantly concerned to detect potentially deviant stratagems. They also include sophisticated cognitive operations which are controlled right down to the forms in which they are expressed and their lexical content. The various experiments we have referred to above have begun to show how the orthodox system compensates for flaws. These flaws may either be created spontaneously within the system or may emerge as effects of internal or external assaults in a complicated interplay between the various levels of its system of social regulation. In particular, it has been possible to show that the evolution of 'rationality' is ultimately beneficial to the system since it can give rise to a reassertion of various social regulations and an increase in their effectiveness.

(b) One is naturally inclined to ask what becomes of an orthodox system, and how the subjects within it are affected, if the set of observations we have just made about them are presented to them and when these observations are authenticated by scientific argument, for example by experimental evidence. In other words, what happens to the social and theoretical epistemology of orthodox subjects when one confronts them with the experimental evidence showing, at least to some degree, that the rational weakness of ideas in their own system is compensated for by the strength of social control?

Once this particular scientific finding had been presented to them, subjects could no longer fall back overtly on the normal system of social control since the artificial basis of the epistemology by which it was legitimised had now been unmasked. In this case the question arose whether subjects who belonged to the orthodox domain were not going to be led to take various social and cognitive risks and to try and establish those ideas on which they regarded their beliefs as being founded upon the basis of more fluid and fragmented cognitive processes, in so far as the experiment provided the means, or history the opportunity, to do so. The system has come to immunise itself against such processes and generally succeeds in controlling, containing or channelling them. For these are social and cognitive processes which occupy precisely the kind of position in which *minority* disputes most often take root. To begin with, at least, the orthodox system would be able, with a view to forming itself into a kind of defensive framework, to take the risk of allowing some localised release of those unstable forces which it is normally capable of controlling. These will probably be vestiges of some troubled or turbulent historical context out of which a set of beliefs has formerly developed.

In a series of experiments, subjects placed in this particular situation, when their beliefs could no longer be founded on the framework of their traditional epistemology, were led (1) to project, in a utopian fashion, ultimate understanding of their beliefs into an imprecisely defined future (N = 29), or (2) to project them into an eschatology whose parameters were clearly not empirical (N = 20). When, in general terms, orthodox language was organised in rhetorically a quite placid fashion, and when its arguments were based on the most sound logical forms, subjects were led to appeal to aesthetic expression (N = 27) or to mystical experience (N = 25) as the basis for their cognitive beliefs. When classical orthodox epistemology was founded on a socially coherent background, orthodox subjects were then more likely to see 'in living and in doing' the place where the true meaning of the beliefs they laid claim to was revealed (N = 20). Others placed a clearer emphasis on the quality of the psychological and material environment in which their beliefs had been experienced as involved in the understanding that they thought they had (N = 16). Yet others were more likely to proclaim that it was only in small and basic communities that one could ever really achieve the deeper meaning of beliefs (N = 20). In other words, we see the entire system moving towards its own periphery, towards the adoption of unstable and more or less anarchic positions which are more usually found at the heart of minority-instigated disputes.

Despite this we still remain within the ideological field over which the orthodox system exercises its control. Moreover, it is significant that in using this experimental paradigm in the same conditions and under the same circumstances we have not succeeded in achieving an artificial synthesis of what might be called the 'secularisation' of belief. For instance, we tried, unsuccessfully, to reinforce the idea that 'in the future, civil society could take over from religious systems the task of leading men to discover the deeper meaning of beliefs'. No more successful was an attempt to increase recourse to the idea that men could, with respect to this or that aspect of their functioning, become believers without knowing it (N = 18), even though it is quite a frequent claim in this type of ideology.

We find ourselves confronted here with careful risk-taking and provisional changes. For at the base there exists in this type of system a kind of institutional programming of the conditions under which these risks can be legitimately taken and the manner according to which it is legitimate to take them. For the subject it is a matter of extracting from the socio-cultural capital controlled by the system this or that residue of its original vitality. It is a matter of reintroducing into his functioning something of the vibrant intuition and social informality which provided its initial historical shape. We were previously able to demonstrate a whole set of lateral balances designed to conceal the structural flaws with which belief may be affected. Here we find ourselves confronted with a kind of movement in depth that tends to produce a selective classification of the mass of cultural and historical data and of data of the collective imagination that the system generates. Thus the risk is taken of reintroducing into the system preliminary representations and meanings, those intuitions which form part of the group's ideological capital but which do not depend on any orthodox logic and which cannot even be described as pre-orthodox when considering what they have become. These are representations, meanings and intuitions that one normally expects to be expressed by isolated, often undisciplined and always suspect subjects, namely *minorities*.

A programmed and careful risk is taken, but all the same a risk. For this area of the system, in which it appeals to unstable contents, is precisely where minority challenges take root, challenges which would break loose from orthodox control, no longer in awe of what might normally be called its perfection. It is therefore a zone of interface between the orthodox minority and the unorthodox minority, or, if one prefers and in the terms of Joachim Wach (1944), between the protest *within* and the protest *without*.

Note

1. By 'doxeme' we mean a self-contained unit of doctrine drawn from the orthodox corpus or potentially inscribable in that corpus.

9. Conformity, innovation and the psychosocial law

SHARON WOLF and BIBB LATANÉ

Since the classic studies of Sherif (1935) and Asch (1951) on the formation and perpetuation of group norms, a vast amount of research has documented the pervasive influence of the group on the individual and of the majority on the minority or subgroup (see Allen, 1965 and Kiesler & Kiesler, 1969 for reviews). This research on conformity has viewed the minority as the passive recipient of influence pressure from the majority. Explanations of majority influence have focused on the majority's superior size, status and power, which afford it a better basis for establishing social reality and greater resources for rewarding those who adopt its viewpoint (Deutsch & Gerard, 1955). Such explanations cannot easily account for influence by a numerically disadvantaged and less powerful minority.

Recent research suggests, however, that individuals can play a role in modifying the attitudes and values of the groups to which they belong and that the minority need not always be the target of social influence (see Moscovici, 1976 and Levine, 1980 for reviews). This research on innovation has viewed the minority as an active source of influence pressure directed towards the majority. When the minority is viewed as a source, rather than as a target, traditional views of the social influence process must be modified. Moscovici (1976; Moscovici & Faucheux, 1972) has argued that minority influence may be explained by the perceptions of confidence and commitment fostered by the minority's consistent behavioural style. The minority's smaller size does not preclude it from exercising influence but rather enhances those perceptions. From this perspective it is difficult to account for influence by a larger and apparently less committed majority.

The conclusion of earlier research on conformity and recent research on innovation would seem to be that majority and minority influence require different explanatory frameworks. Minorities are inherently disadvantaged in terms of size, status and power, the variables hypothesised to mediate majority influence, whereas majorities are at a disadvantage in creating the perceptions of confidence and commitment hypothesised to underlie minority influence. However, neither research tradition has investigated situations in which the influence of majorities and minorities is simultaneous and reciprocal. As a result, explanations of influence by one of the factions often fail to account for influence by the other and little attention has been directed towards finding general laws that govern the social influence process.

There would appear to be theoretical advantages in viewing social influence as a unitary concept. A general model, by considering conformity and innovation as instances of a single process, mediated by a common set of variables, would offer a more parsimonious account of influence data covering a greater variety of influence situations. Social impact theory (Latané, 1981) offers such a unitary perspective. This theory proposes that social influence can be understood as resulting from social forces operating in a social force field and governed by psychosocial laws. Influence by either a majority or a minority will be a multiplicative function of the strength, immediacy and number of its members.

In this chapter we will analyse the social influence situation from the perspective of this new theory. First, the principles of social impact theory will be presented and their application to an understanding of social influence will be specified. Then, findings of previous research on conformity and innovation, as well as some recent research, will be evaluated in light of the theory. Finally, we will argue for the theoretical advantages of viewing social influence as a unitary phenomenon.

1. Social impact theory

Social impact is defined as any of the great variety of changes in physiological states and subjective feelings, motives and emotions, cognitions and beliefs, values and behaviour that occur in an individual as a result of the real, implied or imagined presence of other individuals (Latané, 1981: 343). We describe these effects in terms of social force fields comparable to the physical force fields that govern the transmission of light, sound and gravity.

Figure 1 is an example of a force field, showing the impact of several spotted sources on an individual striped target. Three factors would determine the combined effect of the sources on the target in a physical force field: the strength (S) or intensity of the sources (represented by the area of the circles), their immediacy (I) or proximity to the target, and the number (N) of sources present. Thus, if the sources were lightbulbs, the amount of light they would shed on a surface would be a multiplicative function of their wattage, their closeness to the surface, and the number of bulbs that were lit; or, Impact $= f(SIN)$.

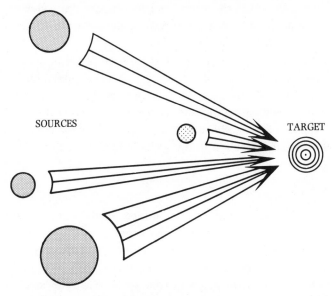

Figure 1. Multiplication of impact: I = f(SIN). (From Latané, 1981. © 1981 by the American Psychological Association. Reprinted by permission of the publisher.)

Analogously, the social impact experienced by a target person should be a function of the strength (in the case of people, such things as status, power and abilities), immediacy (closeness in time or space), and number of source persons in a social force field. As any one of these variables increases, there will be an increase in impact. Further, since these variables are multiplicatively related, the effect of any one variable will be greater, the greater the value of the other variables.

As in the case of physical stimuli, the psychological effect of other people may not be a simple linear function of their strength or number (Stevens, 1975). Rather, we suggest, social impact may obey psycho*social* laws similar to the psycho*physical* laws that govern the subjective impact of light and sound intensity. We propose that the effect on a target person of an increase in the number of sources will be a power function, with each additional source producing less impact than the previous source. This concept is similar to that of marginally decreasing utility in economics. Just as the first dollar you acquire is worth more to you than the hundredth, the first person in a social force field has more impact than the hundredth. Although 100 people have more impact than a single person, we suggest simply that the difference between 99 and 100 is less than the difference between 0 and 1. This principle of marginally decreasing impact is expressed: Impact = sN^t, where s is a scaling constant reflecting the impact of a single person in the situation and t is an exponent with a value of less than one. That the value of the exponent must be less than one implies that impact will grow as some root of the number of source persons.

Latané (1981) describes ten diverse areas of application of social impact theory, including the interest value of news events, social inhibition of responses to emergencies and requests for help, group productivity and crowding in rats. With its few basic propositions, this is clearly a very broad theory, although it does lead to highly specific and verifiable predictions. In this chapter we consider its application to the social influence area.

2. Majority influence

When an individual confronts a unanimous majority, all the social forces acting on him will be experienced as pressure to conform to the majority opinion. Conformity, then, should be a multiplicative function of the strength, immediacy and number of majority members. Further, as majority size increases, conformity should grow as some root of N, with the largest differences in conformity being associated with the first few increments in N.

Ironically, Asch's (1951, 1952, 1956) early research found a very different relationship between majority size and conformity from that predicted by social impact theory. Asch asked students to choose from among three lines the line that was equal in length to a standard. Students did this alone or after one, two, three, four, eight or sixteen other people (actually experimental confederates) had unanimously reported an obviously incorrect response. The students were thus forced to choose between stating a judgment that contradicted the physical evidence or one that contradicted the reported evidence of the other judges. Asch set up a conflict between the physical impact of the stimulus situation and the social impact of from one to 16 other people. He found that majorities of one and two produced very little conformity, conformity was greatest when the majority consisted of three individuals, and increases in majority size beyond three did not lead to increasing amounts of conformity. Asch's results, however, have been called into question by more recent research.

Gerard, Wilhelmy & Conolley (1968) replicated Asch's study with a younger subject population and found that conformity did continue to increase with increases in majority size beyond three. And the first few majority members had the greatest impact. Their data are best described by the power function: Impact $= 14N^{0.46}$, which accounts for 80 per cent of the variance in means. The parameters of this function show that a single confederate induced conformity on 14 per cent of the trials and, as predicted, the exponent is less than one, indicating that conformity grew as about the square root of majority size.

For further evidence on the role of majority size, Latané & Davis (1974) conducted a field experiment in which students were asked to sign a four-page questionnaire concerning the adequacy of local newspapers. Each page had a question about news coverage at the top and two columns labelled 'Yes' and 'No' below and respondents were asked to sign their names on each page in the column that best reflected their opinion. The questionnaires contained a varying number of signatures at the time they were distributed, with one, two, three, six or twelve signatures in one column and none in the other. The signatures were counter-balanced so that they appeared on the 'Yes' and 'No' sides of each issue an equal number of times.

This procedure elicited a high degree of conformity, with 68 per cent of respondents adopting the majority position. Since 50 per cent would have done so even in the absence of the previous signatures, because the majority signatures appeared equally often on both sides of the issue, we can infer that 18 per cent of all respondents were led to conform, or 36 per cent of those who would normally have expressed the opposite opinion from that espoused by the majority. The amount of conformity, further, depended upon the size of the unanimous majority. Conformity increased systematically with the number of signatures up to 12 and the first signature on the questionnaire had more effect than any of the subsequent signatures. The power function: Impact = $24N^{0.38}$ does a good job of describing the relationship between majority size and conformity, accounting for 88 per cent of the variance in means. Conformity on a questionnaire seems to grow as about the cube root of the number of majority signatures.

These results, coupled with those from Gerard, Wilhelmy & Conolley (1968) challenge Asch's conclusion that conformity is unrelated to majority size, both by their demonstration of increases in conformity with increases in majority size beyond three and by the significant amounts of conformity obtained with majorities of one and two. More precisely, they suggest that conformity is related to majority size by a power function, with each additional majority member producing a smaller increment in conformity than the previous member.

3. Minority influence

In the situations just described the social forces were unidirectional, with each influence source contributing to the total pressure on the target person to adopt the majority position. When an individual is the target of influence by others, others who are divided on the issue in question, the force exerted by the larger faction will pull him towards the majority position, while the force of the smaller faction will pull him towards the minority. We propose that the magnitude of each force will be a multiplicative function of the strength, immediacy and number of faction members and that the resultant force on the target will be a simple function of the difference in impact imparted by each. All else being equal, conformity to the majority position should increase as a power function of majority size and decrease as a power function of minority size.

Nemeth, Wachtler & Endicott (1977) investigated parametric variations in minority size by bringing six naive individuals together with one, two, three or four confederates to make a series of perceptual judgments. Their task was to indicate the colour of slides, all of which were objectively blue. The confederates unanimously labelled each slide blue-green. The results showed that three confederates had significantly more influence on the colour judgments of the naive participants than minorities of only one or two, but that a minority of four did not differ from the other conditions. Although Nemeth, Wachtler & Endicott report that the only significant component of the minority size effect was linear, our re-analysis of their data shows that a power function with an exponent of 0.5 achieves a slightly better fit. Unfortunately, a methodological feature of this experiment makes it impossible to obtain a precise estimate of the minority size effect. All of the responses were made publicly and each time a naive participant conformed to the minority position, the majority to minority size ratio changed. The value of their conclusions with respect to minority size, therefore, is limited.

A more precise investigation of the effect of minority size was conducted by Davis & Latané (1974) in the context of a study on social influence in a person perception format. They asked participants to integrate information from several sources in order to form a coherent impression of a target person. Each of up to 24 different persons who knew the target person gave a one-word trait description, either positive or negative, and participants were asked to report how much they would like the person described, on a scale from − 100 to + 100. Each respondent rated 216 different target persons, described by from 1 to 24 different people, with a combination of 0 to 12 extremely positive, and 0 to 12 extremely negative adjectives listed in a single page.

Considering those cases in which people gave either all positive or all negative descriptions, the change in favourability ratings from a no influence baseline increased systematically with the number of descriptions and the first few descriptions had the greatest impact. The positive and negative descriptions were equally influential, although their effects were in opposite directions. The power function: Impact $= 22N^{0.49}$, accounts for 99 per cent of the variance in means, implying that the first person giving a description increased or decreased liking for the target by an average of 22 percentage points, and that impact grew as the square root of the number of people giving descriptions.

When participants were exposed to both positive and negative influences at the same time, the data suggest that they simply subtracted the lesser influence from the greater to form their resultant impression. Holding the number of negative descriptions constant, an increase in the number of people giving positive descriptions led to very regular increases in the favourability of the final impression. Similarly, holding the number of positive descriptions constant, an increase in the number of people giving negative descriptions led to systematic decreases in the favourability of the final impression.

The results of these last two studies indicate that minority influence is a positive, although negatively accelerated, function of minority size. Further, they support the proposition that when exposed to the simultaneous influence of a majority and a minority, conformity to the majority position by an independent target individual will be a function of the majority's impact minus that of the minority.

4. Majority and minority size and strength

In general, the evidence confirms our speculations concerning majority and minority size. Both majority and minority size appear to be related to social influence by a power function with an exponent of less than one. On the other hand, there is little evidence in the social influence literature pertaining to the proposed multiplicative relationship of strength, immediacy and number. Certainly, strength variables, such as attractiveness, power and expertise, have received attention in the literature, but they have not been manipulated in combination with immediacy or number. In order to assess this aspect of social impact theory, then, we developed a new procedure by which to manipulate majority and minority size and strength within the context of a single experiment (Wolf & Latané, 1983).

Social influence research has for the most part employed a single paradigm. A stimulus is presented, participants are exposed to the judgments of the influence sources, they make a response and then the procedure is repeated with a new stimulus. In this paradigm, all of the information relevant to the judgment is presented simultaneously and the distribution of majority and minority viewpoints is immediately apparent. This does not seem to represent

the manner in which people most often learn about the opinions of others. For many issues, information about the opinions of others is acquired over a period of time. Influence requires integrating information, obtained from different people at different points in time, in order to arrive at an estimate of opinion distribution. We attempted to simulate this process of sequential information acquisition in a study on restaurant selection.

Participants were exposed to the restaurant preferences (both likes and dislikes) of two groups of 12 stimulus persons, consisting of both highly expert individuals and individuals with little basis for making restaurant judgments. By integrating the information provided, participants could determine the number of highly- and non-expert individuals who liked and disliked each restaurant. Six levels of majority–minority size (unanimous majorities of one, two, four and six, and holding majority size at four, opposing minorities of one and two), two levels of strength (high and low expertise) and two directions of influence (positive and negative) were created, with a different restaurant assigned to each of the 24 experimental conditions.

This within-subject design allowed us to test several predictions concerning the simultaneous influence of majorities and minorities: (1) influence by either a majority or a minority would be a multiplicative function of the strength (expertise) and number of its members; (2) influence by either a majority or a minority would increase as a power function of its size, with the largest increments in influence being associated with the first few increases in the number of its members; and (3) variations in strength would lead to more pronounced differences for a majority than for a minority, since strength is presumed to be multiplicatively related to the number of influence sources and majorities are, by definition, more numerous.

Each participant completed two experimental booklets. The first described 12 male students at a university in Seattle and the second described 12 male students at a university in Los Angeles. Background information about each student was provided at the top of a separate page. At the bottom of the page were listed the two restaurants the student reportedly liked best in Seattle (Los Angeles) and the two restaurants he liked least. Thus, 48 items of information were provided about the restaurants in each city. Judgments of half of the restaurants were given by expert individuals (students described as having considerable experience dining out in the city), whereas half were given by non-experts (students who had limited off-campus experience). Majority and minority size were manipulated by varying the number of times each restaurant was mentioned positively or negatively. Unanimous majorities of one, two, four and six individuals mentioned liking (or disliking) a given restaurant without opposition. Minorities of one and two individuals mentioned liking (or disliking) a given restaurant in opposition to the expressed opinion of a majority of four. Each size × strength condition was represented in both the Seattle and Los Angeles booklets, with the direction of influence reversed between the two booklets. After completing both booklets, then, each participant had responded to all 24 experimental conditions and additionally, to four no influence controls. A between-subjects variation was also run to control for potential effects of the restaurant names on their perceived attractiveness.

Participants rated both the stimulus persons and the restaurants at the end of each booklet. The primary measure asked participants to imagine that they were moving to Seattle (Los Angeles) and that eating dinner at home would be rated 20. They were to make relative ratings (magnitude estimations) of the desirability of eating at 14 restaurants, 12 of which had been mentioned by the stimulus persons and two of which provided a no influence baseline.

A striking finding of this study is that negative information about the restaurants, whether provided by a majority or a minority, played almost no role in participants' evaluations of the restaurants. Hypotheses concerning majority and minority size and strength, therefore, could be tested only in the positive information conditions, where social influence was clearly obtained.

When restaurants were reportedly liked by a unanimous majority, increases in both the number and strength of influence sources resulted in increased influence and there was marginal evidence that these variables were multiplicatively related. Further, influence was a negatively accelerating function of majority size. The power function: Impact $= 1.75N^{0.20}$, which accounts for 99 per cent of the variance in means, shows that changes in perceived restaurant desirability grew in proportion to the fifth root of majority size, with the first majority member having more influence than any of the subsequent members.

As in the case of the unanimous majorities, minority influence was obtained only when the minority provided positive information about the restaurants (in opposition to a negative majority). Increases in the number of minority members who liked a given restaurant led to increases in the perceived desirability of eating at that restaurant. But, inconsistent with a power function, the second minority member had as much influence as the first. However, this influence was unaffected by minority strength. Where majority influence was obtained, on the other hand, that influence was strongly affected by the expertise of the majority. Taken together, these results demonstrate that strength is a more important determinant of majority influence than of minority influence. Moscovici (1976) has argued that power, status and expertise are not particularly valuable attributes of an innovating minority. Social impact theory and these data suggest, at least, that they are more valuable attributes of a majority.

Where social influence was obtained, the data were generally consistent with the predictions of social impact theory. The surprising aspect of the data is that so little influence was produced when the sources provided negative information. Of course this may have been due to the sequential presentation of information about the restaurants. As the number of individuals who mentioned a given restaurant increased, the number of exposures to the name of the restaurant increased as well. It is possible, therefore, that mere exposure (Zajonc, 1968) increased the attractiveness of the frequently disliked restaurants. The results, then, may reflect a combination of mere exposure and social impact effects.

As Doms & Van Avermaet (1980) have noted, comparisons between conformity and innovation are tenuous because they have seldom been studied in the context of a single experiment. The procedure utilised in this experiment simulates the distribution of majority and minority opinions and assesses the effects of that distribution on a single individual. It permits characteristics of the majority and of the minority to be varied simultaneously and thus it allows for an assessment of the relative importance of those characteristics for the two influence sources. Further, it allows for quantitative comparisons between conformity and innovation. On the other hand, the social forces operating in this experimental context were entirely informational and were directed towards opinion formation rather than opinion change. Thus, this procedure may not be applicable to situations in which group pressure (Festinger, 1950) is a necessary component of influence. We would expect, however, that the addition of normative pressures would enhance the influence of both majorities and minorities.

5. Division of impact

In the situations considered so far, the target individual has been presumed to hold no initial attitude on the issue in question. That is, he has been a member of neither the majority nor the minority. There is another way to view the social influence situation and that is to assume that this individual is a member of either the majority or the minority and is the target of forces coming from the other faction.

Social impact theory defines two types of social situations that result in different kinds of social force fields. In the first, an individual is the target of forces emanating from other people. The impact he experiences, we propose, will be a multiplicative function of the number of people present and

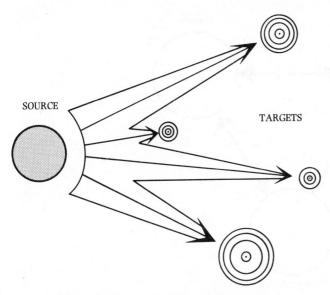

Figure 2. Division of impact: I = f(1/SIN). (Figure from Latané, 1981. © 1981 by the American Psychological Association. Reprinted by permission of the publisher.)

the amount of impact generated by each. In the second situation, an individual stands with others as the target of a social force coming from outside the group. In this case, impact will be diffused or divided among the group members, with each individual feeling less impact than he would if he were alone, as shown in figure 2. As the strength, immediacy or number of other group members increases, the impact of an external source on any individual will decrease, so that in this case: Impact = f(1/SIN).

If we assume an initial attitude on the part of a target individual consistent with that of either the majority or the minority, this individual will be in both a multiplicative and a divisive force field. The impact he experiences will be a direct function of the strength, immediacy and number of people in the opposing group and an inverse function of the strength, immediacy and number of people in his own group, that is: Impact = f(SIN opposing group/SIN own group). This suggests that he will be affected by others in his own subgroup, as well as by those in the other subgroup, and that each subgroup will have an effect upon the other. From this perspective, majority and minority influence may be viewed as simultaneous and reciprocal.

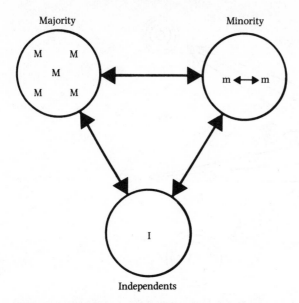

Figure 3. A generalised social force field: M = majority members, m = minority members, I = independents. (Figure from Latané & Wolf, 1981. © 1981 by the American Psychological Association. Reprinted by permission of the publisher.)

6. A general model of social influence

A general model of social influence processes may be described by the social force field depicted in figure 3. Let us assume that this force field represents members of a group who are discussing a relevant issue and that two positions on the issue may be identified, one advocated by a majority and the other by a minority. Let us assume, further, that one or more group members belong to neither the majority nor the minority and may be classified as independent (newcomers to the group, for example). The social force field, then, is composed of three units: majority members (M), minority members (m), and independents (I). In this example, a single individual holding independent status is confronted by a majority of five and a minority of two.

As illustrated by the arrows connecting these units one to another, each unit is a potential source of influence for the other two, as well as a potential recipient of influence from the other two. The magnitude of influence pressure that each unit exerts on the others will be a function of the strength, immediacy and number of individuals in that subgroup. Further, the people in each unit may be affected by others in their own subgroup, as represented by the arrow indicating the reciprocal influence of the two minority members. The impact an individual experiences from others in his own unit may be direct, as when influence by a subgroup leads to the acceptance of new arguments or to a polarisation of its members' opinions. Alternatively, this impact may be indirect, in the form of a diffusion of impact by the other units. The ability of a subgroup to influence its own members or to diffuse influence pressure from outside will be a function of the strength, immediacy and number of its members.

There are two ways to view the social influence situation from the perspective of a single individual. In one case, he may view himself as independent and as the lone recipient of forces generated by the other group members. This perspective would be likely if the individual had no opinion or was neutral on the issue in question, if he were a newcomer to the group, or simply an observer of the interaction between a majority and a minority. The total impact he experiences should be a function of the majority's impact *minus* that of the minority. In the second case, the individual may view himself as a member of either the majority or the minority. The total impact he experiences in this situation should be a function of the other subgroup's impact *divided* by that of his own subgroup.

Social impact theory, then, provides a general framework by which to understand the influence of both majorities and minorities. But while it offers a broad and descriptive, yet precise and testable, model of social influence processes, the model does not specify when or where social influence will occur, nor does it detail the mechanisms by which social influence is transmitted. Rather, it provides general rules, psychosocial laws, that determine the magnitude of influence when it does occur and is most useful when combined with specific theories relevant to each area of application (Latané, 1981).

7. Relationship of the model to earlier models

The present model integrates previous theoretical formulations and empirical findings from research on conformity and innovation. Thus, while there are some points of disagreement, social impact theory has much in common with earlier models of social influence processes.

Previous models of majority influence have stressed the dependence of the minority upon the majority either for information or for material and psychological benefits that the majority can provide (Jones & Gerard, 1967). In contrast, social impact theory suggests that influence may occur even in the absence of an explicit dependence relationship. The simple presence of an individual in a social force field ensures that he will be affected, at least to some extent, by every other individual in that field and that he will simultaneously have some effect upon each of them. Thus, we agree with Moscovici (1976) that single individuals and relatively powerless minorities must inevitably have some influence.

Variables that have traditionally been the focus of conformity research, such as status, power and expertise, are strength variables in the present formulation and variations in their magnitude should lead to corresponding changes in impact. Further, since strength is multiplicatively related to the number of influence sources and majorities are more numerous, these changes should be more pronounced for a majority than for a minority, as the data on restaurant selection have demonstrated (Wolf & Latané, 1983). Thus, it is not surprising that research on conformity has emphasised the role of these variables.

Some properties of the group as a whole, such as group cohesiveness, may also be viewed as strength variables. In line with the proposed multiplicative relationship between strength and number, we would expect variations in cohesiveness to play a larger role in conformity than in innovation settings. Some recent research (Wolf, in press) confirms this speculation. Based on an earlier experimental procedure (Wolf, 1979), female participants interacted in groups of four. These groups were led to be highly cohesive or much less so. During the interaction each participant was exposed to an influence attempt by either a minority of one or a majority of three other group members. The results showed, not surprisingly, that the majority was more influential than the minority. Further, participants in high cohesive groups were influenced to a greater extent than those in low cohesive groups. Finally, there was an interaction such that the effects of the cohesiveness variable were more pronounced when the source of influence was a majority than when it was a minority. These results are consistent with the predictions of social impact theory and with the important role that group cohesiveness has played in the conformity literature (Festinger, 1950; Festinger, Schachter & Back, 1950; Back, 1951).

In keeping with Moscovici's (1976) analysis of minority influence, social impact theory views individuals and minorities as potential sources, as well as recipients, of influence pressure. We suggest, however, that their impact will be proportional to their strength, immediacy and number. It will neither be excessive nor relatively greater than that of a majority.

Research on social support for nonconformity (Allen, 1975) has shown dramatic reductions in conformity with a single dissenter from the majority position. The apparently disproportionate influence of a single deviate may reflect two processes. First, deviates may acquire greater perceived strength and/or immediacy by maintaining their position consistently in the face of negative sanctions and by becoming the focus of increased communication in the group (Schachter, 1951). Secondly, the seemingly excessive influence of a single deviate may simply reflect the power function relating influence to the number of influence sources. The first person in a social force field should always have the greatest impact. Increases in minority size should have a marginally decreasing effect.

The present formulation suggests, though, that whenever a majority and a minority are simultaneously present and of comparable strength (i.e. the minority does not possess special resources or power), the majority will have a greater impact than the minority. Greater strength and/or immediacy, therefore, are necessary components of successful innovation by a numerically disadvantaged minority. Behavioural style may be the only means by which a powerless minority can increase its strength sufficiently to have a noticeable impact. It is not surprising, therefore, that research on innovation has emphasised the role of this variable (Moscovici, Lage & Naffrechoux, 1969; Nemeth, Swedlund & Kanki, 1974).

8. A unitary perspective

The present analysis suggests that minority influence is governed by the same principles and mediated by the same variables as majority influence, the difference between the two sources of influence being purely quantitative. The theoretical value of viewing conformity and innovation as instances of a general social influence process is both parsimony and the ability to account for a wide range of influence phenomena. More importantly, this formulation views the individual and the group as adaptive social agents. An individual may change his mind, move from one position on an issue to another, without having to engage in a new psychological process and without disrupting the ongoing group interaction. Further, neither the majority nor the minority is viewed as the passive recipient of social forces from the other faction. Whatever position an individual assumes on a given issue, he will be an active participant in the influence process. Finally, by analysing the influence situation in terms of a social force field, social impact theory helps to integrate social influence research with the vast body of research on other social phenomena, such as bystander intervention, responses to crowding, group productivity and so forth.

Note

Much of the material in this chapter is abridged from Latané & Wolf (1981).

10. Infra-group, intra-group and inter-group: construing levels of organisation in social influence[1]

VERNON L. ALLEN

This chapter is an unabashedly speculative essay, though tempered by an effort to use rather than abuse or ignore existing theory and empirical data relevant to the topic. Attempting to stimulate thinking on a problem by offering a generous abundance of suggestions and speculations, while at the same time adhering as closely as possible to the existing scientific literature, is to steer a tenuous course indeed – some would say that such a course runs between Scylla and Charybdis. Even so, I shall try to include evidence obtained both from well-controlled laboratory experiments as well as observations from everyday life in the 'real world' which, though not meeting the canons of science, we as psychologists ignore at our peril. Being rather too loose or too rigid would be detrimental to the goal of throwing some light on the dark corners of the old problem of social influence, which has been at the centre stage of social psychology since its beginnings as a science. The ubiquitous impact of social influence on our actions, beliefs and feelings in everyday life is too obvious to require documentation.

With these caveats, I turn directly to problems concerned with the area of social influence exerted by the minority. Several issues will be raised in connection with the general problem, but the basic thrust of the present inquiry is directed towards the consequences of an individual's construing the social environment at different levels of phenomenal organisation. It is argued that the level at which the individual construes the social world will affect the perceived structure and the meaning of the social behaviour. First, I shall offer some introductory comments about the context of research on minority influence; second, the concept of levels of construing the social environment is presented; third, the potential contributions of levels of construal for understanding minority influence are discussed; and finally, some possible determinants of one's level of construal are suggested. The basic theme running through my comments is the proposition that we should not exclude the *group* from our conceptualisations about group influence.

1. The context of minority influence research

Without question, the history of theory and research on social influence reveals a strong tendency for investigators to concentrate on the role of the majority (or the more powerful agent, e.g. prestigeful source) as the basis for changes in the beliefs and behaviour of an individual. Because of the dominance in psychological research of this unidirectional view of social influence, explanations have usually been offered in terms of the majority's superior capacity for dispensing rewards and punishments; and conversely, the individual's relation to the more powerful individual or group is characterised as being that of dependence. Moscovici has made an important contribution to the study of social influence by decisively cutting through the Gordian knot of the prevailing (though tacit) assumptions about the nature of group influence that had long been accepted without significant challenge (Moscovici & Faucheux, 1972; Moscovici, 1976). The study of social influence was redirected in at least three important respects by Moscovici's critique, which included the following points: (1) the minority can and does influence the majority as well as *vice versa*; (2) the theoretical basis for the effectiveness of the minority is by means of the dynamics of cognitive conflict rather than by dependence; (3) the behavioural style of consistency is one important strategy (among others) that the minority can employ to change the majority's position.

The critique of traditional theory and research in social influence, coupled with stimulating suggestions for a theoretical reorientation and for a shift in the empirical questions being posed, without doubt have had an energising effect on subsequent activity in this area. As a consequence, a substantial body of empirical research is now available under the rubric of 'minority influence', which provides a much more comprehensive and valid representation of the rich and variegated processes that constitute the phenomena of social influence than had previously existed in the field.

As stated above, to a great extent the importance of research on minority influence initiated by Moscovici and his colleagues is due to its having clearly revealed the hidden or tacit philosophical and psychological assumptions upon which existing research on majority influence was based. An entire set of taken-for-granted (and therefore unquestioned) ways of thinking about social influence had a pervasive effect on theorising and on all phases of the research process. Such presuppositions are inevitable in any area of scientific endeavour, of course, and perhaps they constitute on a minor scale a 'paradigm' in Kuhn's (1962) sense of the term. But a new research agenda or paradigm is also susceptible to the human proclivity to impose a (different) set of tacit presuppositions. Some of the contextual constraints within which research on minority influence has been conducted will be mentioned now as a prelude to the main topic of this chapter – implications of an individual's construal of the social environment.

In his critique of research and theory in majority influence (conformity), Moscovici (1976) claimed that the existing research conceptualised social influence as being unidirectional – from the majority to the minority – and rightly pointed out that it is a bi-directional process, that the minority also influences the majority. Stressing the opposite direction of influence – from minority to majority – was an important corrective to the traditional point of view. But I strongly doubt that, if pressed, even the most ardent adherent to conformity-to-the-group research would demur from the assertion that social influence is a two-way, reciprocal process. To accept verbally a dynamic, interactional model of social behaviour is, however, a great deal easier than to follow through its implications in concrete empirical studies. Actual research in minority influence (or the typical study) is no exception – the design simply turned on its head the majority influence research paradigm (an Asch-backwards change); that is, still only unidirectional influence is studied, albeit the minority's influence on the majority rather than the opposite is the *raison d'être* of the studies. For obvious reasons of control this procedure has much to commend it, but interaction during the social influence process is still not allowed to operate if the minority members' behaviour is controlled. And the interaction between the minority and majority may play an even more important role in the case of minority than in majority influence. Neglecting the role of social interaction in minority influence is due partly to the nature of the theory, that is, to the psychological processes posited as being responsible for producing change. In the theory emphasis is placed on the cognitive conflict engendered by the minority's consistent advocacy of a position. Employing cognitive dynamics as the central explanatory process tends to prevent (or to distract) us from examining other important elements in the interaction between the majority and minority which may play a crucial role in the influence process. Strongly focusing on intra-individual cognitive processes as the crucial explanatory mechanism tends to discourage the investigation of other potentially important non-cognitive processes (interpersonal and inter-group) that may contribute to successful influence produced by the minority. More will be said about this issue in later sections; suffice it here to point out that the minority influence paradigm, both in its experimental research manifestations and in its choice of explanatory constructs, is captive to its own preconceptions just as was majority influence research. In the case of minority influence, one result is the neglect of the process of dynamic, reciprocal, social interaction, the same neglect for which majority influence research has been justly criticised.

Other important consequences stem from the presuppositions (in theory and research design) inherent in the minority influence paradigm. An overriding interest in the impact of the minority's style of behaviour (primarily consistency) has tended to direct attention away from collateral or alternative modes of behaviour that minority members may use. That is, by turning the focus of our attention in the research paradigm towards the majority (and controlling the minority's behaviour in a predetermined way), we may have overlooked aspects of their behaviour that play a central role in social influence. In fact, some important mechanisms may not have been included in existing theory. For example, minorities do not always lack power and, hence, resort to the tactic of behavioural style in order to influence the majority. Even a cursory observation of events around the world during recent years indicates that minorities do sometimes have access to techniques of power, for example, terrorist acts such as bombing, kidnapping and assassination. To a considerable degree the minority's potential for exerting power and control *vis-à-vis* the majority (and thus its ability to influence the majority) is due to the majority's perception of the minority as reckless and willing to take high or irrational risks to attain its ends. To say that the minority does not have access to power and does not sometimes succeed by the use of sheer power is to ignore a great deal of history. If we take instances of minority influence in the real world as our basic referent cases, we would be well advised to investigate with great care the nature of the minority's actual behaviour in particular situations. Furthermore, valuable insights might be gained by giving attention to a detailed analysis of the minority's behaviour during an extended time period of interaction with the majority.

Related to the last point is another characteristic of the experimental paradigm used in minority influence research that is discrepant from real-life referent cases: the temporal duration of the interaction. To use learning theory terminology, the typical research paradigm consists of massed rather than distributed influence trials, all occurring within a brief time span (less than an hour). By contrast, imagine an experiment in which, for instance, the minority gave a consistent response on a topic once a day for 30 days rather than 30 times in one day. Which of these two examples would be more effective in producing influence? Two elements are involved: the space of time between influence attempts and the total length of the temporal duration. What is the effect of a large number of consistent responses given seriatim by the minority, as opposed to a spaced (distributed) pattern in which different responses are interspersed among the consistent responses (Allen & Wilder, 1978)? Real-life cases of minority influence typically consist of distributed instances of consistent responses. One may speculate that such a temporal spacing pattern could lead to greater influence by allowing time for the gradual changes produced by long-term cognitive work and by providing opportunity for disassociation between the source and the content of the message. A greater total amount of time might contribute to more influence through the same mechanisms and, in addition, might have a greater impact due to the cross-situational character of consistent behaviour which occurs over a span of time (Kelley, 1967).

Another interesting element in cases of minority influence in the real world is not present in the typical experimental situation. In the laboratory members of the majority and minority are usually in face-to-face contact; escape from the conflict produced by the minority is not possible. But if given the opportunity, persons who are being subjected to social pressure will attempt to avoid confronting the opposition (Allen, 1975), which may prevent the attempted influence from succeeding. Thus, it can be suggested that attempted influence by the minority in the broader societal context will be even less effective than it is in the laboratory setting.

Finally, one of the most important consequences of accepting implications implicitly dictated by theory is the neglect of an obvious feature of minority influence in real life – the centrality of the concept of group. Though it may be less evident in laboratory experiments than in actual cases in the real world, the minority's influence on the majority involves psychological processes occurring at the within-group and between-group levels; and much of the meaning of the influence behaviour is lost if not seen in the light of the implications that an act conveys as a social representation of identity and values of the group. In his book, Moscovici (1976) cites many instances in history when a minority position that was consistently advocated by an individual eventually led to its being adopted by the majority. But similarly, one can cite numerous instances in which an individual who began as a lone voice crying in the wilderness remained such forever. Perhaps the explanation for the adoption or non-adoption by others of a lone voice's cry can be accounted for in part by the simple fact that disagreements about physical reality are amenable to being objectively tested and verified. The majority was ultimately converted to Galileo's views because the world does move, as was later determined to the satisfaction of agreed-upon criteria for assessing truth. But barring this category of explanations, the 'correct' position for many other matters cannot be so easily determined. Major religions provide good examples of the consequences of successful influence by an initially very small minority. Yet many other individuals have attempted, long and consistently, to proselytise for their religious beliefs without ever reaping success.

It can be suggested that group factors play an important role in contributing to the success of minority influence. A belief system which is the beneficiary of strong social support from like-minded others can attain profound levels of conviction of the rightness (yea, even righteousness) and truthfulness of one's own position. The intensity of a minority's beliefs and the accompanying eagerness to persuade others to accept its views is bolstered by the psychological reinforcement derived from group membership and by militancy and hostility towards the outgroup majority (Brewer, 1979). Another contribution of group membership is its effect on the majority's perceptions about a given behaviour. When perceived as representing a larger group, an action may be taken more seriously by the majority. The alacrity with which a self-designated 'leader' or 'spokesman' attempts to present his own position as being that of a 'group' (though it may be only a paper organisation) is an example of the use of this tactic. The effect of a person's actions being seen as representing a group was investigated by Blake & Mouton (1962), among others.

In addition to the psychological aspects of group membership, there are also the advantages of all the organisational apparatus being available to promote one's position. If the lone voice crying in the wilderness has at his disposal a competent cadre of speech-writers, a pollster, a public relations agent and press secretary, advance men, emissaries to the majority group, and a hierarchical structure capable of effectively implementing his every desire – in short, if he has all the elements of an organisation – it is very likely that this particular lone voice in the wilderness will soon be joined by a significant number of converts to his cause. Perhaps, then, instead of talking about 'minority group' influence, we should talk about 'minority group' influence – shifting the point of emphasis in research and theory to the group level. (I shall return to this issue in more detail in a later section.)

In summary, in this first section I have tried to place minority group influence in a more general social context in order to point out that a set of tacit assumptions seems to exist which affects, in part, the type of questions asked and the type of research designed to answer these questions. Do not misunderstand the present argument by concluding that my concern is with the problem of the representativeness or the ecological validity of experimental laboratory research in minority influence. That is not the point of the discussion at all; rather, my aim has been to suggest that in this research area, as in others, we often unwittingly impose blinders upon ourselves by accepting implicit assumptions and presuppositions.

2. Levels of construing the social environment

The basic thrust of my comments in this second section is to urge a re-appraisal of the role of the individual in social interaction: that more emphasis be given to the individual's active contribution to the phenomenal structuring of the social situation. From this perspective we can derive a number of implications that may be useful in helping us to understand social influence in general and minority influence in particular. It is obvious, of course, that most social behaviour is potentially ambiguous much of the time, in the sense that it is susceptible to many different meanings which are equally plausible and acceptable. To a very large extent the meaning of a social act depends upon the way it is perceived, defined, interpreted or structured. Perhaps George Kelly's (1955) term 'construed' is the most appropriate word to express this idea, since it captures nicely the essence of the process by focusing attention on the active contribution of the individual to the process of assigning meaning to an action. In this way is a behavioural response transformed into social conduct.

A behavioural response is amenable to being construed by an individual along one of several possible dimensions. For present purposes the size or level of the phenomenal unit of analysis will be the focus of discussion. After a brief presentation of a suggested scheme of organisation for units of analysis, I will illustrate the behavioural consequences that may stem from an individual's construing a standard episode of behaviour at different levels of analysis. Then some speculations will be offered concerning the determinants of construing a sequence of behaviour at different levels of organisation.

In a number of scientific disciplines the notion of different conceptual levels is a well-known and widely accepted point of view. The fields of physics and chemistry have employed very effectively the concept of levels for processes and for manifestations of phenomena. Perhaps closer to the concerns of psychologists is the use of the concept of levels in the field of biology, which resembles psychology in that both deal with processes associated with living organisms; many obvious parallels can be seen in the problems faced by biologists and psychologists. For purposes of illustration, consider the levels of organisation in biology proposed by R. W. Gerard (1958). Starting with the smallest unit and progressing to the largest, he has suggested the following levels of organisation of biological phenomena: (1) molecule, (2) organelle, (3) cell, (4) organ, (5) individual, (6) small group (band), (7) species, (8) community (eco-system, and (9) total biota. With little effort it is possible to assign to these levels analogous behavioural units from the field of psychology. Each of the levels of organisation is considered to have equal epistemological status; each is as 'true' or 'correct' as the others. Since any system of levels of organisation is a product of one's conceptual process, it is easy to shift among different levels of organisation depending upon a number of factors.

In the case of behaviour (as with biological phenomena) a person can readily construe any given act within a hierarchy which ranges from large to small (or coarse to fine) levels of organisation. Implications of the concept of 'levels of organisation' in social behaviour have been discussed by Schneirla (1953) with particular reference to the utility of the concept for integrating existing data concerning the collective behaviour of subhuman organisms. Tolman's (1932) discussion of the importance of the molar–molecular distinction in behaviour can be accepted as being consistent with the present approach, if it is understood that the terms refer to a continuum rather than to a dichotomy.

In short, it is possible for an individual to construe any ongoing social behaviour at any one of several different levels of organisation or analysis. One scheme that I suggest for social behaviour is represented in figure 1. At a given point in time, any ongoing behavioural act may be construed from the perspective of any level within the hierarchical structure encompassed by this broad molar–molecular continuum. Other levels of units could have been added to this scheme or some of these could have been omitted; the precise number and nature of different levels that are necessary and useful in discussing social behaviour remains uncertain.[2] But for purposes of discussion the different levels of organisation described in figure 1 seem to be ones which are worthwhile, since they have the potential for producing differential consequences in behaviour.

In the present section we shall discuss the implications of construing social behaviour at different levels of analysis, with attention being directed primarily to the topic of this chapter. In the three sub-sections to follow, suggestions and interpretation of results will be offered which illustrate the impact of the level of construal on perception and behaviour in the area of minority influence.

For purposes of simplification, the nine levels of organisation depicted in figure 1 will be coalesced into three categories that demarcate the most important distinctions that seem to be worthwhile in the discussion of social influence: infra-group, intra-group and inter-group. The meanings of these three broad categories of levels of organisation are self-evident from the terminology I have employed.

By infra-group, I refer to actions or psychological processes taking place below the level of membership group – at the levels of an aggregate of entities (for example, four persons standing together in an elevator) but not constituting

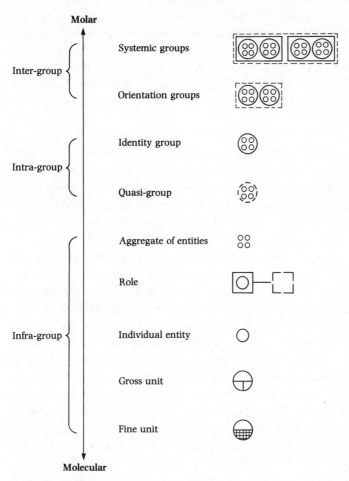

$\circ$ = person

Figure 1. Levels of construal of social behaviour.

a psychological group; a single individual in an individual-situation nexus (i.e. social role); and minute responses or psychological processes occurring within a single individual but short of representing the individual as a goal-directed totality.

By the category called intra-group I mean to include all the psychological phenomena occurring at the level of the psychological group, which is represented by two degrees of 'groupness' in figure 1: the psychological group (bounded entity) and the near-group or quasi-group. The quasi-group contains some of the characteristics of the psychological group but it does not play a central role in the individual's social identity.

The third category I have labelled the inter-group level, which combines two types of inter-group structure, the simple ingroup/outgroup arrangement based on the criterion of categorisation along a single dimension (e.g. Tajfel's minimal group categorisation paradigm) and a more complex ingroup/ outgroup structure in which a group may be based on two or more ascriptive or achieved criteria in the broader society (for example, race and religion, or race, sex and attitude).

2.1. Infra-group. Before discussing minority influence directly in this sub-section, it may be useful first to provide some empirical information to support the general thesis that construal of the social environment at different levels does have important effects on behaviour – even when the two different units of organisation are both contained within the larger 'infra-group' category being discussed here.

Consider the contrast between the two most molecular levels presented in figure 1, those labelled 'fine unit' and 'gross unit'. Data from a doctoral dissertation by one of my former students provides some interesting information about the effects of construing behaviour at these levels (Newtson, 1973). It was predicted that subjects who were instructed to segment an ongoing sequence of motoric behaviour into fine units (as opposed to gross units) would be more confident in their impressions and would form a more differentiated impression about the target person. It was also predicted that construing the behaviour at the fine-unit level would lead to stronger dispositional attributions. The rationale for these predictions was that construing behaviour at a fine-unit level generates a greater quantity of information – that is, it eliminates more uncertainty – than construing the behaviour at a gross unit level of analysis. Results supported the hypotheses. With regard to social influence, these results suggest that when one construes behaviour at the fine-grained (as opposed to the gross) level the initial influence tendency will be strengthened. That is, if the influence source possesses positive characteristics, the result will be greater confidence about one's impressions, greater differentiation of the impressions, and a stronger dispositional attribution – all of which should serve to enhance the effectiveness of any influence attempt. The opposite relation between fine-unit analysis and attempted influence should be found, however, if the influence source possesses negative characteristics.

In another study we used non-verbal responses of children as stimuli to investigate the effect of the level of phenomenal analysis on an observer's judgments about the nature of the behaviour, i.e., whether it was perceived as spontaneous *versus* deliberate or role-played (Allen & Atkinson, 1981). It was predicted that subjects who were instructed to employ a fine-grained level of analysis would be more likely than global-unit observers to believe that the behaviour was deliberate (role-played). Results again supported the predictions. In terms of implications for social influence, these findings suggest that construing ongoing behaviour at the fine-unit (*versus* the gross) level will result in interpreting it as being less spontaneous (more deliberate); hence, influence attempts should be less effective.

Returning to a point that was alluded to briefly in the first section, I suggested there that the explanatory processes offered in minority influence research were located primarily at the infra-group level. The explanation states that by consistently endorsing the same position the minority creates cognitive conflict in the majority. The consistent minority is perceived as being confident and committed, and as a trustworthy source of information. The minority is, moreover, the focus of the majority's attention – the source of conflict – and cannot be ignored by members of the majority. The change in the majority members is mediated by an attempt (not necessarily intentional) to come to grips with the cognitive conflict created by the consistent minority. Evidence suggests that 'latent' change (shift in cognitive coding) may be even greater than overt behavioural change (Moscovici, Lage & Naffrechoux, 1969). Be that as it may, the explanatory mechanism is based on the process of resolving cognitive conflict, which does not involve social or interaction processes at all. Perhaps in laboratory experiments the subject does conceive of the situation as being essentially at the non-social (infra-group) level; as such, the consistent responses presented by the minority constitute basically a cognitive instead of a social problem. The same conflict process could also have been activated by introducing conflicting information from a totally non-social source. The degree to which the situation is viewed as primarily a problem-solving task (with little or no social or interpersonal involvement) will depend upon many factors in the experimental situation, such as instructions, task, prior acquaintance of subjects, expectations about future interaction, etc. Take one of these factors, the nature of the task. Construal at the infra-group level will be more likely with some tasks than with others (for example, with colour-naming tasks rather than jury deliberations). If the social situation is construed as being at the infra-group level it is more likely that the resolution of cognitive conflict will be an important explanatory process accounting for change in the majority members. But we can also expect that other potential explanatory processes based on social instead of cognitive factors will come into play when individuals in the situation are construed as a group instead of as a set of separate individuals (i.e. as an aggregate of entities). Consistent with this interpretation, a study conducted by Wolf (1979) found that the minority exerted less influence on the majority in a low-cohesive condition (which approximates to what I have called 'aggregate of entities') than in a high-cohesive ('group') condition. In this experiment the effectiveness of the minority seems to have been due primarily to the creation of a social conflict – a threat to interpersonal relations – within the group rather than to cognitive conflict; and the majority members resolved the conflict by moving towards the deviant.

2.2. Intra-group. Now we examine a second category of levels depicted in figure 1 which has important implications for social influence: the group level. Four persons who are in close proximity to each other may constitute a simple aggregation of individuals who have congregated for no other reason than their exposure to a common stimulus (for example, all are waiting for a bus); no psychological relationship whatsoever exists among them. By contrast, four persons who constitute a psychological group are interdependent, have common beliefs or values and share a common fate. An observer may construe any given set of entities (for example, four persons) at the level of the individual (an aggregate of four separate entities) or at the level of the group.

A series of studies reported in a doctoral dissertation by another former student of mine explored the consequences of a person's construing behaviour at the level of the individual or the group (Wilder, 1977). In one experiment it was hypothesised that: (a) an aggregate of individuals (multiple entities) would exert more influence than a single group composed of the same number of persons; and (b) that with a constant number of persons the amount of influence would increase as they were categorised into a larger number of groups. Results supported the hypotheses. It should be noted that informational rather than normative influence was primarily operative in this experiment. Results might be different in a strongly normative situation.

Given a majority–minority division between individuals in a face-to-face setting, it would be quite natural in some circumstances to construe this situation at the single-group level. After all, subjects in an experiment usually share many common characteristics – they are similar in age, education, and other background characteristics (and same-sex subjects are often used). In short, their overt commonalities seem greater than their differences, leading to a construal of the situation at the single-group level. What happens when a minority consistently disagrees with the other group members, creating a potential for construal at the level of inter-group or infra-group/intra-group? Even under these circumstances the individual may persist in the group-level construal, seeing the minority as troublesome deviants from the other members but still as being part of the group.

Construing the minority at the single-group level suggests some means by which influence may be exerted on the majority members. Some evidence suggests that recall of information is better when it refers to a group than to a person (Wyer & Gordon, 1982). Also, since the situation is construed at the single-group level, maintenance of good interpersonal relations among the group members is more important than at the aggregate or inter-group level. The majority members might, therefore, compromise by shifting towards the minority's position in the spirit of maintaining group harmony. This interpretation can account for Wolf's (1979) finding that group members moved more towards the deviant in cohesive than in non-cohesive groups. Finally, if the minority members are within the boundary of a single group, their views must be given very serious consideration by the majority members because they are appropriate sources for social comparison.

Is it possible or likely that a majority–minority encounter will be construed at the (single) group level in 'real life'? The answer to this question is clearly affirmative; ample evidence can be seen in contemporary society and history. Where are the minorities of yesteryear? Admittedly, some of them through their success have become indistinguishable from the majority. But often an organisation or society deals with a minority by co-opting it; one way to accomplish this end is to construe the majority and minority at the (single) group level. While admitting, perhaps, that some difference in point of view exists, one single group is seen as encompassing both the majority and the minority ('a family may have its differences but it is still a family' expresses this view). In effect, by construing the minority at the single-group level, it is denied the status of a separate entity. Whether the minority will have more or less effect on other (majority) members when construed as deviants within a single group rather than as a separate group, depends upon many factors which cannot be discussed here. Attempted accommodation by the majority may eventually result in true change occurring; but being construed as part of a group also places pressure on minority members to contribute to smooth social relations within the group. On the other hand, a psychological boundary can be drawn around the 'deviants' in the group, who are then labelled, ignored, or merely tolerated. Organisations do create such 'enclaves' in order to neutralise the effectiveness of deviants who disagree with the majority but who, nevertheless, are still construed as members of the group.

Before moving on to the group-to-group orientation, that is, to the levels in the category that I have designated as 'inter-group', let us pause for a moment to consider the interesting situation that cuts across the infra-group and intra-group categories and thus qualifies as a quasi-inter-group situation. I refer to the asynchrony in the construed level of majority and minority members: one is seen as being a group and the other as a non-group (aggregate). What is likely to be the majority members' level of construal in this situation? Since this is a task-oriented situation, it might be construed initially at the level of an aggregate (separate individuals). As the trials progress, however, a change in the structure becomes obvious due to the minority members consistently agreeing with each other. As the focal point of the situation, the consistent minority soon is construed at the group level while the aggregate level of construal is maintained for the majority members. In any event, this is the simplest transformation that can be effected (changing one of the two, now distinct, elements). The behaviour of some majority members will also help contribute to this type of construal of the situation. On some occasions one (or more) of the majority members will give a response that agrees with the minority. This lack of unanimity among them is likely to contribute to construing the majority at the aggregate (non-group) level, thus creating a condition of an aggregate (individuals in the majority) opposed by a group (the minority). Holding constant the level of the minority (group level), more influence on the majority would be expected when they are construed at the aggregate rather than at the group level. Social support is more uncertain when the majority is construed at the aggregate rather than at the group level; the aggregate situation resembles the conditions of uncertain social support in the desertion condition in conformity research. Group influence is more effective when a social supporter deserts the subject (Allen, 1975). Consistent with this finding are results of a study by Hawkins (1960) using a simulated jury situation. When juries were divided, the side that first lost a member to the opposition never won the final decision (regardless of whether it was initially a majority or minority). We can speculate that lack of uniformity among majority members may be seen as the beginning of an evolution or drift towards the opposition (bandwagon effect), which would also contribute to construing the majority at the aggregate rather than the group level.

The asynchrony of the construal of the majority and the minority (majority as aggregate and minority as group) has a complementary side: construing the majority at the group level and the minority at the aggregate level. When might this occur? When minority members are inconsistent they are more likely to be construed at the aggregate level. In one study the minority agreed only 75 per cent of the time, and they did not influence the majority (Moscovici, Lage & Naffrechoux, 1969). In real-life situations asynchronous construal of levels (of both types) is probably very common; it is a device the majority members can use to discount the validity of the minority. By construing themselves as a group and the minority as an aggregate, majority members can experience social support and solidarity while at the same time

Table 1. *Levels of construal of the majority and minority by their members*

Construal by minority members	Construal by majority members			
	Of the majority		Of the minority	
	Aggregate	Group	Aggregate	Group
Aggregate	1	3	5	7
Group	2	4	6	8

downgrading the minority claim to legitimacy by denying them the status of groupness (they're only 'rabble rousers' or 'a few outsiders').

In accord with my admonition in the first section to devote attention to the minority as well as the majority, it should be explicitly acknowledged that the two asynchronous levels described above should be examined also from the point of view of minority group members (the discussion above took the point of view of majority members). Taking these two perspectives together, interesting possibilities exist for congruence or incongruence in the construals of majority and minority members. A discrepancy between construals of majority and minority members will affect social influence only if one or both sides is aware of the discrepancy. During attempted influence by the minority in everyday life it is likely that communication concerning each side's level of construal will be conveyed to the other. Such discrepant information could affect individuals' reactions, for example, by increasing commitment to one's own level of construal of the situation. The possible patterns of congruence and incongruence for construal across levels is shown in table 1. Agreement between the majority and minority members in cross-level (asynchronous) construal is represented by cells 1 and 8 and cells 4 and 5.

2.3. Inter-group. In real-life instances of minority influence (and also in the experimental paradigm) the situation may very well be construed at the inter-group level. Do individuals tend to construe the minority influence situation at the inter-group level? Before speculating about this possibility, a short tangent will be taken to present some relevant data and speculative analysis in a closely related problem – social support in the conformity situation. Then I shall return to the issue of minority influence. Notice that a strong homology exists between the social support and minority influence situation, in that both involve a confrontation between a majority and a minority.

When the subject in a conformity situation gains a partner the situation can be construed quite differently from before. Rather than there being a discrepancy between the phenomenal level of the opposition and of the subject (group *versus* individual level), the presence of a partner may transform the situation into two equal levels – group *versus* group. Then the subject can face the larger group on a level of psychological equality, as it were – as a member of one group which is opposed by another group. The disparity in size of the two groups (that the subject and partner are only a minority in relation to the majority group) is not a critical factor in the process of the individuals' construal of themselves as a group.

Interestingly, by symbolically evoking other persons as supporters *vis-à-vis* the majority the subject's cognitive structure of the situation undergoes a dramatic change. Rather than a situation in which a group majority opposes a single individual, it is now seen as a group *versus* group situation. In Israel's (1963) experiment several subjects reported that they had invoked non-present supporters. Thus, one subject who resisted conformity pressure stated that she had thought of how her parents wanted her to answer. Another subject said she tried to imagine how her best friends would answer in such a situation. We have shown experimentally that an absentee partner can reduce conformity under certain conditions (Allen & Wilder, 1979).

Do subjects in the conformity experiment actually construe the situation as structured in terms of two opposing groups when a social supporter is present? Indirect evidence suggests a positive answer to this question. Gerard & Hoyt (1974) showed that the smaller the size of the ingroup, the more favourable the evaluation that was given to ingroup members. Inspection of their data indicates that subjects in an ingroup of only two persons evaluated the other ingroup member very positively (relative to an outgroup member), whereas subjects in larger groups (five and eight members) did not show as much favouritism towards another ingroup member. We have consistently found in our research that subjects express very positive affect towards the social supporter. In a recent experiment subjects awarded points to other persons by using the Tajfel matrix (Allen & Sobel, 1979). Subjects who received social support gave their partner significantly more points than subjects in the unanimous-group condition gave to another group member. This result is consistent with findings from studies that have explicitly created a clear ingroup/outgroup situation.

We have attempted an even more direct examination of the subject's construal of the social support situation in another study (Allen & Sobel, 1980). Four experimental conditions were created: no group pressure, conformity pressure, social support, and disagreement among majority members. Subjects received diagrams representing a large number of possible construals of the situation. In the social support condition two-thirds of the subjects designated two of the members as comprising a unit, as compared to only eight per cent in the conformity condition. As crude as this measure is, it suggests that in the presence of a social supporter the subject tends to construe his own behaviour at the group level rather than the individual level – thereby rendering the situation one of group *versus* group rather than group *versus* two individuals.

As mentioned earlier, the social support condition is the obverse of the minority influence paradigm. In minority influence the majority group members are naive subjects who face a smaller though consistent group – the opposite of the social support procedure. In the discussion above it was hypothesised that a subject in a minority position may be likely to construe the situation at the inter-group level. It can be suggested that the majority members in the minority influence condition also construe the situation at the inter-group level. The behavioural consistency displayed by the minority probably plays a critical role in strengthening the majority's construal of the 'groupness' of the minority.

When the minority influence situation is construed at the inter-group level it is reasonable to expect that extant theories and findings from inter-group research in general should also be applicable to this special case. One of the well-known findings in inter-group research is ingroup favouritism at the expense of the outgroup. Ethnocentrism presumably leads to the expression of hostility and to the attribution of negative characteristics towards outgroup members (and a corresponding positive reaction towards ingroup members). Research has shown that mere categorisation of persons into two groups on the basis of a trivial criterion is sufficient to produce discriminatory behaviour towards the outgroup (Tajfel, 1978).

Applying inter-group theory to minority influence seems to imply that neither the majority nor the minority would be able successfully to influence the other, since an influence attempt by one group would result in distortion and resistance by the other group. But a closer look at inter-group research suggests that the typical picture is not entirely accurate. Data from studies of ingroup favouritism (or outgroup discrimination) suggests that two social norms are operating in the experimental situation (and presumably in real life as well): that is, the norm of discrimination against the outgroup and the norm of fairness. Behaviour in the experimental situation seems to be a compromise between these two norms. According to some research the fairness norm exerts an equal, if not greater, effect on behaviour than the discrimination norm (Branthwaite & Jones, 1975; Branthwaite, Doyle & Lightbrown, 1979). More relevant to minority influence is the finding that the norm of fairness is stronger in less cohesive groups and in groups having superior status (Branthwaite, Doyle & Lightbrown, 1979). (Or to state it another way, stronger discrimination is shown by the self-perceived underdog.)

These conditions seem to hold in minority influence experiments when the situation is construed at the inter-group level. As noted earlier, larger groups are less cohesive than smaller ones; and larger size is probably associated with higher status. These conditions should facilitate fairness by the majority towards the minority, as expressed by being objective, receptive to opposing views and accommodating to the minority's (consistently expressed) point of view. Under these conditions influence by the minority would be predicted. In real-life cases the greater status of the majority may lead to deliberate fairness – a *noblesse oblige* attitude towards the minority outgroup – that could lead to change by the majority members.

The general conclusion stated about the ethnocentrism of ingroup/outgroup evaluations is not in complete agreement with empirical results. True, results of most studies show greater attraction and more positive evaluations of ingroup than of outgroup members. At the same time, the degree of ingroup bias is not as strong for measures of respect or perceived achievement as for evaluation (Brewer, 1979). In other words, the congruence is not strong between the two components of 'friendship' and 'respect' in inter-group attitudes. Thus, an outgroup may be disliked and at the same time (perhaps grudgingly) still respected. Applied to minority influence, consistent behaviour may lead to respect for the minority even if the inter-group level of construal produces an evaluative bias against the outgroup. Hence, successful minority influence is not dependent upon the majority (ingroup) expressing positive evaluative reactions towards the minority (outgroup).

In the discussion above I have referred primarily to one of the two levels in the inter-group category, namely, 'orientation groups'. Basically, I have had in mind the simplest type of inter-group situation, one in which two groups are differentiated on a single dimension. Inter-group relations are often more complicated than this, however, and at a higher or systemic level groups may be differentiated along several relevant dimensions. A couple of examples will be given with reference to minority influence.

In most experimental research on minority influence the majority and minority differ on a single dimension such as attitude or some other response. Employing a more complex set of criteria for groupness, a recent study by Maas, Clark & Haberkorn (1982) created a minority group that differed from the majority not only on belief but also on another (ascribed) characteristic (i.e. gender). Results showed that such minorities were less effective, primarily because they were perceived as having a self-interest in the issue (females were supporting a pro-abortion position). Minority groups formed on the basis of multiple criteria need not always be perceived as having a self-interest in a position, so these results should not be generalised. Yet the more complex the bases of the minority's groupness, the easier it is for the majority to attribute ulterior motives for any position whatsoever, thus rendering the minority less acceptable as a social comparison source.

Another aspect of what I have called the systemic level of inter-group relations deals with larger societal norms. How is the minority's position seen in relation to the existing and evolving norms in society, and hence in relation to a potentially broader or new alignment for all groups concerned? In a study relevant to this question, Paicheler (1979) found that minority influence was greater when the norm relevant to the issue was shifting towards the position advocated by the minority. Influence by the minority in this case might be interpreted as anticipatory conformity to a soon-to-be majority position, which has been observed in other contexts (Saltzstein & Sandberg, 1979). In view of the present-day rate of social change and innovation, anticipatory conformity is not an unlikely reaction to a consistent minority. Given the tendency for persons to overestimate the amount of social support from others for their position (Goethals, Allison & Frost, 1979), consistent and sustained advocacy of a position by a minority might elicit the belief that the majority norm is beginning to change.

3. Determinants of the level of construal

Sufficient evidence has been provided, I hope, to support the assertion that the construing of social behaviour at different phenomenal levels of organisation has important consequences. Not all the levels of organisation represented in figure 1 have been discussed; but the three levels that were discussed (infra-group, intra-group and inter-group) appear to have important implications for research on social influence.

Even if the arguments advanced so far are accepted, a very important question still remains: what determines the level at which an individual construes the social environment? Only a few tentative speculations will be offered with regard to this question. In the most general terms, there seems to be a tendency for persons to use a more molecular level of analysis under conditions of high uncertainty. By construing the social environment at a more molecular level one obtains a greater amount of information which can be employed in an attempt to reduce the degree of uncertainty. An unexpected or non-normative or unusual event (perhaps a special case of uncertainty) increases the level of uncertainty in a situation and, therefore, will stimulate a search for more information. By shifting to a more molecular level an individual can obtain a greater amount of information. A study by Newtson (1973) found that a person shifts to a finer-grained level of unitisation of an ongoing stream of behaviour after an unexpected event occurs.

The presence of certain types of cues will increase the probability that individuals will be construed as a group rather than as an aggregate of persons. To start at the most basic level, the *gestalt* principles which contribute to the organisation of physical objects are also applicable to social stimuli, that is, factors such as proximity, similarity, common fate and *prägnanz*. Campbell (1958) has argued that all groups possess boundaries that separate members from non-members, and that these boundaries are created by a process of cognitive organisation of other persons in a way analogous to the organisation of physical objects. In the case of social influence (and especially in experimental studies), similarity of attitude is usually the most salient and relevant dimension available for use in construing individuals as being a group or an aggregate.

We have conducted a simple study to examine the perception of group membership as a function of distance between the attitude of the majority and of one of two other individuals (Safran & Allen, 1978). Results showed an interaction between number of deviates (one person *versus* two) and distance of the deviant position from the majority. At distances near the majority, two individuals were more strongly perceived as being members of the group than was a single individual; but the opposite was found for far distances between the deviant and the majority. Similarity of attitude is not always sufficient, however, to induce a person to construe behaviour at the group level if the attitudinal similarity conflicts with other important personal characteristics central to social identity. For example, we found that a prejudiced white subject tended to move away from his true attitudinal position rather than accept the groupness implied by the expression of agreement with a black social supporter (Boyanowsky & Allen, 1973).

Research on the determinants of the individual's level of construal of social behaviour deserves our careful attention. We need to understand better the internal and external conditions and momentary cues that evoke a shift in the individual's ongoing level of organisation of social behaviour. As stated earlier, we should recognise that individuals are constantly engaged in an active process of construing social behaviour, and this means that different phenomenal levels of organisation form the context for judgments, perceptions, and responses in social situations. Hence, it should be emphasised once again that the individual is not merely a passive recipient of a constant flux of objective stimuli that are invariant in their meaning.

A strong emphasis has been placed throughout this discussion on the proposition that the individual plays an active role in organising and structuring the social environment by the process of construing it as falling at some point along a hierarchy of organisation. It should go without saying, however, that a person will employ all the cues available in the environment during this process. Moreover, there are some instances in which the cues are so clear-cut and compelling that the individual will have little option but to construe the situation at one particular level instead of others. In other words, the extent of the equivocality of a situation will determine the degree of constraint on the individual's viable options during the construal process.

4. Conclusions

Having explored some of the implications of the idea of levels of construing social behaviour, I hope that the potential usefulness of this perspective for research and theory in social influence (and for minority influence) will have become apparent. Not all the possibilities touched upon could be discussed in any detail, of course, nor could straightforward predictions always be made. Only a cursory and unsystematic attempt has been made to discuss the specific processes underlying the impact of the minority. Instead, the goal throughout has been to direct attention to the structural features of the minority influence situation and the implications that this perspective has for better understanding of this problem.

One important implication of the present theoretical perspective is that different mechanisms may be responsible for any social influence produced by the minority, depending upon the individual's construal of the level of organisation of the majority–minority interaction. (Less strongly stated, the relative contribution of different mechanisms to social influence may depend upon the level of construal of the situation.) For example, at the infra-group level the resolution of cognitive conflict may play an especially important role; at the intra-group level social accommodation may be more important; and at the inter-group level perceptual distortion may make a significant contribution.

Several other general points deserve to be mentioned briefly. First, the level of construal employed by the majority and minority members should be assessed for both, since agreement will not always exist between them. Second, the level of construal adopted by an individual will not always be strong and stable. Shifting back and forth across levels is entirely likely in many cases, with one level sometimes being held only tentatively and uncertainly. Third, persons differ in their level of construing a standard social episode due not only to dispositional or personality factors but also to differences in degree of sensitivity and attentiveness to cues that contribute to level of construal. Hence, individuals may differ strongly in the way they construe a standard sequence of social interaction.

In this chapter I have speculated shamelessly about several different facets of minority influence and have meandered across several plots of the social influence landscape; but since this is what I promised to do at the outset, at the very least I can claim the virtue (if not the efficacy) of displaying a high degree of consistency. It is abundantly clear that more questions have been raised in this chapter than have been answered (perhaps more than deserve to be answered); even so, I hope that the discussion will stimulate us to examine closely once more some of the problems connected with the important area of social influence. After all, the word research means 'to look *again*' at a problem – and by doing so perhaps we shall see it more clearly than before.

Notes

1. This article was written while the author was a Fellow at the Netherlands Institute for Advanced Study in the Social Sciences and Humanities, Wassenaar, Netherlands.

2. It is entirely coincidental that figure 1 contains the same number of levels (nine) that Gerard (1958) presented for biological phenomena. I did not attempt to create an analogue to the biological levels, but instead have proposed a scheme that seems to be useful for the analysis of social behaviour.

References

Allen V. L. Situational factors in conformity. In L. Berkowitz (ed.) *Advances in experimental social psychology*, vol. 2. New York: Academic Press, 1965.
—— Social support for nonconformity. In L. Berkowitz (ed.) *Advances in experimental social psychology*, vol. 8. New York: Academic Press, 1975.
Allen, V. L. & Atkinson, M. L. Detection and perception of deception: the role of level of analysis of nonverbal behavior. *Annals of New York Academy of Sciences*, 1981, *364*, 279–91.
Allen, V. L. & Sobel, S. Affective reactions to a social supporter. Unpublished MS. Madison, Wisc.: University of Wisconsin, 1979.
—— The perception of social units in a group setting. Unpublished MS. Madison, Wisc.: University of Wisconsin, 1980.
Allen, V. L. & Wilder, D. A. Perceived persuasiveness as a function of response style: multi-issue consistency over time. *European Journal of Social Psychology*, 1978, *8*, 289–96.
—— Social support in absentia: the effect of an absentee partner on conformity. *Human Relations*, 1979, *32*, 103–11.
Allport, F. H. *Social psychology*. Cambridge, Mass.: Riverside Press, 1924.
Allyn, J. & Festinger, L. The effectiveness of unanticipated persuasive communications. *Journal of Abnormal and Social Psychology*, 1961, *62*, 35–40.
Altman, I., Vinsel, A. & Brown, B. B. Dialectic conceptions in social psychology: an application to social penetration and privacy regulation. In L. Berkowitz (ed.) *Advances in experimental social psychology*, vol. 14. New York: Academic Press, 1981.
Alvarez, R. Informal reactions to deviance in simulated work organizations: a laboratory experiment. *American Sociological Review*, 1968, *33*, 895–912.
Arnold, D. W. & Greenberg, C. I. Deviate rejection within differentially manned groups. *Social Psychology Quarterly*, 1980, *43*, 419–24.
Asch, S. E. Effects of group pressure on the modification and distortion of judgments. In H. Guetzkow (ed.) *Groups, leadership and men*. Pittsburgh: Carnegie, 1951.
—— *Social psychology*. Englewood Cliffs, NJ: Prentice-Hall, 1952.
—— Studies of independence and conformity. A minority of one against a unanimous majority. *Psychological Monographs*, 1956, *70*, No 9.
Back, K. Influence through social communication. *Journal of Abnormal and Social Psychology*, 1951, *46*, 9–23.
Bahro, R. *Je continuerai mon chemin*. Paris: Editions Stock, 1979.

Bateson, N. Familiarization, group discussion, and risk-taking. *Journal of Experimental Social Psychology*, 1966, *2*, 119–29.

Becker, H. S. Outsiders: studies in the sociology of deviance. New York: The Free Press, 1963.

―――― Personal changes in adult life. *Sociometry*, 1964, *27*, 40–53.

Becker, H. S., Geer, B., Hughes, E. C. & Strauss, A. L. *Boys in white: student culture in medical school*. Chicago: University of Chicago Press, 1961.

Berscheid, E. Opinion change and communicator–communicatee similarity and dissimilarity. *Journal of Personality and Social Psychology*, 1966, *4*, 670–80.

Birenbaum, A. & Sagarin, E. *Norms and human behavior*. New York: Praeger, 1976.

Blake, R. R. & Mouton, J. S. Over-evaluation of own group's product in inter-group competition. *Journal of Abnormal and Social Psychology*, 1962, *64*, 237–8.

Boyanowsky, E. O. & Allen, V. L. Ingroup norms and self-identity as determinants of discriminatory behavior. *Journal of Personality and Social Psychology*, 1973, *25*, 408–18.

Branthwaite, A., Doyle, S. & Lightbrown, N. The balance between fairness and discrimination. *European Journal of Social Psychology*, 1979, *9*, 149–63.

Branthwaite, A. & Jones, F. E. Fairness and discrimination: English v. Welsh. *European Journal of Social Psychology*, 1975, *5*, 323–38.

Bray, R. M., Johnson, D. & Chilstrom, J. T. Social influence by group members with minority opinion: a comparison of Hollander and Moscovici. *Journal of Personality and Social Psychology*, 1982, *43*, 78–88.

Brehm, J. W. *A theory of psychological reactance*. New York: Academic Press, 1966.

Brehm, J. W. & Cohen, A. R. *Explorations in cognitive dissonance*. New York: Wiley, 1962.

Brehm, J. W. & Mann, M. Effects of importance of freedom and attraction of group members on influence produced by group pressure. *Journal of Personality and Social Psychology*, 1975, *31*, 816–24.

Brewer, M. The role of ethnocentrism in intergroup conflict. In W. G. Austin & S. Worchel (eds) *The social psychology of intergroup relations*. Monterey, Ca.: Brooks/Cole, 1979.

Buchanan, B. Building organizational commitment: the socialization of managers in work organization. *Administrative Science Quarterly*, 1974, *19*, 533–46.

Burgess, R. L. & Huston, T. L. (eds). *Social exchange in developing relationships*. New York: Academic Press, 1979.

Byrne, D., Ervin, C. & Tamberth, J. Continuity between the experimental study of attraction and real-life computer dating. *Journal of Personality and Social Psychology*, 1970, *16*, 157–65.

Byrne, D. & Rhamey, R. Magnitude of positive and negative reinforcements as determinants of attraction. *Journal of Personality and Social Psychology*, 1965, *2*, 884–9.

Campbell, D. T. Common fate, similarity, and other indices of the status of aggregates of persons as social entities. *Behavioral Sciences*, 1958, *3*, 14–25.

Charters, W. W. Jr. & Newcomb, T. M. Some attitudinal effects of experimentally increased salience of a membership group. In E. E. Maccoby, T. M. Newcomb & E. L. Hartley (eds) *Readings in social psychology* (3rd edn). New York: Holt, Rinehart & Winston, 1958.

Cialdini, R. P., Levy, A., Herman, P., Kozlowski, L. & Petty, R. E. Elastic shifts of opinion: determinants of direction and durability. *Journal of Personality and Social Psychology*, 1976, *34*, 663–72.

Cialdini, R. B. & Richardson, K. D. Two indirect tactics of image management: basking and blasting. *Journal of Personality and Social Psychology*, 1980, *39*, 406–15.

Coch, L. & French, J. R. P. Jr. Overcoming resistance to change. In E. E. Maccoby, T. M. Newcomb & E. L. Hartley (eds) *Readings in social psychology* (3rd edn). New York: Holt, Rinehart & Winston, 1958.

Cohen, A. R., Brehm, J. W. & Latané, B. Choice of strategy and voluntary exposure to information under public and private conditions. *Journal of Personality*, 1959, *27*, 410–22.

Coser, L. *The functions of social conflict*. New York: Free Press, 1956.

—— Some functions of deviant behavior and normative flexibility. *American Journal of Sociology*, 1962, *68*, 172–81.

Darley, J. M. & Cooper, J. The 'clean for Gene' phenomenon: the effects of students' appearance on political campaigning. *Journal of Applied Psychology*, 1972, *2*, 24–33.

Davis, D. & Latané, B. Minority vs. majority influence and impression formation. Unpublished MS, 1974.

De Alarcon, R. The spread of heroin abuse in a community. *Bulletin of Narcotics*, 1969, *21*, 17–22.

Deconchy, J.-P. *L'orthodoxie religieuse. Essai de logique psycho-sociale*. Paris: Editions Ouvrières, 1971.

—— *Orthodoxie religieuse et sciences humaines*. Suivi de: (*Religious*) *Orthodoxy, rationality and scientific knowledge*. La Haye, Paris, New York: Mouton Editeur, 1980.

Dentler, R. A. & Erikson, K. T. The functions of deviance in groups. *Social Problems*, 1959, *7*, 98–107.

Deschamps, J. C. *L'attribution et la catégorisation sociale*. Berne: Lang, 1977.

Deutsch, M. & Gerard, H. B. A study of normative and informational social influences upon individual judgment. *Journal of Abnormal and Social Psychology*, 1955, *51*, 629–36.

Doise, W. Levels of explanation in the *European Journal of Social Psychology*. *European Journal of Social Psychology*, 1980, *10*, 213–31.

Doise, W. & Moscovici, S. Approche et évitement du déviant dans des groupes de cohésion différente. *Bulletin de Psychologie*, 1969–70, *23*, 522–5.

Doms, M. The minority influence effect: an alternative approach. In W. Doise & S. Moscovici (eds) *Current issues in European social psychology*, vol. 1. Cambridge: Cambridge University Press, 1983.

Doms, M. & Van Avermaet, E. Majority influence, minority influence and conversion behavior: a replication. *Journal of Experimental Social Psychology*, 1980, *16*, 283–92.

Duck, S. A topography of relationship disengagement and dissolution. In S. Duck (ed.) *Personal relationships 4: Dissolving personal relationships*. London: Academic Press, 1982.

Duck, S. & Gilmour, R. (eds). *Personal relationships 2: Developing relationships*. London: Academic Press, 1981.

Durkheim, E. *Les règles de la méthode sociologique*. Paris: Alcan, 1895.

Evans, W. M. Peer group interaction and organizational socialization: a study of employee turnover. *American Sociological Review*, 1963, *28*, 436–40.

Evans, G. W. & Crumbaugh, C. M. Effects of prisoner's dilemma format on cooperative behavior. *Journal of Personality and Social Psychology*, 1966, *3*, 486–8.

Faucheux, C. & Moscovici, S. Le style de comportement d'une minorité et son influence sur les réponses d'une majorité. *Bulletin du CERP*, 1967, *16*, 337–60.

Favier, J. Préface. In M. Tillory, G. Audisio & J. Chiffoleau (eds) *Histoire et clandestinité du moyen-âge à la première guerre mondiale*. Albi: Revues du Vivarais. APOSJ, 1979.

Feldbaum, G. L., Christ...ison, T. E. & O'Neal, E. C. An observational study of the assimilation of the newcomer to the preschool. *Child Development*, 1980, *51*, 497–507.

Feldman, D. C. A contingency theory of socialization. *Administrative Science Quarterly*, 1976, *21*, 433–52.

Festinger, L. Informal social communication. *Psychological Review*, 1950, *57*, 217–82.

———— *A theory of cognitive dissonance*. Evanston, Ill.: Row, Peterson, 1957.

Festinger, L. & Maccoby, N. On resistance to persuasive communications. *Journal of Abnormal and Social Psychology*, 1964, *68*, 359–66.

Festinger, L., Schachter, S. & Back, K. *Social pressures in informal groups: a study of human factors in housing*. New York: Harper, 1950.

Fine, G. A. *The effect of a salient newcomer on a small group: a force field analysis*. Paper presented at the meeting of the American Psychological Association, Washington, DC, 1976.

Flanders, J. P. & Thistlethwaite, D. L. Effects of familiarization and group discussion upon risk-taking. *Journal of Personality and Social Psychology*, 1967, *5*, 91–7.

French, J. R. P. & Raven, B. H. The bases of social power. In D. Cartwright (ed.) *Studies in social power*. Ann Arbor: University of Michigan Press, 1959.

Freud, S. *Moïse et le monothéisme*. Paris: Gallimard, 1948. (Publication in French of his 1939 work.)

Gamson, W. A. A theory of coalition formation. *American Sociological Review*, 1961, *26*, 373–82.

———— Experimental studies in coalition formation. In L. Berkowitz (ed.) *Advances in experimental social psychology*, vol. 1. New York: Academic Press, 1964.

Gerard, H. B. The effect of different dimensions of disagreement on the communication process in small groups. *Human Relations*, 1953, *6*, 249–71.

———— Conformity and commitment to the group. *Journal of Abnormal and Social Psychology*, 1964, *68*, 209–11.

———— Deviation, conformity and commitment. In I. D. Steiner & M. Fishbein (eds) *Current studies in social psychology*. New York: Holt, Rinehart & Winston, 1965.

Gerard, H. B. & Folster, S. Social comparison and opinion polarization. Unpublished MS., 1982.

Gerard, H. B. & Hoyt, M. E. Distinctiveness of social categorization and attitude toward ingroup members. *Journal of Personality and Social Psychology*, 1974, *29*, 836–42.

Gerard, H. B., Jackson, T. D. & Conolley, E. S. Social contact in the desegregated classroom. In H. B. Gerard & N. Miller (eds) *School desegregation*. New York: Plenum, 1975.

Gerard, H. B. & Rotter, G. S. Time perspective, consistency of attitude, and social influence. *Journal of Abnormal and Social Psychology*, 1961, *62*, 565–72.

Gerard, H. B. & Wagner, W. Opinion importance, coorientation and social comparison. Unpublished MS., 1984.

Gerard, H. B., Wilhelmy, R. A. & Conolley, E. S. Conformity and group size. *Journal of Personality and Social Psychology*, 1968, *8*, 79–82.

Gerard, R. W. Concepts and principles of biology. *Behavioral Science*, 1958, *3*, 95–102.

Gingerich, O. L'affaire Galilée. *Pour la science*, 1982, *60*, 68–79. (French edition of *Scientific American*.)

Goethals, G. R., Allison, S. J. & Frost, M. Perceptions of the magnitude and diversity of social support. *Journal of Experimental Social Psychology*, 1979, *15*, 570–81.

Gordon, B. F. Influence and social comparison as motives for affiliation. *Journal of Experimental Social Psychology*, 1966, *1*, 55–65.

Gordon, M. E., Philpot, J. W., Burt, R. E., Thompson, C. A. & Spiller, W. E. Commitment to the union: development of a measure and an examination of its correlates. *Journal of Applied Psychology Monograph*, 1980, *65*, 479–99.

Griffitt, W. & Veitsch, R. Preacquaintance attitude similarity and attraction revisited: ten days in a fall-out shelter. *Sociometry*, 1974, *37*, 163–73.

Guillon, M. Influence sociale et 'conformisation' apparenté de l'agent d'influence. Unpublished MS., Nanterre: Université de Paris X, 1977.

—— Stratégies d'influence, traitement de l'information et changement d'attitude. (Doctoral thesis.) Lille (roneo). 1981.

—— Analyse de la dynamique des représentations de sujets cibles en situation d'influence sociale: propositions méthodologiques. Unpublished MS., Université de Lille III, 1982.

Guillon, M. & Personnaz, B. Analyse de la dynamique des représentations au cours d'une interaction d'influence avec une minorité et une majorité. *Cahiers de Psychologie Cognitive*, 1983, *3*.

Harvey, J. H., Ickes, W. H. & Kidd, R. F. (eds). *New directions in attribution research, vol. 1*. Hillsdale, NJ: Erlbaum, 1976.

Hawkins, C. Interaction and coalition realignment in consensus-seeking groups: a study of experimental jury deliberations. Doctoral dissertation, University of Chicago, 1960.

Heisenberg, W. *Across the Frontiers*. New York: Harper Torch Books, 1975.

Heiss, J. & Nash, D. The stranger in laboratory culture revisited. *Human Organization*, 1967, *26*, 47–51.

Hollander, E. P. Conformity, status, and idiosyncrasy credit. *Psychological Review*, 1958, *65*, 117–27.

—— Competence and conformity in the acceptance of influence. *Journal of Abnormal and Social Psychology*, 1960, *61*, 365–9.

—— *Leaders, groups and influence*. New York: Oxford, 1964.

Hollander, E. P. & Willis, R. H. Some current issues in the psychology of conformity and nonconformity. *Psychological Bulletin*, 1967, *68*, 62–76.

Homans, G. C. *Social behavior: its elementary forms* (rev. edn). New York: Harcourt, 1974.

Horai, J., Naccari, N. & Fatoullah, E. The effects of expertise and physical attractiveness upon opinion agreement and liking. *Sociometry*, 1974, *37*, 601–6.

Hovland, C. I. & Weiss, W. The influence of source credibility on communicator effectiveness. *Public Opinion Quarterly*, 1951, *15*, 635–50.

Hughes, P. H. & Crawford, G. A. A contagious disease model for researching and intervening in heroin epidemics. *Archives of General Biology*, 1972, *27*, 149–55.

Israel, J. Experimental change of attitude using the Asch-effect. *Acta Sociologica*, 1963, *7*, 95–104.

Jackson, J. Structural characteristics of norms. In I. D. Steiner & M. Fishbein (eds) *Current studies in social psychology*. New York: Holt, Rinehart & Winston, 1965.

———— A conceptual and measurement model for norms and roles. *Pacific Sociological Review*, 1966, 9, 35–47.

Jones, E. E. *Ingratiation: a social psychological analysis.* New York: Appleton-Century-Crofts. 1964.

Jones, E. E. & Gerard, H. B. *Foundations of social psychology.* New York: Wiley, 1967.

Julian, J. W., Bishop, D. W. & Fiedler, F. E. Quasi-therapeutic effects of intergroup competition. *Journal of Personality and Social Psychology*, 1966, 3, 321–7.

Kanter, R. M. Commitment and social organization: a study of commitment mechanisms. *American Sociological Review*, 1968, 33, 499–516.

———— *Commitment and community: communes and utopias in sociological perspective.* Cambridge, Mass.: Harvard University Press, 1972.

Katz, D. The functional approach to the study of attitudes. *Public Opinion Quarterly*, 1960, 24, 163–204.

Kaufmann, A. *Introduction à la théorie des sous-ensembles flous III. Applications à la classification et à la reconnaissance des formes, aux automates et aux systèmes, au choix des critères.* Paris: Masson, 1975.

Kelley, H. H. Salience of membership and resistance to change of group-anchored attitudes. *Human Relations*, 1955, 8, 275–90.

———— A classroom study of the dilemmas in interpersonal negotiations. In K. Archibald (ed.) *Strategic interaction and conflict.* Berkeley: University of California, 1966.

———— Attribution in social psychology. In D. Levine (ed.) *Nebraska symposium on motivation.* Lincoln, Nebraska: University of Nebraska Press, 1967.

Kelley, H. H. & Shapiro, M. M. An experiment on conformity to group norms where conformity is detrimental to group achievement. *American Sociological Review*, 1954, 19, 667–77.

Kelley, H. H. & Thibaut, J. W. Group problem-solving. In G. Lindzey & E. Aronson (eds) *Handbook of social psychology.* Reading, Mass.: Addison-Wesley, 1968.

Kelly, G. *The psychology of personal constructs.* New York: Norton, 1955.

Kelman, H. C. Compliance, identification and internalization: three processes of attitude change. *Journal of Conflict Resolution*, 1958, 2, 51–60.

Kiesler, C. A. & Kiesler, S. B. *Conformity.* Reading, Mass.: Addison-Wesley, 1969.

Kiesler, C. A. & Pallak, M. S. Minority influence: the effect of majority reactionaries and defectors, and minority and majority compromisers upon majority opinion and attraction. *European Journal of Social Psychology*, 1975, 5, 237–56.

Komorita, S. S. & Brenner, A. R. Bargaining and concession making under bilateral monopoly. *Journal of Personality and Social Psychology*, 1968, 9, 15–20.

Kuhn, T. S. *The structure of scientific revolutions.* Chicago: University of Chicago Press, 1962.

———— *The essential tension.* Chicago: University of Chicago Press, 1977.

Lage, E. Innovation et influence minoritaire. (Doctoral thesis.) Paris: Ecole Pratique des Hautes Etudes, Laboratoire de psychologie sociale, 1973.

Larsen, K. S. Social cost, belief incongruence and race: Experiments in choice behavior. *Journal of Social Psychology*, 1974, 94, 253–67.

Latané, B. Psychology of social impact. *American Psychologist*, 1981, 36, 343–56.

Latané, B. & Davis, D. Social impact and the effect of majority influence on attitudes toward the news media. Unpublished MS., 1974.

Latané, B. & Nida, S. Social impact theory and group influence: a social engineering perspective. In P. B. Paulus (ed.) *Psychology of group influence.* Hillsdale, NJ: Lawrence Erlbaum Associates, 1980.

Latané, B. & Wolf, S. The social impact of majorities and minorities. *Psychological Review*, 1981, *88*, 438–53.

Lemaine, G. Social differentiation and social originality. *European Journal of Social Psychology*, 1974, *4*, 17–52.

Lemaine, G., Kastersztein, J. & Personnaz, B. Social differentiation. In H. Tajfel (ed.) *Differentiation between social groups: studies in the social psychology of intergroup relations*. London: Academic Press, 1979.

Lemaine, G., Lasch, E. & Ricateau, P. L'influence sociale et les systèmes d'action: les effets d'attraction et de répulsion dans une expérience de normalisation avec l'allocinétique. *Bulletin de Psychologie*, 1971–2, *25*, 482–93.

Levine, J. M. Reaction to opinion deviance in small groups. In P. B. Paulus (ed.) *Psychology of group influence*. Hillsdale, NJ: Lawrence Erlbaum Associates, 1980.

Levinger, G. Toward the analysis of close relationships. *Journal of Experimental Social Psychology*, 1980, *16*, 510–44.

Levinger, G. & Huesmann, R. L. An 'incremental exchange' perspective on the pair relationship: interpersonal reward and level of involvement. In K. J. Gergen, M. S. Greenberg & R. H. Willis (eds) *Social exchange: advances in theory and research*. New York: Plenum, 1980.

Lewin, K., Lippitt, R. & White, R. K. Patterns of aggressive behavior in experimentally created social climates. *Journal of Social Psychology*, 1939, *10*, 271–99.

Maas, A., Clark, R. D. III & Haberkorn, G. The effects of differential ascribed category membership and normal on minority influence. *European Journal of Social Psychology*, 1982, *12*, 89–104.

McGrath, J. E. Small group research. *American Behavioral Scientist*, 1978, *21*, 651–74.

McGuire, W. J. The nature of attitudes and attitude change. In G. Lindzey & E. Aronson (eds) *Handbook of social psychology, vol. IV*. Reading, Mass.: Addison-Wesley, 1969.

Merei, F. Group leadership and institutionalization. *Human Relations*, 1949, *2*, 23–39.

Merton, R. K. *Social theory and social structure*. Glencoe, Ill.: Free Press, 1957.

Meyers, A. E. Team competition, success, and adjustment of group members. *Journal of Abnormal and Social Psychology*, 1962, *65*, 325–32.

Middlebrook, P. N. *Social psychology and modern life*. New York: Alfred A. Knopf Publishing Company, 1980.

Milet, J. *Gabriel Tarde et la philosophie de l'histoire*. Paris: Vrin, 1970.

Milgram, S. *Obedience to authority*. New York: Harper & Row, 1966.

Mills, J. & Aronson, E. Opinion change as a function of communicator's attractiveness and desire to influence. *Journal of Personality and Social Psychology*, 1965, *1*, 173–7.

Mills, J. & Jellison, J. M. Effect on opinion change of how desirable communication is to the audience the communicator addressed. *Journal of Personality and Social Psychology*, 1968, *6*, 98–101.

Montmollin, G. de. *L'influence sociale: phénomènes, facteurs et théories*. Paris: Presses Universitaires de France, 1977.

Moreland, R. L. Social categorization and the assimilation of 'new' group members. Unpublished doctoral dissertation, University of Michigan, 1978.

Moreland, R. L. & Levine, J. M. Socialization in small groups: temporal changes in individual–group relations. In L. Berkowitz (ed.) *Advances in experimental social psychology*, vol. 15. New York: Academic Press, 1982.

Morley, I. & Stephenson, G. *The social psychology of bargaining*. London: George Allen & Unwin Ltd., 1977.

Morris, W. N. & Miller, R. S. Impressions of dissenters and conformers: an attributional analysis. *Sociometry*, 1975, *38*, 327–39.

Moscovici, S. Social influence I: Conformity. In C. Nemeth (ed.) *Social psychology: classic and contemporary integrations*. Chicago: Rand McNally, 1974.

———— Reply to a critical note on two studies of minority influence. *European Journal of Social Psychology*, 1975, *5*, 261–3.

———— *Social influence and social change*. London: Academic Press, 1976.

———— *La psychologie des minorités actives*. Paris: Presses Universitaires de France, 1979.

———— Toward a theory of conversion behavior. In L. Berkowitz (ed.) *Advances in experimental social psychology, vol. 13*. New York: Academic Press, 1980.

———— *L'age des foules*. Paris: Fayard, 1981.

Moscovici, S. & Doms, M. Compliance and conversion in a situation of sensory deprivation. *Basic and Applied Social Psychology*, 1982, *3*, 81–94.

Moscovici, S. & Faucheux, C. Social influence, conformity bias, and the study of active minorities. In L. Berkowitz (ed.) *Advances in experimental social psychology, vol. 6*. New York: Academic Press, 1972.

Moscovici, S. & Lage, E. Studies in social influence III: Majority versus minority influence in a group. *European Journal of Social Psychology*, 1976, *6*, 149–74.

———— Studies in social influence IV: Minority influence in a context of originality judgments. *European Journal of Social Psychology*, 1978, *8*, 349–65.

Moscovici, S., Lage, E. & Naffrechoux, M. Influence of a consistent minority on the responses of a majority in a color perception task. *Sociometry*, 1969, *32*, 365–80.

Moscovici, S. & Mugny, G. Minority influence. In P. B. Paulus (ed.) *Basic group processes*. New York: Springer-Verlag, 1983.

Moscovici, S., Mugny, G. & Papastamou, S. 'Sleeper effect' et/ou effet minoritaire. Etude théorique et expérimentale de l'influence sociale à retardement. *Cahiers de Psychologie Cognitive*, 1981, *1*, 199–221.

Moscovici, S. & Nemeth, C. Social influence II: Minority influence. In C. Nemeth (ed.) *Social psychology: classic and contemporary integrations*. Chicago: Rand McNally, 1974.

Moscovici, S. & Neve, P. Studies in social influence I: Those absent are in right: convergence and polarization of answers in the course of social interaction. *European Journal of Social Psychology*, 1971, *1*, 201–14.

———— Studies in social influence II: Instrumental and symbolic influence. *European Journal of Social Psychology*, 1973, *3*, 461–71.

Moscovici, S. & Paicheler, G. Social comparison and social recognition: two complementary processes of identification. In H. Tajfel (ed.) *Differentiation between social groups*. London: Academic Press, 1978.

Moscovici, S. & Personnaz, B. Studies in social influence V: Minority influence and conversion behavior in a perceptual task. *Journal of Experimental Social Psychology*, 1980, *16*, 270–82.

Moscovici, S. & Ricateau, P. Conformité, minorité et influence sociale. In S. Moscovici (ed.) *Introduction à la psychologie sociale*. Paris: Larousse, 1972.

Mowday, R. T., Steers, R. M. & Porter, L. W. The measurement of organizational commitment. *Journal of Vocational Behavior*, 1979, *14*, 224–47.

Mugny, G. Majorité et minorité: le niveau de leur influence. *Bulletin de Psychologie*, 1974–5, *28*, 831–5.

—— Negotiations, image of the other and the process of minority influence. *European Journal of Social Psychology*, 1975, *5*, 209–28.

—— Quelle influence majoritaire? Quelle influence minoritaire? Influence comparée d'une majorité et d'une minorité sur les niveaux de réponse des individus. *Revue Suisse de Psychologie Pure et Appliquée*, 1976, *4*, 255–68.

—— *The power of minorities*. London: Academic Press, 1982.

Mugny, G. & Doise, W. Niveaux d'analyse dans l'étude expérimentale des processus d'influence sociale. *Social Science Information*, 1979, *18*, 819–76.

Mugny, G., Kaiser, C. & Papastamou, S. Influence minoritaire, identification et relations entre groupes: étude expérimentale autour d'une vocation. *Cahiers de Psychologie Sociale*, 1983, 19.

Mugny, G. & Papastamou, S. A propos du 'crédit idiosynchrastique' chez Hollander: conformisme initial ou négociation? *Bulletin de Psychologie*, 1975–6, *29*, 970–6.

—— When rigidity does not fail. *European Journal of Social Psychology*, 1980, *10*, 43–61.

—— Minority influence and psycho-social identity. *European Journal of Social Psychology*, 1982, *12*, 379–94.

Mugny, G., Pierrehumbert, B. & Zubel, R. Le style d'interaction comme facteur de l'influence sociale. *Bulletin de Psychologie*, 1972–3, *26*, 789–93.

Mugny, G., Rilliet, D. & Papastamou, S. Influence minoritaire et identification sociale dans des contextes d'originalité et de déviance. *Revue Suisse de Psychologie*, 1981, *40*, 314–32.

Namer, E. *L'affaire Galilée*. Paris: Gallimard-Julliard, 1975.

Nash, D. & Heiss, J. Sources of anxiety in laboratory strangers. *Sociological Quarterly*, 1967, *8*, 215–21.

Nash, D. & Wolfe, A. W. The stranger in laboratory culture. *American Sociological Review*, 1957, *22*, 400–5.

Nemeth, C. *A comparison between conformity and minority influence*. Paper presented at the XXIst International congress of psychology, Paris, 1976.

—— The role of an active minority in intergroup relations. In W. G. Austin & S. Worchel (eds) *The psychology of intergroup relations*. Belmont, Ca.: Brooks/Cole, 1980.

Nemeth, C. & Brilmayer, A. Negotiation vs. influence. *Social Psychology* (formerly *Sociometry*), 1982, see review.

Nemeth, C., Swedlund, M. & Kanki, B. Patterning of the minority's responses and their influence on the majority. *European Journal of Social Psychology*, 1974, *4*, 53–64.

Nemeth, C. & Wachtler, J. Consistency and modification of judgment. *Journal of Experimental Social Psychology*, 1973, *9*, 65–79.

—— Creating perceptions of consistency and confidence: a necessary condition for minority influence. *Sociometry*, 1974, *37*, 529–40.

—— Creative problem solving as a result of majority versus minority influence. Unpublished MS., 1982.

Nemeth, C., Wachtler, J. & Endicott, J. Increasing the size of the minority: some gains and some losses. *European Journal of Social Psychology*, 1977, *7*, 15–27.

Newcomb, T. M. *Personality and social change: attitude formation in a student community*. New York: Holt, Rinehart & Winston, 1943.

Newell, A. & Simon, H. A. *Human problem solving*. New York: Prentice Hall, 1972.

Newtson, D. Attribution and the unit of perception of ongoing behavior. *Journal of Personality and Social Psychology*, 1973, *28*, 28–38.

Orive, R. *Minority status and opinion extremity.* Unpublished MS., 1982.

Osgood, C. E. A case for graduated unilateral disengagement. *Bulletin of the Atomic Scientists*, 1967, *16*, 127–31.

Osgood, C. E. & Tannenbaum, P. H. The principle of congruity in the prediction of attitude change. *Psychological Review*, 1955, *66*, 42–55.

Paicheler, G. Norms and attitude change I: Polarization and styles of behavior. *European Journal of Social Psychology*, 1976, *6*, 405–27.

――― Norms and attitude change II: The phenomenon of bipolarization. *European Journal of Social Psychology*, 1977, *7*, 5–14.

――― Polarization of attitudes in homogeneous and heterogeneous groups. *European Journal of Social Psychology*, 1979, *9*, 85–96.

Papastamou, S. Stratégies d'influence minoritaires et majoritaires. Doctoral thesis, EGESS, 1979.

――― Strategies of minority and majority influence. In W. Doise & S. Moscovici (eds) *Current issues in European social psychology*, vol. 1. Cambridge: Cambridge University Press, 1983.

Papastamou, S., Mugny, G. & Kaiser, C. Echec à l'influence minoritaire: la psychologisation. *Recherches de Psychologie Sociale*, 1980, *2*, 41–56.

Pecheux, M. Etude expérimentale de conditions déterminant la plausibilité d'une théorie psychologique. *Bulletin de Psychologie*, 1972, *25*, 102–18.

Peirce, C. S. *Collected papers.* Cambridge, Mass.: Harvard University Press, 1934.

Pepitone, A. Lessons from the history of social psychology. *American Psychologist*, 1981, *36*, 972–85.

Pepitone, A. & Reichling, G. Group cohesiveness and the expression of hostility. *Human Relations*, 1955, *8*, 327–37.

Personnaz, B. Conformité, consensus et référents clandestins. La dépendance en tant que processus annulateur et l'influence. *Bulletin de Psychologie*, 1976, *29*, 230–42.

――― Niveau de résistance à l'influence de réponses nomiques et anomiques. Etude des phénomènes de référents clandestins et de conversion. *Recherches de Psychologie Sociale*, 1979, *1*, 3–26.

――― Study in social influence using the spectrometer method: dynamics of the phenomena of conversion and covertness in perceptual responses. *European Journal of Social Psychology*, 1981, *11*, 431–8.

Personnaz, M. La conformité comme source d'influence. Unpublished MS., Université Paris X Nanterre, 1976.

Platt, M. Recruiting new members: A theoretical framework for group selection procedures. Unpublished MS., University of Michigan, 1974.

Proust, M. *Remembrance of things past*, vol. 2: *Cities of the plain*. New York: Vintage Books, Random House Press, 1981.

Pruitt, D. G. & Johnson, D. I. Mediation as an aid to face saving in negotiation. *Journal of Personality and Social Psychology*, 1970, *14*, 239–46.

Putallaz, M. & Gottman, J. M. An interactional model of children's entry into peer groups. *Child Development*, 1981, *52*, 986–94.

Raven, H. H. & Kruglanski, A. Conflict and power. In R. Swingle (ed.) *The structure of conflict.* New York: Academic Press, 1970.

Riba, D. & Mugny, G. Consistencia y rigidez: reinterpretación. *Cuadernos de Psicología*, 1981, *2*, 37–56.

Ricateau, P. Processus de catégorisation d'autrui et les mécanismes d'influence sociale. *Bulletin de Psychologie*, 1970–1, *24*, 909–19.

Ridgeway, C. L. Conformity, group-oriented motivation, and status attainment in small groups. *Social Psychology*, 1978, *41*, 175–88.

—— Nonconformity, competence, and influence in groups: a test of two theories. *American Sociological Review*, 1981, *46*, 333–47.

Rokeach, M. *The open and closed mind. Investigations into the nature of belief and personality systems.* New York: Basic Books, 1960.

Rosenblatt, P. C. Needed research on commitment in marriage. In G. Levinger & H. L. Rausch (eds) *Close relationships: perspectives in the meaning of intimacy.* Amherst: University of Massachusetts Press, 1977.

Rubin, J. Z. & Brown, B. R. *The social psychology of bargaining and negotiation.* New York: Academic Press, 1975.

Safran, S. & Allen, V. L. Perception of group membership. Unpublished MS., University of Wisconsin, 1978.

Saltzstein, H. H. & Sandberg, L. Indirect social influence: change in judgmental process or anticipatory conformity? *Journal of Experimental Social Psychology*, 1979, *15*, 209–16.

Santee, R. T. & Maslach, C. To agree or not to agree: personal dissent amid social pressure to conform. *Journal of Personality and Social Psychology*, 1982.

Schachter, S. Deviation, rejection, and communication. *Journal of Abnormal and Social Psychology*, 1951, *46*, 190–207.

Schein, E. H. Organizational socialization and the profession of management. *Industrial Management Review*, 1968, *9*, 1–16.

—— The individual, the organization, and the career: a conceptual scheme. *Journal of Applied Behavioral Science*, 1971, *7*, 401–26.

Schneider, D. J. *Social psychology.* Reading, Mass.: Addison-Wesley, 1976.

Schneirla, T. C. The concepts of levels in the study of social phenomena. In M. Sherif & C. W. Sherif (eds) *Groups in harmony and tension.* New York: Harper, 1953.

Schuetz, A. The stranger: an essay in social psychology. *American Journal of Sociology*, 1944, *49*, 499–507.

Shelling, J. C. An essay on bargaining. *American Economic Review*, 1956, *46*, 281ff.

—— *The strategy of conflict.* London, Oxford, New York: Oxford University Press, 1975.

Sherif, M. A study of some human factors in perception. *Archives of Psychology*, 1935, *22*, No 187.

Sherif, M. & Hovland, C. I. *Social judgment: assimilation and contrast effects in communication and attitude change.* New Haven, Conn.: Yale University Press, 1961.

Simmel, G. *The sociology of George Simmel.* (Ed. K. Wolff.) Glencoe, Ill.: Free Press, 1950.

—— *Conflict and the web of group affiliations.* Glencoe, Ill.: Free Press, 1955.

Smith, C. E. A study of the automatic excitation resulting from the interaction of individual opinions and groups opinions. *Journal of Abnormal and Social Psychology*, 1936, *30*, 136–64.

Smith, M. B., Bruner, J. S. & White, R. W. *Opinion and personality.* New York: Wiley, 1956.

Snyder, C. R. & Fromkin, H. L. *Uniqueness: the human pursuit of difference.* New York: Plenum, 1980.

Snyder, E. C. The supreme court as a small group. *Social Forces*, 1958, *36*, 232–8.

Sorrentino, R. M., King, G. & Leo, G. The influence of the minority on perception: a note on a possible alternative explanation. *Journal of Experimental Social Psychology*, 1980, *16*, 293–301.

Staw, B. M. The consequences of turnover. *Journal of Occupational Behaviour*, 1980, *1*, 253–73.

Steiner, I. Whatever happened to the group in social psychology? *Journal of Experimental Social Psychology*, 1974, *10*, 93–108.

Stevens, S. S. *Psychophysics: introduction to its perceptual, and social prospects.* New York, Wiley, 1975.

Suchner, R. W. & Jackson, D. Responsibility and status: a causal or only a spurious relationship? *Sociometry*, 1976, *39*, 243–56.

Tajfel, H. Experiments in intergroup discrimination. *Scientific American*, 1970, *223*, 96–102.

——— La catégorisation sociale. In S. Moscovici (ed.) *Introduction à la psychologie sociale*. Paris: Larousse, 1972.

——— *Differentiation between social groups: studies in the social psychology of intergroup relations.* London: Academic Press, 1978.

Tajfel, H., Billig, M., Bundy, R. P. & Flament, C. Social categorization and intergroup behaviour. *European Journal of Social Psychology*, 1971, *1*, 149–78.

Tarde, G. *Les lois de l'imitation*. Paris: Alcan, 1890.

Tedeschi, J., Lesnick, S. & Gahagan, J. Feedback and 'washout' effects in the Prisoner's Dilemma game. *Journal of Personality and Social Psychology*, 1968, *10*, 31–4.

Tesser, A. Self-generated attitude change. In L. Berkowitz (ed.) *Advances in experimental social psychology*, vol. 11. New York: Academic Press, 1978.

Thibaut, J. W. & Kelley, H. H. *The social psychology of groups.* New York: Wiley, 1967.

Thibaut, J. W. & Strickland, L. H. Psychological set and social conformity. *Journal of Personality*, 1956, *25*, 115–29.

Tolman, E. C. *Purposive behavior in animals and men.* New York: Appleton-Century, 1932.

Turner, J. C. Towards a cognitive redefinition of the social group. *Cahiers de Psychologie Cognitive*, 1981, *1*, 93–118.

Turner, R. H. The public perception of protest. *American Sociological Review*, 1969, *34*, 815–31.

Upmeyer, A. Social perception and signal detectability theory: group influence on discrimination and usage of scale. *Psychologische Forschung*, 1971, *34*, 283–94.

Van Gennep, A. *The rites of passage* (trans. M. B. Vizedom & G. L. Caffee). Chicago: University of Chicago Press, 1969. (Originally published, 1908.)

Van Maanen, J. Breaking in: socialization to work. In R. Dubin (ed.) *Handbook of work, organization, and society*. Chicago: Rand-McNally, 1976.

——— People processing: strategies of organizational socialization. *Organizational Dynamics*, 1978, *7*, 18–36.

Van Maanen, J. & Schein, E. H. Toward a theory of organizational socialization. In B. Staw (ed.) *Research in organizational behavior: an annual series of analytic essays and critical reviews*, vol. 1. Greenwich, Conn.: JAI Press, 1979.

Veblen, T. *Essays in our changing order.* New York: Viking Press, 1934.

Wach, J. *Sociology of religion.* Chicago: University of Chicago Press, 1944.

Wagner, W. & Gerard, H. B. Similarity of comparison group, opinions about facts and values and social projection. *Archives of Psychology*, 1983.

Wahrman, R. Status, deviance, and sanctions. *Pacific Sociological Review*, 1970, *13*, 229–40.

Wahrman, R. & Pugh, M. D. Competence and conformity: another look at Hollander's study. *Sociometry*, 1972, *35*, 376–86.

—— Sex, nonconformity and influence. *Sociometry*, 1974, *37*, 137–47.

Waller, W. W. & Hill, R. *The family: a dynamic interpretation*. New York: Dryden, 1951.

Wanous, J. P. Organizational entry: newcomers moving from outside to inside. *Psychological Bulletin*, 1977, *84*, 601–18.

—— *Organizational entry: recruitment, selection, and socialization of newcomers*. Reading, Mass.: Addison-Wesley, 1980.

Wheeler, S. The structure of formally organized socialization settings. In O. G. Brim & S. Wheeler (eds) *Socialization after childhood: two essays*. New York: Wiley, 1966.

Wicklund, R. A. Objective self-awareness. In L. Berkowitz (ed.) *Advances in experimental social psychology*, vol. 8. New York: Academic Press, 1975.

Wiggins, J. A., Dill, F. & Schwartz, R. D. On 'status-liability'. *Sociometry*, 1965, *28*, 197–209.

Wilder, D. A. Perception of groups, size of opposition, and social influence. *Journal of Experimental Social Psychology*, 1977, *13*, 253–68.

Wilson, K. V. A distribution-free test of analysis of variance hypotheses. *Psychological Bulletin*, 1956, *53*, 96–101.

Wolf, S. Behavioural style and group cohesiveness as sources of minority influence. *European Journal of Social Psychology*, 1979, *9*, 381–95.

—— The manifest and latent influence of majorities and minorities. *Journal of Personality and Social Psychology*, in press.

Wolf, S. & Latané, B. Majority and minority influence on restaurant preferences. *Journal of Personality and Social Psychology*, 1983, *45*, 282–92.

Wyer, R. S. Jr. & Gordon, J. E. The recall of information about persons and groups. *Journal of Experimental Social Psychology*, 1982, *18*, 128–64.

Zajonc, R. B. Attitudinal effects of mere exposure. *Journal of Personality and Social Psychology*, 1968, Monograph Supplement, *9*, 1–29.

Zaleska, M. & Chalot, C. Réponses exprimées et inexprimées en fonction de l'extrémisme de l'attitude, du degré d'implication et de l'information. *Bulletin de Psychologie*, 1980, *23*, 795–805.

Zander, A. The study of group behaviour during four decades. *Journal of Applied Behavioral Science*, 1979, *15*, 272–82.

Ziller, R. C. Individuation and socialization: a theory of assimilation in large organizations. *Human Relations*, 1964, *17*, 341–60.

—— Toward a theory of open and closed groups. *Psychological Bulletin*, 1965, *64*, 164–82.

—— Group dialectics. *Human Development*, 1977, *20*, 293–308.

Ziller, R. C. & Behringer, R. D. Assimilation of the knowledgeable newcomer under conditions of group success and failure. *Journal of Abnormal and Social Psychology*, 1960, *60*, 288–91.

Subject index

Author index